SECRET PLACES, HIDDEN SANCTUARIES

SECRET PLACES, HIDDEN SANCTUARIES

Uncovering Mysterious Sites, Symbols, and Societies

STEPHEN KLIMCZUK
and
GERALD WARNER
of CRAIGENMADDIE

STERLING ETHOS
An imprint of Sterling Publishing Co., Inc.

New York / London
www.sterlingpublishing.com

STERLING and the distinctive Sterling logo are registered trademarks of Sterling Publishing Co., Inc.

PICTURE CREDITS
Corbis: 61: Himmler Addressing his Troops at Wewelsburg Castle

Courtesy Wikimedia Commons: 7: Vauxhall Cross; 27: Yasukuni Shrine/Author: Fg2; 45: Valencia Cathedral sanctuary/Author: Felivet; 79: Teutonic Order's coat of arms/Author: Böhringer Friedrich; 98: Passetto di Borgo/Author: Raja Patnaik, post-processed and uploaded by Alessio Damato (with permission of the author); 119: RAF Menwith Hill radome; 139: Montecristo/Author: Allumeur; 159: Sancta Sanctorum; 176: Hungarian crown jewels; 197: Queen's bankers' Coutts & Co. HQ in London; 212: Yale's Scroll and Key; 233: Front of Boodle's Club

Library of Congress Cataloging-in-Publication Data
Klimczuk, Stephen.
Secret places, hidden sanctuaries : uncovering mysterious sites, symbols, and societies /by Stephen Klimczuk and Warner of Craigenmaddie, Gerald.
p. cm.
Includes index.
ISBN 978-1-4027-6207-9
1. Parapsychology. 2. Occultism. 3. Antiquities. 4. Sacred sites. 5. Curiosities and wonders. I. Warner, Gerald. II. Title.
BF1031.K55 2009
001.9--dc22
2009013420

2 4 6 8 10 9 7 5 3 1

Published by Sterling Publishing Co., Inc.
387 Park Avenue South, New York, NY 10016
© 2009 by Stephen Klimczuk and Gerald Warner of Craigenmaddie
Distributed in Canada by Sterling Publishing
c/o Canadian Manda Group, 165 Dufferin Street
Toronto, Ontario, Canada M6K 3H6
Distributed in the United Kingdom by GMC Distribution Services
Castle Place, 166 High Street, Lewes, East Sussex, England BN7 1XU
Distributed in Australia by Capricorn Link (Australia) Pty. Ltd.
P.O. Box 704, Windsor, NSW 2756, Australia

Design and layout by Chris Welch

Manufactured in the United States
All rights reserved

Sterling ISBN 978-1-4027-6207-9

For information about custom editions, special sales, premium and
corporate purchases, please contact Sterling Special Sales
Department at 800-805-5489 or specialsales@sterlingpublishing.com.

"And I will give thee the treasures of darkness, and hidden riches of secret places." (Isaiah 45:3)

CONTENTS

Introduction   1

Chapter 1 🪷 MYSTERIOUS HERITAGE   7

Investigating (and, where necessary, debunking) the "Usual Suspects"

Rosslyn Chapel, Midlothian, Scotland   8

Rennes-le-Château, France: Wholly Bunk, Hoary Tale   12

Villa Tevere: The Headquarters of Opus Dei in Rome   16

The Hotel de Bilderberg and the Bilderberg Group, The Netherlands   19

Vauxhall Cross: London's Secret Intelligence Service (MI6)
    Headquarters   22

Rosicrucian Park, San José, and Club 33, Anaheim, California   24

Chapter 2 🪷 SHRINES AND SANCTUARIES,
ANCIENT AND MODERN   27

*Places of primordial spiritual impulses and folklore—and a psychedelic
West Coast enclave*

Ise Shrine, Japan   28

Yasukuni Shrine, Tokyo   31

Jokhang Temple, Lhasa, Tibet   34

The Shrine of the Oracle at Delphi, Greece   36

The Esalen Institute, Big Sur, California   41

Chapter 3 ✿ THE TEMPLE, THE ARK, AND
THE GRAIL 45

*Undeniable surprises on the sober trail of Knights Templars, Freemasons,
Holy Grail hunters, and Gnostics*

The Bååtska Palace, Stockholm 46

The Chapel of the Ark, Aksum, Ethiopia 53

The Chapel of the Holy Grail, Valencia Cathedral, Spain 54

Significant Masonic Temples from Rome and Paris to Washington and
Pushkin (Russia) 55

Gnosticism Today 59

Chapter 4 ✿ GOTHIC NIGHTMARE 61

*Himmler's "Black Camelot" and Nazi spiritual center, with side trips to
other Germanic esoteric sites*

Wewelsburg Castle, Westphalia, Germany 62

The Goetheanum, Dornach, Switzerland 71

Bollingen Tower, Lake Zurich, Switzerland 74

Chapter 5 ✿ CITADELS OF CHIVALRY 79

*Remaining outposts of ancient noble and charitable brotherhoods at the
service of humanity*

The Knights of Malta, Rome 81

The Tuscan Order of St. Stephen Pope and Martyr, Pisa 88

The Teutonic Order 93

Chapter 6 ✿ GROTTOES AND GROTESQUES 98

Strange and historic passageways, caverns, and hiding places

The Passetto di Borgo, Rome 99

The Magic Door, Rome 105

The Grotto of the Beati Paoli, Palermo, Sicily 109

Priest Holes in England 112

Chapter 7 ❀ MODERN-DAY BOLT-HOLES 119

Secret government installations, well-oiled for use in time of war or crisis

Mount Weather Emergency Operations Center, Bluemont, Virginia 120

The Federal Relocation Arc 128

Area 51: The Facility That Does Not Exist, Nevada 129

RAF Menwith Hill, Yorkshire, England 134

Chapter 8 ❀ ISLANDS OF MYSTERY 139

Five special island sanctuaries with their unique treasure hoards,
inaccessibility, or spiritual significance

Montecristo: The Forbidden Island, Off the Italian Coast 141

Easter Island: Mysterious Graven Images 150

Isle of Lewis, Scottish Hebrides 153

Iona: St. Columba's Scottish Island Sanctuary 155

Svalbard: Norway's Arctic Eden 156

Chapter 9 ❀ HOLIES OF HOLIES 159

Places on the trail of a higher reality, ultimate human destiny—and
according to some, Apocalypse

Sancta Sanctorum, Rome's Lateran Palace 161

The Pauline Chapel, The Vatican's Apostolic Palace 163

   The "Prophecies" of St. Malachy 164

The Monastery of St. Catherine of Sinai, Egypt 165

The Autonomous Monastic Republic of Holy Mount Athos, Greece 167

The Abbey of Sainte-Madeleine du Barroux, France 169

The Hagia Sophia, Istanbul, Turkey 171

Her Majesty's Chapels Royal of the Mohawks, Ontario, Canada   172
    Counterfactual History: The Eternal "What If . . . ?"   175

Chapter 10 ❧ HIDDEN TOTEMS   176
    Treasured objects or talismans of great antiquity

The Stone of Destiny   177
The Holy Crown of St. Stephen of Hungary   183
The British and Polish Crown Jewels in Canada   188
The Holy Ampoule of the Kings of France   190
Joyeuse, the Sword of Charlemagne   192
The Holy Lance of St. Longinus: The "Spear of Destiny"   193
Oliver Cromwell's Head   195

Chapter 11 ❧ (VERY) PRIVATE BANKING   197
    *A discreet tour through the great temples of high finance and private
    wealth management*

Rothschilds, London   198
Banks That Are No More   199
The Great Survivors: Goldman Sachs and the House of Lazard   201
The Wealth Managers, Including Coutts & Co.—the Queen's
    Bankers   202
The Swiss Banks: Models of Discretion   204
The German Private Banks: Oppenheim, Warburg, and Others   207
A Well-Connected American House: Brown Brothers
    Harriman & Co.   209
    C. Hoare & Co.   210
The Enduring Allure of Gold   210

Chapter 12 🔖 UNIVERSITY SECRET SOCIETIES
AND DUELING CORPS 212

*Inside the closely guarded doors of fraternities and societies for
the future elite*

The Apostles of Cambridge and the Bullingdon Club of Oxford 213

Princeton's Eating Clubs 215

Harvard's Final Clubs 216

Yale's Senior Societies: Skull and Bones and Its Rivals 217

Rivals to Skull and Bones 221

The German University "Corps" 224

The Mensur 229

Chapter 13 🔖 JOLLY GOOD FELLOWSHIP 233

*The lore, elegance, humor, and eccentricities of the great private clubs of
London and the world*

London's Private Clubs 235

White's: The Oldest Club 235

Boodle's, Brooks's, and Others of Distinction 238

Other London Clubs of Distinction 240

Clubs Outside London and in Europe 245

America's Private Clubs 247

Sanctuaries: The Enduring Tradition 251

Index 253

About the Authors 259

INTRODUCTION

What is the origin of the basic human instinct to hide away in obscure places, to seek privacy in secret sanctuaries, and to congregate in select groups in venues from which the rest of humanity is excluded? Is it some subconscious attempt to return to the womb? Whatever the explanation, this phenomenon cannot be denied. It can be observed in the behavior of toddlers who will happily crawl into an empty cardboard box or conceal themselves behind furniture. Even in the age of computer games, young children still love to play hide-and-seek and are seldom happier than when they are crouched in a cupboard beneath the stairs, hoping to escape discovery. Later, when they huddle with friends in tree houses or huts, the discerning parent may recognize that the fraternity house, with its close-knit camaraderie and cabalistic Greek initials (those esoteric Phis and Kappas and Gammas), is only a few years down the road.

This book takes a close but wide-ranging look at such behavior, both in the past and present, by casting the light of day on a rich variety of highly private enclaves in which groups have gathered to worship, to conspire, to defend themselves, and, in one gruesome instance, to plan one of the most shocking mass murders in the history of the world. In a lighter vein, we also explore a large number of secretive and exclusive venues that exist for the purpose of good fellowship and unabashed enjoyment. Such a broad undertaking necessarily means that the book is eclectic in its range of subjects, with strongly contrasting topics in different chapters. We venture to hope that this is one of its strengths and appeals. This is the first time that these varied interests have been brought together between one set of covers, and some of the material will be a revelation to readers.

If there is one key word that summarizes the subject matter of this book it is *sanctuary*. That is the common feature of contrasting studies that investigate shrines, the headquarters of secret societies, and convivial but exclusive private clubs. In every instance, those involved have sought sanctuary from public scrutiny or the pressures of the outside world. Interest in the hidden and the esoteric has grown exponentially in recent years, fueled by such publications as *The Holy Blood and the Holy Grail* and *The Da Vinci Code,* to name just two books that have spearheaded the growth of a specialized literary genre. In recognition of this, we have begun our study, in Chapter 1, with a review of the "usual suspects," the sites uppermost in the public consciousness when it comes to the mysterious and the esoteric. That is not to say that we endorse the mythology surrounding these places. There are intriguing aspects to Rosslyn Chapel in Midlothian, Scotland, but much of the furor surrounding it is artificial. Is there a great Templar treasure, or a devastating secret that would threaten Christianity, concealed at Rennes-le-Château? Having studied the case, we don't think so. We also take an unfashionable view, again dictated by the evidence, of the guilt of the Templars. The Opus Dei headquarters in Rome and the famous Hotel de Bilderberg in the Netherlands similarly exhibit characteristics of downright ordinariness—though in the latter instance we do not discount the possibility of a significant power nexus being involved.

But this book is by no means an exercise in debunking the secrets of mysterious places—quite the opposite. We want to direct attention to the many sites that deserve more interest and attention than they have received. Readers will find more to intrigue them in these pages than to disillusion them. With regard to religious sites, our investigations range from the Ise Shrine in Japan, the Jokhang Temple in Tibet, and the Sanctuary of the Delphic Oracle in Greece, to the alleged resting place of the Ark of the Covenant in Ethiopia and the former chapter house of Valencia Cathedral in Spain, where it is claimed the Holy Grail is safeguarded—and many more besides.

The darkest chapter in the book (Chapter 4, Gothic Nightmare) addresses the topic of Wewelsburg Castle in Germany, where Heinrich

Himmler created a "Black Camelot" to provide his SS murderers with a pseudoreligion and a kitschy parody of knighthood to inspire them in their task of extermination. This site, distasteful as it may be, is arguably the most important of all those surveyed, because it actually provides answers to crucial questions. Any normal human being, informed of the details of the mass murder of the Jews and other victims of the Third Reich, is moved to ask: How were the perpetrators capable of such conduct? How could they remain immune to all the instincts of conscience and compassion? What drove them? Those are among the most important questions arising from the history of the twentieth century and the answers are to be found behind the towering, grim battlements of Wewelsburg. Those answers are disconcerting, insofar as they betray the level of mummery and crass naiveté that lay behind the Final Solution—a farrago of esoteric nonsense that would have been utterly laughable if it had not produced such appalling consequences. That makes them all the more important to uncover.

The succeeding chapter provides an antidote to the nasty taste left in the mouth by Nazi mysticism, examining as it does the remaining outposts of genuine Christian chivalry belonging to the great military orders of the Knights of Malta, the Teutonic Order, and the Knights of St. Stephen of Tuscany—ancient noble and charitable brotherhoods at the service of humanity, representing a medieval ideal updated to the twenty-first century. Their surviving strongholds—private sanctuaries of chivalry and aristocratic charity—are described in detail. Then we look at a series of intriguing secret passages, grottoes, and hiding places, including the Passetto di Borgo, the tunnel at the Vatican down which popes fled to safety when their lives were in danger and restored to fame recently in Dan Brown's novel *Angels and Demons;* the cavern of the Beati Paoli, a black-robed and hooded secret society of assassins in Palermo, Sicily; and the priest holes in England in which Catholic priests were concealed from the Protestant authorities hunting them down. This theme is updated in Chapter 7, which investigates modern-day secret installations, such as Mount Weather in Virginia, and Area 51 near Las Vegas.

Islands are naturally secluded and secretive places. So we take a fresh and penetrating look at the fabled treasure island of Montecristo and conclude, on the basis of the evidence, that this is one place that has, if anything, been underrated even by researchers, and that it may well conceal the secret of great wealth to this day. In this instance, therefore, rather than discrediting the mystery and legends associated with Montecristo, we proclaim the island's enduring significance. We also visit other insular sanctuaries, some of which served as refuges for saints and hermits—such as Iona, off the west coast of Scotland—and finally describe Svalbard, the "Arctic Eden," where the seeds of all the world's varieties of plants are stored as a precaution against ecological disaster. Under the headings "Holies of Holies" and "Hidden Totems," we record further secret sanctuaries and concealed objects of great historical and mystical significance. But, of course, people often seek privacy for material motives, with the rich anxious to protect their fortunes from the greedy attention of governments. The world of Swiss banking and similarly discreet financial services have long intrigued the curious. Under "(Very) Private Banking" we disclose some of the secrets that lie behind the discreetly worded and highly polished brass plates of private banks in Geneva and elsewhere.

Exclusive retreats are by no means the preserve of the middle-aged and elderly. In Chapter 12 we pass through the closely guarded doors of America's legendary university secret societies, homes to the nation's youthful elite—the movers and shakers of the future—and the enclosed fraternities whose influence shaped many of the present leaders of American society. These societies represent the distinctive American contribution to private student conviviality. So we examine Harvard's Porcellian Club, its Hasty Pudding and Lampoon, while Yale's Skull and Bones and a host of other "senior" societies are also investigated.

Then, moving on to the corresponding organizations in Europe, we enter the world of the famous but secretive German university dueling fraternities—over two hundred of them, meeting behind closed doors to inflict and receive dueling scars and observe centuries-old rituals, secluded from the disapproving eyes of contemporaries. Not all the fraternities duel, but they all wear colorful uniforms (mostly among themselves, in discreet privacy) and have a lively social life. We visit such evocative sites as the ruined Rudelsburg Castle, annual meeting place of the oldest federation of German student corps; the Borussia House, Bonn, headquarters of the old-line Corps Borussia; and the turreted gothic house of the Corps Hannovera (to which Bismarck belonged), among other places, where the clash of steel still defiantly proclaims the survival of the values of an earlier age.

Finally, to end on a congenial note, the last chapter outlines the histories, characters, and rich anecdotage of those ultimate impenetrable sanctuaries: private clubs. Since this phenomenon was originally native to Britain, we first chronicle the imposing array of aristocratic and highly eccentric clubs established in London, beginning with the most famous and exclusive of all—White's, founded in 1693 and still maintaining its effortless superiority over all others. The fund of lore, elegance, and humor residing in the still-flourishing clubs of London, including such celebrated sanctuaries of gentility as Boodle's, Brooks's, and Pratt's, provides highly entertaining material. Since the institution of the private club has spread around the world, creating a social version of the British Empire, we also look at similar establishments in Paris and Rome, before turning the spotlight on American clubs. These range from the exclusive Knickerbocker in New York to less formal convivial societies, notably those where American show-business personalities have traditionally congregated and created an enduring legacy of humorous anecdotes and long-remembered witticisms—usually at one another's expense.

Even the vast range of sites described in this book cannot claim to be an exhaustive survey of every secretive place and institution thriving today. Although we live in an age of mass communication that has shrunk the planet, with the ever-intrusive media shedding often unwelcome light in previously dark corners, there is a growing awareness that there is much going on beneath the surface of our seemingly open societies. It is not necessary to join the ranks of conspiracy theorists to recognize that some of this activity is sinister. On the other hand, just because an organization or venue shuns publicity, that does not necessarily mean its activities are antisocial. Privacy is a human right, like any other. There are occasions when "the people's right to know" is not a right at all, but an erosion of somebody else's rights. Much suspicion of private groups and discreet activity today stems from an unfounded paranoia, used to justify intrusion into the reasonable privacy enjoyed by clubs and societies for legitimate purposes. At the same time, organizations whose purposes are criminal or truly subversive deserve to be exposed. The challenge is to tread the fine line that separates these two categories.

One of the primordial human instincts is for men (women's societies have a lesser survival rate) to bond together and form associations reflecting shared interests. It is safe to prophesy that, as long as the human race endures, small sections of it will congregate privately to pursue some purpose, good or evil. Such groups inevitably arouse the curiosity or suspicion of those who are excluded. That, too, is a fundamental human instinct: to see a locked door or a curtained chamber and ask indignantly, "Why am I not allowed in there?" Today, through the pages of this book, you are allowed in, by being offered the key to the door in the wall and transported into the secret places of the world.

Chapter 1

MYSTERIOUS HERITAGE

*T*o begin our investigation of the world's secret sanctuaries and hidden places, it is worth looking first at some well-known sites and associated organizations that come to most people's minds whenever this topic is mentioned. We might just as well have called this chapter "The Usual Suspects," since the places and institutions examined here are mostly household names. As we shall demonstrate, however, celebrity is no guarantee of authenticity. Thanks to the popularity of books like *The Da Vinci Code* and, before it, *The Holy Blood and the Holy Grail*, discussion of all things esoteric has come to be dominated by theories about the Knights Templar. The Freemasons follow close behind them in popularity. Then there is the more specialized interest—born of the age of technology—in UFOs, extraterrestrial aliens, and government cover-ups. As the public palate becomes more jaded, the purveyors of conspiracy theories increasingly feel impelled to cross-fertilize these elements, so that it is now commonplace to find both Templars and Masons appearing within the same scenario—since some Masons also claim to be Templars. Unfortunately, we didn't unearth any conspiracy theory that involved the Templars, the Masons, *and* aliens landing from UFOs, but it can surely only be a matter of time before one evolves.

Rosslyn Chapel, Midlothian, Scotland

The natural starting point, therefore, for a review of secret sites is to look at the two places most closely associated in the public mind with theories about the survival of the Templars centuries after their suppression by the Church. The first, made notorious by Dan Brown's novel *The Da Vinci Code* (the film of the book was also partly shot on location there), is Rosslyn Chapel in Scotland. It is situated on a small hill overlooking Roslin Glen, close to the village of Roslin, in Midlothian, six miles south of Edinburgh. It was founded in 1456 by William Sinclair, or St. Clair, first Earl of Caithness, as the Collegiate Church of St. Matthew, one of nearly forty such collegiate churches in Scotland before the Reformation, and housed up to six canons (priests) and two boy choristers. Its purpose was to celebrate the Divine Office daily and to sing Masses for the repose of the souls of the dead, particularly deceased members of the St. Clair family. There was a permanent endowment to support this establishment, which endured until the Reformation in Scotland (1560). The provost was then driven out and the altars were smashed. In the seventeenth century, when Oliver Cromwell invaded Scotland, his troops used the chapel as a stable, but they left its many rich carvings largely intact. In 1861 it once again became a place of worship, this time under the aegis of the Scottish Episcopal Church, as it remains today.

That is the factual history of Rosslyn Chapel. But this chronicle of unsensational Christian worship has been overlaid with a massive deposit of unsubstantiated mythology—and downright bunk—that has turned it into a place of pilgrimage for tens of thousands of visitors who have imposed their own fantasies, or rather the fantasies they have been fed, on the building. The chief allegations are that its founder, William St. Clair, was a Knight Templar; that the building is a rich lode of Templar lore; that its stone carvings illustrate many cabalistic Templar and Masonic secrets; and—to pile insanity upon distortion of history—that its vault conceals a buried secret of cosmic significance, variously claimed as the treasure of the Templars, the Holy Grail, or even the head of Christ. It is further asserted that the St. Clairs, in their seafaring role as princes of Orkney, discovered America before Columbus and that medieval carvings in the chapel illustrate a type of corn found only in the New World at that time. Wishful thinking based on such delusions has generated a vast literature of competing claims, each further removed from the truth than its predecessor.

These fabrications are based on features of the building that are indeed striking, but all of which can be explained in conventional terms. The chapel is supported by fourteen pillars that form twelve arches on three sides of the nave. The three pillars at the east end are now known as the Master Pillar, the Journeyman Pillar, and the Apprentice Pillar. The Apprentice Pillar is named after a legend that the stonemason in charge of crafting it delegated the work to an apprentice who wrought better carving than he was capable of producing, whereupon the jealous master murdered him. This has prompted commentators to attach a Masonic significance to the pillars. In fact, the apprentice story was made up as late as the eighteenth century, about the same time as these Masonic-sounding names were attached to the columns. The three pillars' original, medieval names were the Earl's Pillar (self-explanatory, the chapel's founder being the Earl of Caithness), the Shekinah (meaning "the presence of God," a traditional Christian usage from biblical sources and a natural attribution for the east end of a church where Mass was celebrated *ad orientem*), and the Prince's Pillar (the St. Clairs were also princes of Orkney), sometimes known as "Matthew's Staff," since it upheld a chapel dedicated to St. Matthew.

Those theorists grasping at esoteric straws would claim that the notion of *Shekinah* derives originally from the Temple of Solomon at Jerusalem, which has a Templar resonance, and advance claims that Rosslyn is modeled on the layout of the original Temple. That is not the case. The chapel was designed as a much larger, cruciform church, of which the existing building was intended to be only the choir and Lady Chapel: The foundations of the unbuilt nave and transepts, extending for ninety feet (27m) beyond the present structure, were discovered in the nineteenth century. So far from being modeled on the Temple, the two most informed critics of such legends, the historians Mark Oxbrow and Ian Robertson, in their book *Rosslyn and the Grail,* have proved conclusively that it is a replica of the choir of

Glasgow Cathedral. Their withering conclusion is: "Rosslyn Chapel bears no more resemblance to Solomon's or Herod's Temple than a house brick does to a paperback book."

These authors and other serious commentators have systematically discredited the fantasies of the esotericists. To summarize briefly the refutations that scholarship has made against superstition, the principal points are as follows. So far from being Templars, the St. Clair family was among the forty-one witnesses who testified against the Order at the trial of its Scottish Knights in the Abbey of Holyrood in Edinburgh, in December 1309. At that time there were only two Knights Templar in Scotland: Sir Walter de Clifton, the Preceptor of Balintradoch, the Templars' Scottish headquarters, just five miles (8km) from Rosslyn, and Sir William de Middleton, both of whom were beyond the age of military service. Giving evidence against the order, Henry St. Clair and his son William declared that "if the Templars had been faithful Christians they would in no way have lost the Holy Land." So far from championing his neighbors, the then-head of the St. Clair family denounced them—possibly in the hope of acquiring some of their confiscated land. The two Templars were acquitted for lack of evidence, but their order was dissolved in Scotland, as elsewhere. Nor was there ever a scintilla of evidence of an underground survival of the Order in Scotland (starting from the meager foundation of just two elderly knights) in medieval times. So there is no reason to suppose that, when the descendant of their enemies, the St. Clairs, set up a chapel to pray for the salvation of his family 147 years later, he had any thought of the long-forgotten Templars—still less of the Freemasons, who had yet to invent themselves.

At no point does the Templar legend hold water. The Templar "rose" on the founder's tomb is actually the wheel emblem of St. Catherine, his patron saint, rather than a Rosicrucian sign. There is a carving at the base of a statue niche representing two knights on one horse (or possibly just a knight and his squire), which was a Templar symbol. But, unfortunately for conspiracy theorists, it was not the Order's emblem in the British Isles, where a paschal lamb was the Templar seal. Then we come to the green men. These are not extraterrestrials, but a series of carvings—more than 110 in all—of human heads surrounded by greenery. In fact, they simply depict the progression through life to death, moving from east to west in the chapel, the first carvings illustrating youth and spring, the final ones reduced to skulls. These carvings, too, are an imitation of ornamentation in Glasgow Cathedral. Similarly, the supposed New World corn shown in the carvings has been interpreted by medieval scholars as stylized representations of native wheat and strawberries or lilies, as rendered in heraldic art. As for the Star of David carved into the floor, described in *The Da Vinci Code*, no such symbol exists. In one or two instances, it might just be possible to place a Masonic interpretation on carvings, but that is unsurprising, since they were restored in the 1860s by David Bryce, an Edinburgh architect who was a prominent Freemason. The interpretation of the patterns on 213 boxes in the chapel's stonework as a musical notation is surely a triumph of imagination over reality.

It speaks volumes about human credulity that, on the basis of so much nonevidence, addicts of bizarre theorizing can confidently proclaim that the burial vault beneath Rosslyn Chapel holds the Holy Grail, or the treasure of the Templars (who cunningly buried it among the tombs of a family that was testifying against them), or—more dementedly and blasphemously—the head of Christ. Yet sensible people should not on that account be deterred from visiting an interesting medieval church decorated with artwork of considerable accomplishment, on the realistic premise that, at Rosslyn, what you see is what you actually get. That is more than can be said for the second "Templar" site we shall now investigate.

Rennes-le-Château, France: Wholly Bunk, Hoary Tale

Even the far-fetched distortions of history and leaps of the imagination associated with Rosslyn Chapel pale into insignificance beside the farrago of nonsense surrounding the massive confidence trick that is the legend of Rennes-le-Château, originating in the inventions of a hard-up restaurateur trying to make a fast buck—or, since he was French, a fast franc. That enterprising fabrication has now taken on a life of its own, begetting countless offspring delusions and generating an entire industry based on fantasy, false history, and a lie deeply offensive to all Christians, which, if perpetrated against the Prophet Muhammad, would almost certainly have resulted in a fatwah.

To delve beneath the layers of misinformation and present the true facts, here is what actually happened. Bérenger Saunière, a Frenchman of rebellious temperament, entered the Church and served as parish priest of the poor village of Rennes-le-Château, in the Aude region of France, from 1885 to 1909. After some time, despite his known poverty and that of his parishioners, he became noticeably affluent and embarked on a number of building projects around the village. These included renovation of his church and presbytery, the construction of a handsome villa for himself, and a tower roughly modeled on the *Migdal David* (Tower of David) in Jerusalem, called in French the *Tour Magdala,* which served as his private library. Eventually, the Church authorities became concerned about how a dirt-poor parish priest in a village of three hundred souls could afford to live in this lavish style, so they launched an investigation. The answer was simple: Saunière was a crook. He had been selling Masses—thousands of them, most of which had never been celebrated. He had done so by employing modern marketing methods—advertising his services and receiving stipends by mail. Some people sent a sizable sum, to ensure the celebration of a number of Masses for the repose of the souls of loved ones. Over years, this scam had netted Saunière a good income. He was convicted of fraud in the Episcopal Court of Carcassonne in 1910. His guilt was not in doubt—he had listed his crooked transactions in account books. On August 23, 1910, the court recorded that he had amassed, over twenty-five years, 193,150 francs (more than a million dollars in today's money) for thousands of unsaid Masses. There was no mystery about his wealth, which was already exhausted: He eked out a precarious existence for the remainder of his days, selling rosaries and religious medals.

Obviously, a scandal involving their parish priest provided

considerable grist for gossip and speculation among the local population, so after his death an aura of mystery surrounded Saunière, even as the memory of the prosaic and squalid scandal in which he had actually been involved faded. In the 1940s a man named Noël Corbu bought the small estate the priest had created with his ill-gotten gains, and in 1955 set up a restaurant there. Since Rennes-le-Château was off the beaten track, customers were hard to come by, so Corbu set out to embellish the legends surrounding Saunière in hopes of creating a tourist trade. Early in 1956 he gave an interview to the local newspaper in which he claimed that, while renovating his church, Saunière had discovered parchments revealing the whereabouts of a treasure belonging to Queen Blanche of Castile, the wife of King Louis VIII of France. Thus began the exponential growth of the legend of Rennes-le-Château. The claim was spotlighted in a French television documentary, after which much more ambitious mythmakers than Corbu carried the story forward.

That same year, 1956, a French draftsman named Pierre Plantard, who had already served a prison sentence for fraud, set up an organization called the Priory of Sion in the town of Annemasse on the Swiss-French border. It had no Templar significance at the time: The *Sion* in the title referred to a nearby mountain. Plantard heard about Corbu's story, met him a few years later, and intruded himself into the mythology by claiming the parchments found by Saunière supported his claim to be the modern descendant of the last Merovingian king of France, Dagobert II. He also changed his name to Plantard de St.-Clair. Even at this stage the nonsense might easily have been contained, had not Plantard teamed up with Philippe de Chérisey, who, besides having a career as a writer, radio humorist, and actor, was also a brilliant forger whose work has excited admiration even among the scholars who have exposed it, and the writer Gérard de Sède. Chérisey concocted cleverly forged documents, some of which the conspirators contrived to plant in the Bibliothèque nationale in Paris. Meanwhile, Gérard de Sède wrote a book called *L'Or de Rennes* (The Gold of Rennes), based on these documents, which would later be "discovered." It was a highly skilled and successful hoax. The documents looked convincing, although analysis of them some time ago proved them to be then only forty years old.

The final combustion was triggered when three coauthors—Michael Baigent, Richard Leigh, and Henry Lincoln—published a book in 1982 titled *The Holy Blood and the Holy Grail,* later abbreviated to *Holy Blood Holy Grail.* By this stage, the story had taken on a distasteful and offensive aspect with the claim that Christ had married St. Mary Magdalen (the church at Rennes-le-Château was dedicated to her) and left as his bloodline descendants by her the Merovingian royal line. Since the church at Rennes-le-Château was not as rich in symbolism as Rosslyn Chapel, much was made of the inscription above the door: *Terribilis est locus iste* (Terrible is this place—surely a sign of dark mystery). In fact, it is a phrase drawn from the formal Dedication of a Church, more lengthily reading: "This is a place of awe; this is the house of God, the gate of heaven . . ." (Genesis 28:17). It can be seen in other churches as well. The authors threw everything into the ragout—Merovingians, Templars, treasure, even the painting *Et in Arcadia Ego* by Nicolas Poussin. Eventually, it turned out to be too rich a concoction even for Plantard, grand master of the Priory of Sion, which was now revealed as the manipulative power behind the Templars over centuries (even though it had only been founded in 1956), who broke ranks with the authors in 1986 and denounced the documents and the Merovingians. Plantard died in 2000, thus missing out on the climactic consequence of his hoax—the publication three years later of Dan Brown's novel *The Da Vinci Code.*

At least Brown had the grace to purvey his material as fiction, unlike previous peddlers of Templar/Merovingian/Masonic exotica and blasphemous fabrications regarding Christ. The innumerable mistakes and solecisms in the book, which makes solemn claims as to its accuracy, have caused much hilarity among its more literate reviewers. One much-quoted phrase is a reference to "the misty hills of Kent spreading wide beneath the descending plane." Considering that the county of Kent is known as the "garden of England," with its flat acres of hop fields, this suggests that, although Brown may be privy to much esoteric knowledge, that gnosis does not include the basic geography of Britain. A frightening survey suggested that six million people in Britain believed *The Da Vinci Code* was true, which lends weight to the remark often attributed to G. K. Chesterton that when people stop believing in God, they won't believe in nothing— they will believe in anything. One Oxbridge academic has plausibly suggested that much of the popularity of *The Da Vinci Code* in Anglo-Saxon countries can be attributed to its tapping into the anti-Catholic prejudice that is never far below the surface in those societies.

That readership must particularly enjoy the new player that Brown brings to the table to refresh the clichéd Templars and Priory of Sion: the Catholic prelature Opus Dei, caricatured in the novel as a band of monkish assassins. Ironically, not only did Opus Dei experience a marked rise in interest in membership as a result of the novel and film (much of it surely counterproductive, if inquirers were hoping to sign up for a spot of murder), but the "elegant understatement" of its measured refutation of Brown's portrayal of the organization is now studied in American journalism schools as a model of good PR. So what exactly is Opus Dei and where do its members hang out?

Villa Tevere: The Headquarters of Opus Dei in Rome

Opus Dei (Work of God) is something of a contemporary Rorschach inkblot test, with people tending to see whatever they are looking for, including every type of wickedness, from "uncovered extravagant religious practices, alleged corruption, and authoritarianism" to global conspiracy. Visitors to the Villa Tevere, Opus Dei's now-famous world headquarters in Rome, may be puzzled by the conventional, business-like atmosphere there, similar to that of a large law or management consulting firm. Perhaps that is unsurprising, since the majority of members are laypeople currently working as executives, academics, and journalists. In a city positively bursting with ancient artifacts and florid symbolism, nothing of that kind is in evidence inside this rather ordinary and unadorned villa at 75 Viale Bruno Buozzi, which incorporates part of a former Hungarian embassy.

The only place of note inside is the crypt where Opus Dei's founder was initially entombed under a simple slab with a cross and the words *El Padre,* though after his canonization in 2002 his remains were transferred to a more substantial altar there. St. Josemaría Escrivá de Balaguer y Albás (to give him his full name) remains a bogeyman figure to many both within and outside the Church, and perhaps provides evidence that saints are sometimes known by the embarrassment and annoyance they provoke. Father Escrivá was, among other things, known for his intense Spanish energy, effervescence, and joke-cracking; but diocesan bureaucrats were rarely amused—and considered his group suspect in its early years. Later, after the Second Vatican Council and without regard for political correctness, he complained about the banalization of the liturgy, and prophetically told priests to hang onto their old missals and vestments, as they would be needed again someday (turns out he was correct). A further embarrassment to many was his reclaiming of an old noble title for his family, in recognition of both its heritage and the sacrifices it had made for him, a priest who liked to rock the boat. In 1968, he was confirmed as the rightful Marquis de Peralta, a title that later passed to his brother.

His successors in "The Work" (as members refer to the organization) rarely like to talk about these vignettes, as Opus Dei's culture combines orthodoxy with an avoidance of anything that might be perceived as eccentric. In the area of membership expansion, it continues to have all the energy and spit-and-polish of a U.S. Marine Corps recruiting operation. By an irony likely to have been enjoyed by its witty founder, the Opus Dei headquarters is on a street named after a trade union leader who was notably hostile to the Church. (The current headquarters of the Italian Democratic Socialist Party is only a couple of doors down too, at number 87.)

Aficionados of *The Da Vinci Code,* however, who lurk outside the villa in Viale Bruno Buozzi in the hope of sighting sinister monkish assassins are doomed to disappointment. For this is another target of conspiracy theorists that does not make the cut. Opus Dei is a genuine Catholic devotional organization seeking the sanctification of its members. It was founded in Spain in 1928 and that origin has given it a cultural orientation that is largely foreign to Anglo-Saxon societies; hence the misunderstanding of its character. It has no "monks," but rather members who are divided among supernumeraries (usually married men or women with careers), accounting for 70 percent of the membership; numeraries (living celibate lives in Opus Dei centers while also pursuing careers), representing about 20 percent of the members; numerary assistants (celibate female members, without careers, who look after the running of the centers); and associates (also celibate, but not based in centers and usually having family or professional commitments). The spiritual needs of these members are served by the priests who belong to the prelature and comprise 2 percent of the membership. The total membership is around 87,000.

Opus Dei is called a prelature because it is under the jurisdiction of a prelate appointed by the pope, rather than local diocesan bishops. It has attracted much hostility within the Catholic Church because of its privileged position. Contrary to popular superstition, it is not particularly secretive, beyond the discretion that most organizations observe regarding their affairs (how much does the public know—or want to know—about the internal workings of, say, Rotary International?). Members may not advertise their affiliation to Opus Dei among office colleagues; but if they did it might be regarded as a sign of eccentricity or a pose of moral superiority. Opus Dei is distrusted in the modern, secular world because it is what the Church calls "a sign of contradiction": It swims against the current of modern, morally relativist society—it does not go with the flow. Its self-discipline is regarded as sinister in a post-Freudian culture that has been taught to distrust "repression." Much has been made of the organization's penitential practices. The most "extreme" is the *cilice,* a small metal chain with inwardly pointing spikes worn around the thigh that chafes the flesh but does not draw blood. It might not be to everybody's taste, but mortification and penance have a long tradition in many religions.

That, with apologies to Dan Brown fans, is as medieval as it gets. As a sinister, murderous, secret society seeking world domination, Opus Dei simply doesn't cut it.

The Hotel de Bilderberg and the Bilderberg Group, The Netherlands

In case readers are by now feeling that their cherished illusions of esoteric conspiracies and underground nexuses of power are being relentlessly dispelled by prosaic reality, here is a shadowy entity on which the jury at least is still out: the Bilderberg Group. Its precise agenda is a matter of speculation and bitter contention; its meetings are totally private; and whether its influence is good, bad, or neutral is a matter of dispute. But one thing is certain: There is no way it can be written off as lacking power and influence, considering its membership and the attendees it attracts to its meetings: They are not bogus Templars or esoteric fantasists—these are heavy hitters.

In a wooded part of the Dutch countryside, close to Arnhem, where the ill-fated Allied airborne assault in World War II went so badly wrong, stands the luxurious Hotel de Bilderberg, from which the publicity-shy group takes its name. You will not find any armed guards there, however, nor will you sight world statesmen or conspirators strolling its elegant grounds: You would be more than half a century too late for that—they all left in 1954, taking with them the name of the hotel where they first met as an informal group. Insofar as the "Bilderbergers" have any kind of headquarters, it is minimalist in the extreme: P.O. Box 3017, 2301 DA, Leiden, The Netherlands. A call to the Leiden office will produce in response only an automated voice inviting you to leave a message. That will not be entirely unproductive: The group has thawed sufficiently in its attitude toward publicity to send out a free pamphlet to inquirers. Nowadays, the Bilderberg Group also issues a brief press release at the time of its yearly meeting, and a list of attendees is available by faxed request. The list is not a comprehensive identification of everybody involved, since new attendees are brought in at each meeting while others take a pass, but there is a steering committee composed of two representatives each from around eighteen countries. Bilderberg attendees represent the crème de la crème of international politics, defense, banking, and multinational corporations.

The group was the brainchild of Józef Retinger, a cosmopolitan Polish intellectual and political adviser whose best friend was the Polish writer Joseph Conrad and who was an inveterate intriguer who mysteriously had the ear of some of the most powerful people in Europe. During the Second World War, Retinger made his way to London, where he worked as an aide to General Sikorski, the Polish prime minister in exile. Under the code name "Salamander," he parachuted into Nazi-occupied Poland on a covert intelligence mission—despite having never undertaken a practice jump. He survived the war, including at least one assassination attempt. By the early 1950s, Retinger had become concerned about increasing anti-American feeling throughout Europe, so he set up an informal but highly secret meeting of senior politicians in an apartment in Paris in 1952. It was regarded as useful, so in 1954 it was organized on a more formal basis at the Hotel de Bilderberg in the Netherlands. By a touch of genius, Retinger induced the clubbable Prince Bernhard of the Netherlands to chair the meetings, which he did until 1976 when his disgrace in the Lockheed bribery scandal forced his resignation and the cancellation of that year's Bilderberg conference. Retinger died in 1960, but his legacy, the Bilderberg Group, has gone from strength to strength, still meeting in a luxury hotel in a different country each year, usually with around 120 people attending. (Of a similar elite cachet is the annual meeting of the World Economic Forum in Davos, Switzerland, but the extroverted, publicity-generating buzz of Davos is entirely different, with some three thousand participants and accompanying guests, public webcasts, and large battalions of invited journalists.)

Over the years Bilderberg has hosted such luminaries as Denis Healey, later British chancellor of the exchequer; David Rockefeller; Henry Kissinger; Margaret Thatcher; Donald Rumsfeld; Paul Wolfowitz, former head of the World Bank; Crown Prince Philippe of Belgium; and a host of chief executives of corporations, such as Nokia, BP, Unilever, Daimler, and Pepsi. Bilderberg stands accused of securing the promotion of its protégés to high office; but the fact that both Bill Clinton and Tony Blair took over the governance of their countries shortly after attending a Bilderberg meeting more likely indicates informed talent scouting by the organization and a keenness to bring onboard those who are clearly headed for positions of power under their own steam. Bilderberg has fierce critics, among them journalist James P. "Big Jim" Tucker, of *American Free Press,* who has stalked the organization since 1975 to try to penetrate its secrecy, and Russian-born Daniel Estulin, author of the book *The True Story of the Bilderberg Group.* To such critics Bilderberg is a secretive nexus of power and influence promoting globalization and a new world order.

They make some telling points, but there is a chicken-and-egg dilemma here: Do these individuals hold increased power because of their Bilderberg affiliation, or are they simply invited to meetings because they are powerful? Is Bilderberg not just the institutionalization of an existing reality—that elites will always rule, if only because any alternative is anarchical? It was implausible, in its formative years, to suppose that Bilderberg had a defined left or right agenda, since politicians of all stripes attended. At the founding meeting in Paris, both Antoine Pinay, France's conservative prime minister, and Guy Mollet, of the Socialist opposition, attended—a fact that had to be kept secret. In recent times, however, ideology has largely dissolved and politics in the Western world has become more consensual. Politicians are never more dangerous than when they are in agreement with one another, and arrayed against the interests of electorates. In this climate it is likely that Bilderberg does not set an agenda, but simply creates an atmosphere of consensus—the most effective kind of influence that can be exerted—favoring whatever ideas or policy thrusts are currently in vogue among elites. If that is so, it is of concern to democratic societies. One thing is certain: Unlike the Priory of Sion and others of their ilk, the individuals in this group could not avoid being massively powerful, even if they tried.

Vauxhall Cross: London's Secret Intelligence Service (MI6) Headquarters

One of the sensational (and partly substantiated) claims regarding Bilderberg founder Józef Retinger that surfaced after his death was that he had been an agent of Britain's Secret Intelligence Service, popularly known as MI6. Of the two masters Retinger allegedly served, it is an irony that the allegedly democratic forum he founded, despite its influence, has no visible headquarters, whereas the Secret Service now occupies one of the most high-profile buildings in London. The headquarters of SIS, or MI6, at 85 Vauxhall Cross, Albert Embankment, on the south bank of the Thames beside Vauxhall Bridge, is something of a tourist attraction (though, unlike the CIA, it offers no museum or public tours, by appointment or otherwise). Designed by Sir Terry Farrell on a dramatic riverside location on the Thames, it is a Ziggurat-like, ultramodern structure, with between nine and twelve visible stories—it's not possible to tell for certain. It was built at a total cost of almost £153 million ($226 million), of which £17 million ($25 million) was due to the special inbuilt security features, including bomb-blast protection, bulletproof walls, triple glazing to block electronic eavesdropping and jamming, vast computer suites, emergency backup systems, reinforced doors, and—in more traditional defensive mode—two moats. One of the difficulties attending its construction and funding was that, in those days (1988–1995) the British government did not acknowledge the existence of MI6, until it was "placed on a statutory footing by the Intelligence Services Act 1994," to use the wonderful phraseology of the civil service.

The security precautions proved necessary on September 20, 2000, when the building was attacked by the Real IRA (RIRA) terrorist group, using a Russian-built RPG-22 antitank missile, which hit the eighth floor, but did little damage. The attack on the building that has probably remained more firmly lodged in the public imagination was the fictitious explosion there in the precredits sequence of the James Bond film *The World is Not Enough*. Initially, the government refused permission to film there, on security grounds, but then agreed. Robin Cook, the then–foreign secretary, observed: "After all Bond has done for Britain, it was the least we could do for Bond." The building, occupied since 1995, is known to those who work there as "Legoland." Some details of its construction remain classified, but much of its space is underground and there is strongly rumored to be a tunnel leading from it, under the Thames, to government ministries in Whitehall.

Britain's intelligence apparatus was originally founded in 1909 as the Secret Service Bureau. At the outbreak of World War I the Bureau's foreign section became the Directorate of Military Intelligence Section 6 (MI6), under the direction of Captain Sir George Mansfield Smith-Cumming, a gentleman spy in the John Buchan amateur mold who successfully traveled through Germany and the Balkans posing as a high-powered German businessman—despite not speaking a word of German. Smith-Cumming initialed documents simply as "C." Since then, the head of MI6 has been code-named "C" (translated to "M" by Ian Fleming in his James Bond novels). After World War I, MI6 was housed at 54 Broadway, off Victoria Street, London SW1, from 1924 to 1966 (though its chiefs operated from St. James's Street, the heart of London's clubland, from which its members were mostly recruited), then at Century House, 100 Westminster Bridge Road, Lambeth, from 1966 to 1995.

The secretive existence of MI6 contrasted with the high-profile headquarters of other intelligence agencies, such as the spine-chilling Moscow base of the KGB (with the public statue of its sinister founder Felix Dzerzhinsky) at the Lubyanka Prison and the iconic Langley, Virginia campus of the CIA. In compensation, MI6 and the domestic counterintelligence service MI5 made frequent operational use of other people's sanctuaries around the globe, both louche and luxurious. These included such comfortable way stations for the world's rich and powerful as Claridge's, the famous London hotel, located on Mayfair's Brook Street. As Peter Wright, former domestic intelligence operative of *Spycatcher* fame, revealed: "This London hotel was a favourite among distinguished visitors. For convenience, it had all rooms permanently bugged. This sensible arrangement saved us at MI5 a great deal of trouble going to and fro." Today, MI6 has joined the open market, with its own online Web site (which is more than the security-conscious Bilderberg Group condescends to do), including an application form for aspiring spooks and a specimen "cover story" to be memorized within two minutes as an aptitude test. Sir Mansfield Smith-Cumming—the original "C"—would not have been impressed.

Rosicrucian Park, San José, and Club 33, Anaheim, California

No offense to the citizens of the Golden State, but most of them would freely admit that, in the kookiness stakes, California is a major-league contender. Here we look at a couple of sanctuaries sited in California, one of which is classically esoteric, the other more conventionally catering to an exclusive clientele, its chief point of interest being that it is situated in the most unlikely of places—in fact, within one of the world's leading temples of frivolity.

Considering California's wealth of supposedly mystical sites, users of the American Automobile Association guidebooks must occasionally find themselves frustrated—especially if they are engaged in a desperate search for hidden knowledge and revelations of long-held secrets. The AAA Tourbook, for example, recommends visiting Rosicrucian Park, the world headquarters of the Ancient Mystical Order Rosae Crucis (AMORC) in San José. Visitors probably won't find much in the way of mind-blowing illumination, but the campus-like buildings and grounds, including an Egyptian museum and planetarium, have a delightfully kitsch 1930s feel about them. The whole ensemble encompasses a city block in what is now Silicon Valley, but as one wag has suggested, the Rose-Croix University on the premises probably doesn't provide course transfer credits to Stanford. The outfit was the brainchild of New Jersey–born H. Spencer Lewis, who claimed he "crossed the threshold" in Toulouse in 1909 and was invested with the momentous secrets of the age-old Rosicrucian brotherhood. An illustrator by trade, Lewis pioneered the use of mass-market advertising for mail-order Rosicrucian correspondence courses (one of whose distance learning students turned out to be Sirhan Sirhan, later the assassin of Bobby Kennedy). Lewis is also credited with inventing three devices: the Luxatone (or "Color Organ"), the Cosmic Ray Coincidence Counter, and the Sympathetic Vibration Harp. AMORC has operated worldwide for some seven decades, and also claims a special knowledge of Atlantis. According to its key documents, it alternates between "108-year cycles of activity and inactivity." Perhaps one should visit while there is still time.

If some of the more far-fetched conspiracy theories have a flavor of Disneyland, that is exactly where one such myth is based. Spinners of urban legends sometimes claim that the body of Walt Disney was cryonically frozen at the time of his death in 1966, with his body "cryopreserved" in a low-temperature chamber beneath Disneyland's Pirates of the Caribbean ride. It is true that cryonics became a crackpot fad in the mid-1960s, based on the scientifically suspect idea that human remains might be resuscitated at some point in the future, perhaps hundreds or thousands of years from now when medicine is infinitely more advanced. Woody Allen's film *Sleeper* poked fun at the concept, while West Point dropout and psychedelic guru Dr. Timothy Leary made arrangements to have himself frozen—before deciding that was one ultimate trip he didn't want to take, saying, "I was worried that I would wake up in fifty years surrounded by humorless people with clipboards."

The Walt Disney cryonics legend is in fact pure hokum, as he had a relatively traditional burial at Forest Lawn Memorial Park in Glendale, California. Fans can pay their respects at his gravesite in a quiet corner of the cemetery, itself a kind of theme park concept satirized by Evelyn Waugh in his wickedly funny 1948 novella about the Los Angeles funeral business—*The Loved One.*

Disneyland did, however, have a couple of strictly private

sanctuaries, the surviving one of which is the little-known and exclusive Club 33. Walt Disney maintained a secret apartment above the Fire Station on "Main Street, USA," from which he'd monitor crowd numbers and watch the gleeful expressions of children and their parents in what he dubbed "the happiest place on earth." But his other secret retreat survives today, concealed behind a very discreet house number ("33") and buzzer within the New Orleans Square section of the park—at 33 Rue Royale. Prior to his death, Disney had worked intensively on a personal project to create a secret club within Disneyland where visiting dignitaries could be stylishly entertained in private amid his best movie memorabilia, with fine dining and good wines (the theme park being otherwise dry). Club 33 opened in 1967 and remains officially nonexistent to passersby among the paying guests of Disneyland, who are blissfully unaware of the lavish Victorian-style interiors filled with valuable Disneyana behind the façade. Its membership waiting list is said to be fourteen years long.

So there are plenty of authentic and sinister mysteries remaining to be explored in these pages, but, as we have already shown, some secret sanctuaries and their devotees are pure Mickey Mouse.

Chapter 2

SHRINES AND SANCTUARIES,
ANCIENT AND MODERN

H. G. Wells and Philip K. Dick were just two of many science-fiction writers who have been drawn to the theme of time travel. Actually there is a time machine in existence, and it is called Japan—which is at once a place of the near future and of the distant past. Visitors can encounter a putative version of their own life a few years from now, with domestic robots, astonishingly computerized bathrooms, voice-activated sensors, and sleek visual displays at every turn. But a trip to Japan is also a trip down memory lane—to what are arguably humanity's oldest political forms and deepest spiritual impulses. Almost all human societies began with some form of sacral kingship, with the monarch as father, priest, and governor. Likewise, the search by the human race for meaning and transcendence began with primitive animism and folklore. Japan's Ise Shrine is a unique fusion of both dimensions, a kind of time capsule like no other on earth, as described below.

Ise Shrine, Japan

The Ise Jingu is the most sacred shrine in Japan, situated in the small city of Ise in the Mie Prefecture on southern Honshu Island, 87 miles (140km) southeast of Kyoto and 100 miles (161km) southeast of Osaka, within the Ise-Shima National Park. Altogether there are around 120 small shrines, but the two important ones are the Geku, or Outer Shrine, dedicated to Toyouke no Omikami, the goddess of the harvest, while the Naiku, or Inner Shrine, the most sacred of all, is dedicated to the sun goddess Amaterasu, from whom the Japanese imperial family claims descent. A peculiarity of the site is that, although it is very ancient, dating back to AD 478, in the case of the Outer Shrine, the structure is ceremonially demolished every twenty years and replaced with similar buildings. This rebuilding was first carried out in 690 and the sixty-first restructuring was finished in 1993, so the next replacement will occur in 2013. This has resulted in very ancient carpentry and construction skills that might not otherwise have survived being passed down among craftsmen from father to son to service the shrines.

The Outer Shrine is approached via a wooden bridge over a river, then the path through the trees (it is situated within a forest of more than 200 acres [80ha] in extent) leads to a *torii* gateway, a standard feature of Shinto temples consisting of two uprights joined above by two crossbeams. After passing various ancillary buildings, the pilgrim arrives at a thatched gatehouse set in a fence made of cedar. There are four concentric fences guarding the sacred compound, but the others are academic as far as more than 99 percent of visitors are concerned: Only the emperor, members of his family, and the Ise-Jingu priests are allowed to pass beyond the gateway in the second fence, where the way to the sacred compound is obscured by a white curtain. The roofs of the three buildings can be glimpsed: two small structures for housing ceremonial accessories and vestments and a larger edifice called the Shoden, twenty feet (6m) high, resting on pillars and with a thatched roof hanging from one long timber running the length of the building. The three structures are made of unvarnished cypress, without any nails, using traditional joinery techniques instead.

The approach to the Inner Shrine, situated three miles (4.8km) to the southeast, is similar: Again, visitors traverse a bridge and enter through a *torii* gate, but with the addition of steps leading down to a beach where they wash their hands and mouths and, if they wish, pause to feed the sacred carp. Then, after passing the stables housing the sacred horses of the Ise Jingu and the equally sacred cowshed, the pilgrims (there are six million of them every year) arrive at stone steps leading to another gatehouse with a symbolic curtain of exclusion, at which point the journey ends. The layout of this compound is similar to the first, but the inner sanctum has the special distinction of housing one of the three great treasures of the imperial house: the Yata no Kagami, a sacred bronze mirror that is a replica of the one said to have been given by the sun goddess to the founder of the dynasty. Without it and the other two treasures—a sword called the Kusanagi no Tsurugi, kept at a shrine in Nagoya, and the Yasakani no Magatama, or crown jewels, held in the imperial palace in Tokyo—no emperor can succeed to the throne. That is the doctrine of the descent from Amaterasu on which the legitimacy of the dynasty depends.

Divine bloodlines seem to be a popular subject these days, given *The Da Vinci Code* and other best sellers, but the Japanese imperial family "clarified" its position in 1945, sidestepping any earlier attributions of semidivine status. Their ancestry is, of course, understood to be mythical, much as the austere beauty of Ise and other key Shinto shrines represents a connection more to national folklore than to what theologians of other faiths would call "truth claims" about the nature of existence. The late Georgetown University professor Cyril Toumanoff was perhaps the leading expert on families with mythical divine status. According to his lifelong study, he found that, apart from the Japanese imperial family, only a small handful of still-existing Balto-Slavic, Scandinavian, Celtic, and Armeno-Georgian noble families could claim any similar status. Scholarly literature in Europe refers to these families as "dynastic princes," who gave up their godlike status when they became Christian (and whose titled descendants now live in such decidedly worldly places as New York and London). Toumanoff's description could just as easily have been applied to the Japanese imperial family: ". . . these dynasts incarnated sovereignty once diffused in an entire tribe and were, according to pagan belief, theophanic, sprung from the gods and by reason of their 'divine blood'—their *ichor*—set apart from other men." (In a different category, of course, are those Asian rulers who claim, or claimed, semidivine status through reincarnation rather than ancestry.)

At the end of the Second World War, there were vigorous debates within the Truman administration about the pros and cons of abolishing the Japanese monarchy, including the possibility of putting on trial (and perhaps even hanging) Emperor Hirohito (now referred to after his death as the "Showa Emperor"). The better part of wisdom turned out to be allowing the imperial family to stay on, given its potential influence as a role model and stabilizing force—an argument also advanced by Winston Churchill, who noted that the demise of the Imperial German Crown after World War I provided a convenient vacuum for Hitler and other lowlife types to fill. General Douglas MacArthur, who exercised supreme authority over Japan from 1945 to 1951, didn't need a great deal of convincing; as it turns out he was, in private, a lifelong monarchist (and even a member of the Royal Stuart Society in the UK). Debate will never end on the question of the Showa Emperor's responsibility for the war in its various aspects, but there is little doubt that effective control of Japanese policy was for many years in the hands of a junta of hard-line army generals (who were very different from their less bellicose—and less powerful—navy colleagues). When it came to what Japan chose to do, the army brass called the shots. But these are still sensitive subjects in Japan, and probably not good topics to bring up in casual conversation with the Japanese clients you just met over a round of martinis at the historic Frank Lloyd Wright–designed bar of the Imperial Hotel in Tokyo, just around the corner from the palace.

Yasukuni Shrine, Tokyo

Arguably the most controversial place in Japan is the Yasukuni Shrine in Tokyo, which commemorates as "enshrined divinities" some 2.5 million Japanese war dead since the nineteenth century. As these include 1,068 individuals convicted of war crimes, among them twelve "class A" war criminals and a further two suspected of that status, visits to the shrine by senior Japanese politicians have sparked international controversy. The ceremonies and military museum at the shrine constitute a painfully sore point and a continuing irritant with China and Korea, in particular, although Australia and some other Asia-Pacific countries have also expressed their displeasure. Yasukuni is not an ancient shrine, but it nonetheless captures the primordial animism of Shinto and the warrior code of the Samurai. It is situated in the capital Tokyo on a fifteen-acre (6ha) site within a built-up area, with some subordinate structures standing on a ten-acre (4ha) causeway. Despite its currently controversial character, the shrine was originally built in 1869 by the Meiji emperor, in the wake of the restoration of his power; for centuries the emperors had been mere ciphers, with authority residing in the hands of the Shogun. After the Meiji Restoration in 1868, however, the imperial authority was restored, with a view toward modernizing Japan. Imperialists who had been killed during the Restoration struggle (the Boshin War of 1868–1869) were the first to be commemorated there. Since 1879 it has been known as the Yasukuni Jinja, the term meaning "Peaceful Country," a quotation from a classical Chinese text.

Even apart from the thorny political issues it raises, the Yasukuni is noticeably different from other Shinto shrines. As the visitor moves through the grounds in a westward direction, the first gate encountered is a massive *torii*—called the *Daiichi*—the largest in Japan, built not of wood, as at Ise, but of steel. Similarly, the next *torii*—the *Daini*—is made of bronze and is the biggest of that metal in the country. The following two gates are made of cypress, leading eventually to the *haiden*, or main prayer hall, dating from 1901 and hung with white screens. The heart of the shrine complex, however, is the *honden*, where the *kami* (souls of the fallen) are enshrined and where religious rites are performed by Shinto priests in strict privacy, with the public excluded. It is a steep-roofed, traditional structure with, to the rear of it on its eastern side, a building called the Reijibo Hoanden. Here the priority is security rather than aesthetics: To resist earthquakes the structure was built in concrete with money given for that express purpose by Emperor Hirohito. In Japanese folklore, deceased ancestors are revered as minor deities— spirit beings, if you will—and the shrine is said to provide a permanent residence for the spirits whose names are recorded on the handmade Symbolic Registry of Divinities, which is kept in this building.

The grounds of the shrine also incorporate various other memorials and buildings, including the unique Irei no Izumi monument—dedicated to soldiers who suffered from or died of thirst in battle—as well as a dovecote (where some three hundred white doves are kept) and a sumo ring for the periodic wrestling matches held there. The controversial military collection in the grounds—the Yushukan—is Japan's oldest museum, founded in 1882 but closed down after the Second World War. It reopened in 1985, and both China and Korea have described the exhibits as intolerable, saying that Europe, for example, would not tolerate a museum that justified—and glorified—Nazi Germany's war aims. The point of view expressed throughout the museum's well-presented exhibits is that Japan's war actions were justified by self-defense, given what it portrays as the bullying of the United States and the European colonial powers. To quote from one of the English-language displays on exhibit at the museum (which are sometimes revised because of external pressure):

> When President Franklin D. Roosevelt first took office, the U.S. was in the throes of the Great Depression; the economy still had not recovered when his third term began. Early on, Roosevelt had anticipated a major conflict. In 1939, he had resolved to join Great Britain in the war against Germany, but was hampered by American public opinion, which was strongly antiwar. The only option open to Roosevelt, who had been moving forward with his "Plan Victory," was to use embargoes to force resource-poor Japan into war. The U.S. economy made a complete recovery once the Americans entered the war.

Such sentiments are typical of those put forward at Yasukuni, but also on offer are various commemorations of bravery in the context of *bushido,* the country's famous warrior code. A statue and several exhibits recall the "Special Attack Heroes" (i.e., Kamikaze pilots) with these words: "These utterly pure and noble spirits who gave their lives for our country should be honored and remembered equally by our nation, and their stories should forever be passed on to future generations." The Japanese treated captured soldiers and civilian populations with appalling severity because their own view was that human beings worthy of the name would die rather than surrender. On this principle, some Japanese soldiers continued the fight into the 1970s, as strange, geriatric "holdouts" living in remote jungle locations in Southeast Asia—"the Emperor's last soldiers." The final Japanese officer to be captured was Captain Fumio Nakahira of the Imperial Army, who was apprehended on Mount Halcon on Mindoro Island in the Philippines in April, 1980.

Jokhang Temple, Lhasa, Tibet

Much more peaceful in character than the Yasukuni Shrine, but almost as ancient as the Ise Jingu, is the Jokhang Temple in Lhasa, the capital of Tibet. This is the most sacred shrine of Tibetan Buddhism, housing the Jowo Shakyamuni Buddha statue, the most revered religious object in the country. The Jokhang (House of the Buddha) Temple stands in Barkhor Square in central Lhasa, covering an area of around 27,000 square yards (22,575.5m^2). It is four stories high, its rooftops and pinnacles covered in gilded bronze tiles, and its signature emblem is the large dharma wheel flanked by two golden deer that dominates its frontage. The Jokhang dates from 642–647, when it was built by King Songtsan Gampo with the original name of the Rasa Tulnang Tsuklakang (The Magical Emanation at Rasa). *Rasa,* meaning "place of the goats," was the original name of the Tibetan capital, changed to Lhasa, "place of the gods," as a result of its emergence as a spiritual center. The Jokhang is surrounded by the Kora, a holy path of prayer around which pilgrims circulate throughout the day in a clockwise direction to earn spiritual merit. In doing so they intermingle with a residential area and a market, interspersed with small temples displaying prayer wheels and prayer poles. In front of the Jokhang there is a walled enclosure with some willow trees known as the Jowo Utra (Hair of the Jowo) and containing a stele (pillar) set up by the Chinese in the eighteenth century to combat a smallpox epidemic, and another with an inscription commemorating the ancient treaty made between Tibet and China in 822:

> Tibet and China shall abide by the frontiers they now occupy. Everything to the east is the country of Great China, and everything to the west is, unquestionably, the country of Great Tibet. Henceforth on neither side shall there be waging of war nor seizing of territory. If any person arouses suspicion he shall be detained, his business shall be investigated and he shall be escorted back.

According to legend, the construction of the temple came about when King Songtsan Gampo married two wives: Princess Bhrikuti of Nepal and Princess Wencheng of the Chinese Tang dynasty. Both wives brought a statue of Buddha to Tibet. To house the Chinese statue the king built the Little Jokhang, which provoked the jealousy of his Nepalese wife, who demanded similar honors for her own statue. So the king built the Jokhang for her, creating a temple complex in 647, at a time when he and his court, rather than residing in settled buildings, lived a nomadic existence in sumptuous tents. The Jokhang was built on the dried-up bed of a lake, said to be sited just above a sleeping demoness whose heart was imprisoned in the nether regions by having the temple constructed exactly above it. It is a wooden structure whose mix of architectural styles reflects the different influences brought to bear on Tibet during Songtsan Gampo's reign and long after. It combines the Indian vihara with Chinese Tang and Nepalese styles. Much of the existing structure dates back no further than the seventeenth century, when the complex was greatly expanded by the Fifth Dalai Lama, and the murals largely date from the eighteenth and nineteenth centuries; but the core parts of the Jokhang are very ancient indeed. Wood carving done by specialist Newar carpenters from the Nepal Valley can be dated stylistically back to the founding of the temple in 647, while radiocarbon dating of the columns in front of the main shrine, as well as later tests on a carved wood cornice lion, have established a seventh-century origin, confirming tradition.

The main hall of the Jokhang, therefore, is more than thirteen centuries old. It is approached from the east end of the enclosure in front of the temple, from which lines of votive lights provide a glowing flare path leading the visitor into the Jokhang. The devout prostrate themselves before entering. Passing beneath the famous dharma wheel and through the entrance, the passage leading into the great hall is lined with murals portraying the building of the temple. Then, in the center of the main hall, the visitor or pilgrim finds the heavily gilded and jeweled statue of Sakyamuni at the age of twelve, brought to Tibet by Princess Wencheng, on her marriage to the Tibetan monarch. This is the heart of the Jokhang and its raison d'être.

The remainder of the building is an elaborate complex of shrines containing some other famous statues. On the second floor are statues of the three individuals to whom the Jokhang owes its existence: King Songtsan Gampo and his two wives, Princess Wencheng, who converted him to Buddhism, and Princess Bhrikuti. Other well-known statues in the temple include representations of Chenresig (the embodiment of compassion in Tibetan Buddhism) and Padmasambhava (the historical teacher said to have converted Tibet to Buddhism). Unfortunately, although the Jokhang building survived depredation by the Mongols on several occasions, much of its statuary was smashed during the more recent Cultural Revolution and has had to be reproduced, though often incorporating fragments from the originals. The fourth floor is open, on the roof, and features four tile tops covered in gilded bronze. They are unmistakably Tang in influence. Overall, it is estimated to take a good two hours to do justice to the Jokhang, even simply as a sightseer with no religious duties to perform.

The Shrine of the Oracle at Delphi, Greece

The three shrines we have looked at so far, whether benevolent or malign, all have one thing in common: They are still very much in business. Yet there is one shrine that, for centuries, attracted pilgrims, was regarded as the spiritual focus of a highly evolved culture, and yet today lies in ruins, its spiritual authority a dead letter. Despite that reversal of its fortunes, by a kind of irony it is now drawing far more people to it than it attracted even in its heyday. The difference is that, whereas powerful kings once waited anxiously there to learn their fate, today's visitors are not believers but camera-clicking tourists. The Oracle of Apollo at Delphi was once the center of the civilized Western world; today, its beautiful location and picturesque ruins are crowded with so many people that an ancient Greek, if he were to revisit the site, would probably assume that popular beliefs were unchanged and Apollo was attracting more devotees than ever.

Situated on the southern slopes of Mount Parnassus in Greece, overlooking a valley lush with olive trees sweeping down toward the Gulf of Corinth—the "wine-dark sea" of classical Greek poetry that is more often turquoise blue—it is easy to understand why the ancients believed this to be the home of the gods. According to mythology, Zeus, the father of the gods, released two eagles from the extremities of the earth—east and west—and at the point where they met he cast a sacred stone to identify the center ("the navel") of the world. Apollo, son of Zeus, later slew the snakelike dragon Python that guarded this site and, in the form of a dolphin (hence the name *Delphi*), captured some sailors to serve as the first priests of his temple. This belief that Delphi was the center of the earth had many parallels in other mythologies, even, as we shall see later (in Chapter 4), in a perverted Nazi esotericism in modern times. In the preclassical era, it seems that this site was already imbued with religious significance, dedicated to an earth goddess whose cult was supplanted by the arrival of Greeks who replaced it with worship of Apollo. But the shrine that grew up here was not simply a place of worship but, more notably, of prophecy. Yet it was also a vital cultural center with theater and athletics strongly featured as well. Its growth began in the eighth century BC; by the sixth century BC, the shrine at Delphi had become the religious center of the Greek world, with a fame that reached beyond even that broad culture. This was mostly due to the celebrated Oracle of Apollo at Delphi, the system of augury and prophecy that fascinated the wisest philosophers of the ancient world.

From its substantial ruins and the writings of the ancients, it is possible to reconstruct what life was like at Delphi twenty-five centuries ago. The complex was set within a walled compound, the chief feature of which was the Temple of Apollo. Built in the familiar Doric style of classical architecture in the fourth century, this building was where the famous prophecies were delivered. The oracle—also known as a "Pythia"—was a woman over fifty years of age, chosen from among the peasants of the area for her impeccable character. Her forecasts were couched in language so ambiguous that all but the most naive must have concluded that she was hedging her bets. Nevertheless, the operation was conducted in a very sophisticated way. It is thought that, at one point, the Delphic Oracle had the most far-flung intelligence service in the Hellenic world—and beyond—gleaning information about politics, wars, and other topics so that the prophecies could be as grounded in real events as possible. She delivered her verdict seated on a tripod over a fissure in the ground from which some kind of vapors arose that were said to induce a trancelike condition, facilitating the oracle's prophetic gifts. As a preliminary, she would bathe in the nearby Kastalian Spring, dress in ceremonial robes, then receive the questions of the devout.

The seekers of advice (all men, since women were excluded) would also go through the preliminaries of registering, paying a fee, and purifying themselves in the Kastalian Spring (the bathing trough can still be seen). Then they would proceed along the Sacred Way, a tortuous stone-flagged path lined with statues and votive offerings, until they reached the Temple of Apollo. There they would sacrifice a sheep or a goat whose intestines would be inspected by the priests in search of omens. Unless some appalling augury had been detected, each pilgrim would then repair to a waiting room where he would hand over his question, inscribed on a lead tablet, to a priest. He would pass on the query to the Pythia who, inhaling the sulfurous vapors rising up from the crevice in the ground, would go into a trance, and utter sounds that the priest would translate into verses that amounted to riddles. This response would then be conveyed to the inquirer.

Not all clients were satisfied customers. The most notorious victim of the oracle's cryptic advice was the famously rich King Croesus of Lydia (now western Turkey). In 550 BC, when he was contemplating a war of aggression against Cyrus the Great of Persia, he thought it a sensible precaution, before attacking so formidable a potentate, to get a prediction as to the outcome from the Delphic Oracle. If anyone had a right to expect first-class service from the establishment at Delphi it was Croesus. As a sweetener to both Apollo and his representatives on Parnassus, Croesus sacrificed three hundred cattle to the god, besides sending 117 gold and silver bricks, jewels, sculptures, and a golden bowl weighing a quarter of a ton (227kg) to the priests at Delphi. His question was: Should he invade Persia? The Pythia sent the reassuring response that, if he crossed a river, "Croesus will destroy a great empire." Emboldened by this, Croesus marched across the River Halys into the territory of Cyrus the Great, only to be routed in battle, after which the Persians in turn invaded Lydia, sacked his capital of Sardis, and took Croesus prisoner. Later, Croesus reproachfully sent his chains to the oracle and demanded to know: "Why did you lie to me?" The cool response was that the prophecy had been accurate: Croesus had crossed a river and duly destroyed a great empire—his own kingdom of Lydia.

Above the portico of the Temple of Apollo was inscribed in gold letters the injunction that summarized the wisdom and philosophy of Delphi: "Know thyself." This advice was variously attributed to several sages, among them Pythagoras and Solon of Athens. For the Greek philosophers were greatly engaged with the shrine at Delphi. Plutarch, who had served as a priest at the shrine, wrote: "There are two sentences inscribed upon the Delphic Oracle, hugely accommodated to the usage of man's life: 'Know thyself' and 'Nothing too much'; and upon these all other precepts depend." But there was more than prophecy and philosophy going on at Delphi. Here, every four years, were held the Pythian Games, one of the four major sporting and dramatic festivals of classical Greece. The nearby sports stadium could seat seven thousand spectators and an open-air amphitheater for drama festivals with thirty-three tiers of seats that could accommodate five thousand people still stands, strikingly intact, beside the ruins of the Temple of Apollo.

Another great cultural feature of Delphi was the composition of hymns or "paeans" in honor of Apollo, an art form that reached its zenith in the second century BC. In 1893, French archaeologists discovered paeans to Apollo engraved on stone at Delphi; they have since been performed again, more than two millennia after their composition.

The decline of Delphi began with its occupation by the Romans in 191 BC. The oracle survived in a limited capacity, but political utterances were forbidden; only personal advice on such matters as love and travel, like a modern astrology column in a newspaper, were permitted. The Roman commander Sulla looted the shrine in 86 BC; but worse damage was done by the rapacious Emperor Nero who allegedly stole some five hundred bronze statues, leaving Delphi denuded of art. The neglected sanctuary became increasingly irrelevant with the spread of Christianity. Late in the fourth century AD, Emperor Julian the Apostate tried to revive paganism and ordered the restoration of Delphi; but, despite the imperial command, the oracle merely uttered a wailing sound and would not give prophecy. Shortly after, with the defeat and death of Julian, whose famous last words were "Galilean, thou hast conquered!" the Christian Emperor Theodosius the Great finally closed down the shrine in 390. A few years later the by-then-dilapidated temple was destroyed by the Emperor Arcadius in 398.

Today, the substantial remains at Delphi include the massive foundations of the temple, the base of its altar, and half a dozen columns still upright. The adjacent circular theater is well preserved and it is a curious experience for modern visitors to sit among its tiers and relive in their imagination the scenes of the past. But the jewel of Delphi is the small but well-preserved building known as the Treasury of the

Athenians, which housed offerings to Apollo. Formerly, a number of such treasuries stood in the sanctuary complex to hold the gifts sent to the priests at Delphi from cities and states across Greece. The Athenian Treasury alone has survived as an architectural gem, built in 490 BC to commemorate Athens' victory at the Battle of Marathon and regarded by antiquarians as a masterpiece of Doric design. The Kastalian Spring, too, can still be seen to the east of the site. Curiously, the one thing that is missing and that has caused disputes among scholars, despite its perfectly natural character, is the source of the geological gases that allegedly intoxicated the oracle. Some have discounted the story, though it is attested to by many witnesses. Modern research has detected geological faults beneath the temple that could historically have produced hydrocarbon gases generated by bituminous limestone, which would have had the described effects on somebody seated above the crevice.

What gives the visitor the most striking insight into the past artistic glories of the site is the Museum of Delphi, where all the surviving artifacts are displayed. Foremost among these is the heavily engraved "navel of the world," the omphalos stone. Other wonders include the famous "Charioteer" statue in bronze, a representation of the sphinx that demonstrates that this personification of the riddle (which Delphi turned into an industry) was not restricted to Egyptian culture, and the head of Dionysos. To gaze on these and the many other superb exhibits, and then to stand beside the temple ruins and look out toward the Gulf of Corinth is to travel back in time, for here at Delphi the past is always present.

The Esalen Institute, Big Sur, California

Close to the Temple of Apollo at Delphi is a site that the guardians of Greek culture are not so keen for tourists to visit: the Corycian Cave, dedicated to the less respectable god Pan, where every November rites were celebrated that amounted to drunken sexual orgies. This illustrates the way in which sanctuaries supposedly devoted to higher things may often gain a reputation for debauchery. That ambiguity has survived into modern times and you could not ask for a better example than California's most celebrated contribution to the counterculture, the Esalen Institute at Big Sur. Admittedly, connoisseurs of the sex, drugs, and rock 'n' roll tradition claim that Esalen today is a shadow of its former notoriety. But, in its heyday, this was a place of pilgrimage for the Beat generation, whose habitués may have regarded it as a modern Delphi, and it gave rise to as much scandal as the Corycian Cave in classical times.

Located on California's central coast about a four-hour drive south of San Francisco, Esalen stands on 120 acres (48ha) of land formerly belonging to the Esselen Indians, hence its name. Like Delphi, it overlooks the sea, on an idyllic cliff-top perch, with acres of spectacular gardens featuring a dazzling variety of flowers and an equally sumptuous array of vegetables to enrich the menu. The resemblance to Delphi is enhanced by Esalen's principal feature: hot springs pumping geothermal water at a temperature of 119 degrees Fahrenheit (48°C) into the baths where visitors bathe (mostly) in the nude—a reassuring throwback to the countercultural behavior that once made this place notorious. Though much tamer now, it still attracts ten thousand visitors a year.

Esalen was the brainchild of Michael Murphy and Richard Price, who met in a meditation workshop in San Francisco in 1960, just at the beginning of the hippie era. Both were influenced by the ideas of Aldous Huxley, in particular his notion of "human potentialities." They also wanted to incorporate into their thinking the less disciplined aspects of Eastern mysticism. The outcome was Esalen, established at Big Sur as a haven for Tantric thought and practice. It embodied what Frederic Spiegelberg, another strong influence on Murphy and Price, called the "religion of no religion." From this they derived the Esalen motto, "No one captures the flag," meaning that no one religion or philosophy must ever be allowed to dominate. This was a recipe for chaos and there was plenty of that in Esalen's early days, when celebrities of the hippie culture mixed with every variety of dropout and

Zen enthusiast. Instead of the hydrocarbon gases that had intoxicated the prophetesses at Delphi, Esalen had much more heady narcotics. Sexual license became a byword of existence there. The iconic comedy film about middle-class Americans struggling with the new "liberated" counterculture, *Bob & Carol & Ted & Alice,* released in 1969, had its opening scene set at Esalen—or a faithful parody of the institute. Jack Kerouac, not normally regarded as fastidious, registered a strong complaint about sperm and a dead otter in the baths. Even Esalen's live-and-let-live Zen tolerance had its limits.

In 1961, in an episode that became celebrated as "The Night of the Dobermans," Murphy and Price, assisted by folk singer Joan Baez and three Doberman Pinschers, evicted a group from San Francisco from the baths, where they were having an orgy. That did not mean that Esalen became tame and conventional for the remainder of the 1960s and 1970s: Participants were more often seen naked than clothed. Women who were diagnosed as suffering from fear of their private parts were invited to display them to fellow workshop members: Reticence was not regarded as a virtue at Esalen. The community had its own VD clinic, which suggests a healthy demand for such services. Massage—the signature "holistic" activity at Esalen—was given by naked masseuses to naked patients—six of them kneading a single individual on one reported occasion.

Countercultural celebrities abounded: Jane Fonda worked in the kitchen at one time; Hunter S. Thompson was a security guard, beaten up by some of the orgiasts frequenting the baths. Once the Beatles had earned enough money to reject the real world and immerse themselves in Eastern mysticism, George Harrison was to be found singing among the Tantric devotees, as was Bob Dylan. Allen Ginsberg looked in from time to time. Susan Sontag was a patron and, while Esalen never got its head around politics in any concrete way, one strongly suspects that, despite his California roots, Ronald Reagan did not pick up a lot of votes here.

One thing Esalen was not immune to was fashion. Zen gave way to Gestalt therapy in the psychological realm and to Rolfing—an extremely robust form of massage or "deep tissue bodywork" that effectively tore up the Geneva Convention as far as treatment of patients on the table was concerned—in the physical dimension. On the intellectual plane, Esalen never failed to furnish material for those who dismissed its ideas as "kooky," as when Terence McKenna, who taught there, interpreted extraterrestrial phenomena as "the human soul exteriorized into three-dimensional space as a religious experience."

A sign of the changing times was Esalen's program of "citizen diplomacy" sponsoring Soviet-American contacts—most notably Boris Yeltsin's trip to America in September 1989. The institute used to conduct workshops on such contentious topics as "The Value of Psychotic Experience"; today an unmistakable subtext of boardroom preoccupations and management-speak has entered its curriculum. Perhaps economic recession, in turn, will drive it back to its countercultural roots.

The institute has been far from trouble-free in recent years. In 1998 El Niño devastated the cliff-top baths and a landslide nearly destroyed the hot springs. It cost $5 million to renovate this focal amenity: Five hundred massive steel rods had to be inserted into the cliff, with a network of iron mesh to stabilize the site. The new bathhouse, whatever its functional merits, is certainly not classical in design.

The Esalen Institute defines its purpose as "to promote the harmonious development of the whole person. It is a learning organization dedicated to continual exploration of the human potential, and resists religious, scientific and other dogmas." A dissenting, contrarian graffito daubed on the institute's welcome sign famously offered an alternative analysis: "Jive s*** for rich white folk." Presumably the author had issues about getting in touch with his inner child and would have benefited from a good Rolfing. It must be conceded that that graffito expressed the skeptical majority view of Esalen, the chief sanctuary of fading New Age illusions. If you feel that its history and practices are radically different from your own daily experience of hometown America, remember that it isn't America—it's California.

Chapter 3

THE TEMPLE, THE ARK, AND
THE GRAIL

hat has been the fastest-growing industry of the past decade? While the online social networking business represented by Facebook and MySpace springs immediately to mind, the answer—as we've suggested already—might well be the manufacture of new (and frequently outlandish) theories about the Templars. The narrative tends to go like this: The Templars survived their unfair suppression, having gone underground to act as custodians of important hidden spiritual knowledge and devastating secrets. In many cases, Freemasonry, the Holy Grail, and even the Ark of the Covenant get woven into the story line. However, most serious scholars have dismissed such claims as the product of overheated imaginations marketed to gullible consumers, having assumed that the Templars were innocent, had their valuable property ripped off, and then were wiped out for good. Perhaps it might take a Nobel laureate or two to untangle fact from fiction.

The Bååtska Palace, Stockholm

The Nobel Prize actually has some relevance here, as each December newly named Nobel laureates arrive in the cold, dark, but rather atmospheric Swedish capital of Stockholm to receive their medals, diplomas, and hefty cash prizes. As always, they are put up across the water from the Royal Palace in the Grand Hotel, a posh place owned by the Wallenbergs—"the Rockefellers of Sweden"—where Ingrid Bergman and other jet-setters used to enjoy the smorgasbord in the glamorous Veranda restaurant. You can imagine a famous physicist or

economist feeling a bit dreamy after nibbling the lunch buffet of her-
ring, gravlax, and filet of reindeer, with views—in good weather—of
steam yachts bobbing up and down on the water outside the hotel.
You could also forgive such a scholar for totally overlooking the
rather mysterious Baroque palace right next door that appears to be
flying a Templar flag—a place known as the Bååtska Palace, arguably
one of the world's key jumping-off points for real exploration of the
Templar myth. As we shall see, truth can be stranger than fiction,
for contrary to the "reasoned" view that the Templars were innocent
of the charges made against them in the fourteenth century and no
longer exist, the startling reality appears to be exactly the opposite:
Some Templars may have been guilty, and they still exist—though
not in a way you would expect.

Admittedly, Stockholm would not seem to be immediately rel-
evant to the study of the Order of the Temple (as it should more
correctly be known). However, the country is a good place to begin
exploding conventional wisdom, as in the land of IKEA, the North
American stereotype of Swedes as blond, sensual, egalitarian Socialists
meets the reality of a people who are actually more typically bru-
nette, painfully reserved, title-conscious, and private sector–ori-
ented. It may also come as a surprise that modern Sweden has the
headquarters of the only "serious" institution in the world claiming
direct historical and spiritual descent from the Knights Templars and
even earlier antecedents. This is the *Svenska Frimurare Orden* (Swedish
Order of Freemasons) under the patronage of its High Protector, His
Majesty King Carl XVI Gustaf, and operating from the Bååtska Palace
on Blasieholmsgatan adjacent to Stockholm's Grand Hotel. Arguably
the most magnificent Masonic building in the world, the palace would
not be recognized as such by most Masons elsewhere, as such typical
symbols as the square and compasses are largely absent. It represents
a totally different stream of Freemasonry from that which exists in
most countries, since the Swedish Rite (as it is called) is in some sense
a royal and Lutheran confraternity—with its highest-ranking members receiving civil knighthoods from their king and high protector.

According to its secretariat, the palace itself was built in 1666 and "acquired and carefully reconstructed to Masonic specifications" in 1874. It contains various lodge rooms, dining and ceremonial spaces, offices, subterranean vaults, and even a throne room—the (King) Oscar Hall.

Austrian Masonic scholar Eugen Lenhoff called the Swedish Rite "a revival of the Christian mysticism of the Middle Ages cloaked in Masonic forms"—and he didn't mean that as a compliment, as in his view the whole structure was an ill-conceived departure from the Masonic purity of nonreligious, Enlightenment values and stonemasons' guild symbols. The famous "Third Degree" in most Masonic rituals around the world is based on something called the Hiramic legend, with ceremonies involving the dramatized ritual death and resurrection of the obscure, possibly Old Testament figure Hiram Abiff. But Hiram Abiff is absent from the Swedish Rite, which is based on other figures and on other legends. As one Anglo-Saxon Freemason has described it, on the basis of his many visits to lodges in Stockholm: "The Swedish lodge room . . . is a mysterious and gloomy place, lit only by massive candles, where figures appear from the shadows to deliver their charges, then fade away in the darkness. A Swedish working is an intensely solemn and almost mystical experience. The symbols and ritual of a Swedish degree are somewhat more explicit than our own, further reinforcing the other-worldly atmosphere and heightening the shared experience." The rite involves an initiation system of eleven degrees, which are probably the only Masonic rituals not easily found or acquired on the Internet, in major libraries, or from publishers (although enterprising researchers will find them)—such is the discretion of the Swedish grand lodge. Members wear aprons, sashes, and swords in some of the first seven degrees, though daggers are worn in the fourth and fifth degrees. Where possible, some of the degrees are conferred in specially constructed vaults, cellars, or sepulchral chambers, with coffins, skulls, bones, and similar symbols designed to impress certain "life lessons" on candidates and to emphasize the idea of rebirth into a new spiritual life and fellowship within the Order.

So what does all this have to do with the Templars? By the eighth degree, the Masonic aprons are set aside and the initiate dons a Templar habit, takes a new adoptive name in the form of a Latin motto, is given a golden "Ring of Profession" to be worn ever afterwards on the middle finger of his right hand—and has a coat of arms designed for him if he doesn't already have one, later to be painted on a shield and hung in one of the Order's buildings. In this degree and the remaining ones, the Swedish Rite makes the hushed but astounding claim that it is not merely doing this in honor of the Templars, but that the rite is actually the true, legal successor to the Templars through a secret line of succession from Jacques de Molay's nephew, the Count de Beaujeu. As this inner doctrine is revealed in full, initiates are told they are also the legal and spiritual heirs to a "shadow priesthood" and illumination that the Templar Knights discovered at the Church of the Holy Sepulchre, a hidden tradition that was earlier transmitted by the pre-Christian sect of the Essenes from its origins with the priest Melchizedek himself. No other mainstream Masonic body anywhere makes such Gnostic claims, either publicly or privately. The United Grand Lodge of England—the "world's mother grand lodge"—itself is quick to assert publicly that Freemasonry ". . . has no theological doctrine . . . does not claim to lead to salvation by works, by secret knowledge or by any other means. The secrets of Freemasonry are concerned with modes of recognition. . ." (passwords and the like). Many bishops and clergy of the official (if now no longer established state) Church of Sweden were and are high-ranking Swedish Rite Freemasons, and how they can square this esotericism with their externally professed Lutheran faith is certainly a question. A more interesting question is simply whether these claims have any basis in fact whatsoever.

In order to blow the lid off the whole story, one has to be aware that Templar mythology is now the research subject of increasing numbers of academic scholars at top universities, whose foreign-language skills, access to early manuscripts and archives, and professional knowledge are yielding important new—and previously unknown—information. The doyen in this field has for many years been the distinguished Cambridge University professor Jonathan Riley-Smith, a graduate of Eton and Trinity College, Cambridge who went on to hold that university's principal named chair in ecclesiastical history until 2005. Given his eminence in the study of the knightly military-religious orders, *The Economist* magazine asked him to write a rare bylined article on the meaning of the Crusades for its fat year-end issue in 1995—a piece that turned out to be rather timely, given both the coming of 9/11 and Al-Qaeda's frequent references to "Crusaders," as well as the eventual arrival of *The Da Vinci Code* on the world's bookstore shelves. His research has led him to a number of academically verifiable conclusions, including:

> The Templar myth was an eighteenth-century scam. It was thought up by two charlatans, a German pastor who called himself Samuel Rosa and a man who went under the assumed name of George Frederick Johnson and claimed to be a Scottish nobleman with direct access to Templar secrets. They were joined by an unworldly lunatic, Karl Gotthelf von Hund, who was a substantial landowner in Saxony. These men exploited the fashion for Freemasonry in Germany, which was resisting the egalitarian and rationalist thrust of Masonic thought elsewhere. The German Masons wanted something which was more acceptable to conservative views and to Gothic taste. The mythmakers provided it.

Lunacy or otherwise, Baron von Hund's contribution has been especially enduring, as his Rite of Strict Observance with its Templar-Essene myths and sinister references to "unknown superiors" fed directly into the creation of the Swedish Rite, which in time spread to most of Scandinavia and to parts of Germany. Much of it also got injected into another Masonic system still practiced in some countries: the Rectified Scottish Rite, also called the CBCS *(Chevaliers Bienfaisants de la Cité Sainte)*—with its own claims to hidden knowledge that "Greek and Egyptian sages subscribed to a religious dogma identical to Christianity." (Go figure.)

One of the most dearly held views among contemporary Templar enthusiasts in the "rejected-knowledge" movement is that the Order of the Temple surely did survive somewhere, if only in Scotland. However, there is not a shred of evidence that it survived anywhere, either there or via some hidden transmission mechanism of the kind claimed by the Swedish Rite. It is true that in Portugal some Templars joined the newly founded Order of Christ, which later got involved in Portuguese exploration and colonization overseas—but it was not a continuation of the Temple in any reasonable sense.

The one question that both enthusiasts and serious scholars have tended to agree on, until recently, is the innocence of the Templars, who were believed to have been falsely accused of various serious charges so that the rapacious French king, Philip the Fair, could get his hands on their rich properties. While he was undoubtedly greedy (the epithet *fair* refers to his appearance rather than his moral compass), new research has tipped academic opinion in the other direction. To quote Professor Riley-Smith:

> The general view among scholars . . . is under revision, with some historians, including myself, coming to believe that at some receptions into the order postulants were being forced into a blasphemous rite of passage . . . The most serious accusation levelled at the Templars was that at their reception they were being called upon to deny Christ—sometimes being told he was a false prophet who could not redeem mankind—and to spit, stamp or urinate upon a cross or crucifix. After reading the surviving records of the interrogations I have come to the view that in some commanderies postulants were indeed being forced to [do so] at the time of, or shortly after, their reception. This practice—astonishing in an Order the raison d'être of which was the defence of Christianity—was probably to be found in a minority of commanderies and among a few preceptors in France, but it was not confined to them. It looks as though brothers who believed these demands were customary had carried them to Italy and the Levant . . . [An Italian brother] testified that for much of the time he did not understand what was going on, because so many words were spoken to him in *galico*.

Just why some Templar bodies might have embraced blasphemous rites is a research question likely to keep a new generation of scholars busy for years, in far-flung archives and collections from Paris and Rome to the Middle East. One can speculate that such rituals could have been used to intensify the bond between new members and their commandery—"No turning back now"—much as criminal gangs and secret societies sometimes insist on some notorious act to solidify a member's entry into their midst. Postulants might have found the requests startling and unnerving but, still, the prestige of being a Templar was very great, and they could have reassured themselves that other members had also undertaken the same customary acts in private. Above all, it could perhaps have signified the development of a Gnostic mentality and sense of superiority, even if outward conformity to Catholic doctrine remained in place.

In short, some Templars were probably guilty, but what about the reference at the beginning of this chapter to their continued existence? The Order didn't survive, but it does exist—thanks to the royal and state authority of the Swedish Crown and the patronage and membership of several generations of Swedish (and also Danish, Norwegian, and Prussian) royalty. In effect, the Crown created and legitimized a new Templar brotherhood that begins with "Craft" Freemasonry, continues with higher degrees of what one might call "spiritual Templary," and then culminates in the civil knighthood of the Order of Carl XIII bestowed by the king of Sweden, which is restricted to thirty-three full members who are dubbed Knights and recognized as such by their government. The legends and doctrines involving de Molay's nephew, the Essenes, and the priest Melchizedek appear to be purely invented, but that does not render the Crown's recognition invalid. The Swedish Rite may be a form of Western esotericism with no authentic direct link whatsoever to the original Templars, but it has acquired legitimacy through the acts of a sovereign *fons honorum* (fount of honor). The Knights of Carl XIII, who wear their Templar-like decoration on Sweden's military uniforms or formal civil dress, are in some sense the last Templars in existence. They also sometimes wear a special habit with hat, tunic, mantle, pantaloons, and tall black leather boots—but you won't find many photographs of them in this garb, as the ceremonies in which they are worn are secret. If you ever meet one by chance in the lobby of Stockholm's Grand Hotel, you can ask him whether he believes in the hidden doctrines of his Order.

The Chapel of the Ark, Aksum, Ethiopia

Having addressed the guilt and continued existence of the Templars, what can one say about fanciful claims that Templar Knights were also secret caretakers of the Ark of the Covenant—perhaps even having brought it to England where it remains near Shakespeare's birthplace? Here, too, there is no persuasive evidence of any kind to link the Templars with the Ark, which would admittedly be the most amazing surviving historical and religious object of all time, if it still exists. (Professor Indiana Jones, call your office?) The most intriguing (and plausible) possibility is that the Ark has been in Ethiopia for eons, in the custody of the Ethiopian Orthodox Church, at the Chapel of the Ark in Aksum. Ethiopian Orthodox liturgy is a deeply resonant fusion of Coptic and Judaic elements, and the Ethiopians themselves remain a highly spiritual people—as the psalmist wrote, "Ethiopia shall reach her hand unto God." Even a jaded young Evelyn Waugh seemed taken with it all when dispatched to the Ethiopian capital of Addis Ababa in 1930 as a special correspondent, writing about the arduous all-night coronation vigil "amid continous chanting, beating of drums and the brandishing of brass rattles"—"a spectacle of extreme splendour."

The Chapel of the Ark in Aksum is a relatively silent place, given that only one person on earth is allowed to see its most precious contents. No one other than the priest appointed for life to be the guardian of the Ark is permitted to lay eyes on it, not so much because of its sacredness but because it is simply considered "too dangerous" for those spiritually unprepared to see it—such are the powers attributed to it. Not even the last emperor, Haile Selassie, was allowed inside the chapel to see the Ark. At the moment, until such time as these claims can be verified, the chapel at Aksum remains a closed (if tantalizing) hidden sanctuary.

The Chapel of the Holy Grail, Valencia Cathedral, Spain

As for the Holy Grail, it has been called "the greatest and most enduring literary invention of all time, far outweighing lesser ones like Sherlock Holmes." From twelfth-century Arthurian stories to such nineteenth-century British romantics as Mallory and Tennyson, the legend of the survival, search for, and healing powers of Christ's cup from the Last Supper has fired the imagination of both writers and audiences for centuries. This was no less true in Germany, where Richard Wagner's operas *Lohengrin* and *Parsifal* were smash hits of their day. As Cambridge's Professor Riley-Smith has also explained:

> Aficionados did not really want the Grail to be discovered; it had much more attraction for them as a hidden object, embodying a secret tradition and harnessed in various ways to the history of the Templars or sometimes to that of the Cathar heretics in Languedoc. The latter association is absurd, because a feature of Cathar belief had been the rejection of anything material about Christ, including the reality of the Crucifixion and the Eucharist.

The modern claim that some Templars got hold of the grail and took it to Rosslyn Chapel in Scotland, or to some other hiding place, is surely bogus. If the cup used by Christ at the Last Supper has survived, the most plausible existing object is the Holy Chalice of Valencia, which is normally kept in the former chapter-house of Valencia Cathedral in Spain, now rededicated as a special chapel to house the cup. Pope Benedict XVI used this chalice at Mass during his last visit to the country, but the Church makes no claim about its authenticity. Unlike some icons, relics, and religious objects, which are said to be associated with supernatural, mystical, or miraculous phenomena, no such claims are associated with this chalice. Perhaps this should come as no surprise, given Catholic and Orthodox belief that every chalice used at Mass (or at Orthodox divine liturgy) essentially *is* the Holy Grail, as time and space are rendered obsolete in the mystery of the Eucharist. In this respect, the original holy cup, should it still exist, is no more or less exalted than any other consecrated chalice used around the world today.

Significant Masonic Temples from Rome and Paris to Washington and Pushkin (Russia)

Freemasonry in its Swedish Rite form has already been explored in this chapter, but it is a much bigger subject, which deserves further elaboration. Vast libraries are filled with books on it, many of them badly written and inadequately researched pro- and anti-Masonic polemics. As for its sanctuaries, both public and hidden, any comprehensive tour of the world's key Masonic temples would probably include visits to the well-known grand lodge buildings in Edinburgh, Dublin, Philadelphia, New York, Copenhagen, Oslo, and perhaps especially in London, with its large art deco grand lodge building on Great Queen Street known formally as the Masonic Peace Memorial (though typically referred to by Londoners as "Freemasons' Hall"). Offering rather more conspiratorial buzz and frisson is the former seat of the Grand Orient of Italy, which for many years was based discreetly at the Palazzo Giustiniani around the corner from the Pantheon in Rome, with its entrance at Via Guistiniani 5—which still feels more like a dark alleyway than a full-fledged thoroughfare. The Italian Grand Orient hit the world's newswires in a big way in the 1980s, when it turned out that some members of a highly clandestine and renegade lodge on its roll—P2 or "Propaganda Due"—were involved in political plots, fraud, bribery, and murder. One of P2's members, prominent international banker Roberto Calvi, was found hanging from scaffolding underneath London's highly symbolic Blackfriars Bridge. The membership list turned out to be an eye-popping *Who's Who* of Italy's political, financial, industrial, military, and even Catholic dignitaries; some

P2 members later defended their membership by claiming that it was not a Masonic lodge in any conventional sense, but rather a vehicle to provide for alternative leadership and continuity of government in the event that the country veered further left toward communism or anarchic Euroterrorism, or both.

A different energy emanates from 16 Rue Cadet in Paris, the long-time headquarters of the even more overtly political Grand Orient of France—one of the largest Masonic organizations in Europe. Long known for its militant secularism (and even strident atheism) and for a close connection with the leadership of France's Socialist Party, the Grand Orient is not recognized as "regular" by Anglo-American grand lodges. Its bookstore has a bizarre blend of rationalist and occultist works, combining enthusiasm for Richard Dawkins's *The God Delusion* alongside tomes on Tarot cards. Its prominent members in recent decades have included Roland Dumas, a top Socialist cabinet minister and later president of France's Constitutional Council; prosecuted for misappropriating funds, he received a suspended sentence. Unique among Masonic organizations, the Grand Orient has its members join left-wing street marches in Masonic regalia; afterward, they typically join in the singing of the "Internationale"—the hymn that the Soviet Union adopted as its national anthem in 1944. Researchers looking for inflammatory comments from Grand Orient officials over the years will find no shortage, including Senator Auguste Delpech's 1902 anti-Christian diatribe, in which he said: "The triumph of the Galilean has lasted twenty centuries; he is dying in his turn." The Grand Orient's museum includes a framed photograph of Marxist-leaning Chilean president Salvador Allende wearing his Masonic apron; but Freemasonry is nothing if not complicated, and it is worth noting that Allende's nemesis, General Augusto Pinochet, also joined a Chilean lodge as a young officer—something that was reasonably common in South American military and patriotic circles of the period.

It is difficult, therefore, to characterize in a simple way a heterogeneous worldwide movement and brotherhood whose members have ranged from Mozart to Count Basie, Gerald Ford to Giuseppe

Garibaldi—and from the Duke of Wellington to Duke Ellington. In the seventeenth and eighteenth centuries, a time when craft guilds were dying out across Europe, few could have guessed that a new and highly fashionable club would be created out of the remains of the medieval stonemasons' guilds. (Only in Zurich and in the city of London did traditional craft guilds retain their importance as social, charitable, and municipal government bodies, right up to the present day.) In the British Isles and on the Continent, Masonic lodges became popular places for men of different classes, professions, and political views to meet. Some became hotbeds of radical thinking, while others embraced clerical members and even such noted later reactionaries as Joseph de Maistre. The Scottish Rite (*Rite Ecossais*), later famous in some countries for its anti-Catholic orientation, actually originated with Catholic, royalist, Jacobite Scottish exiles in France. Some speculate, with interesting factual evidence, that Baron von Hund's "unknown superiors" were actually Bonnie Prince Charlie and the Stuarts, rather than some Illuminist puppet masters or shadowy members of a supposed "great white brotherhood" in the Himalayas.

Objections to Freemasonry among churchmen and political leaders over the past two centuries have stemmed from the brotherhood's Deistic, Gnostic, and antireligious tendencies (as seen clearly in some times and places) and also its use by some members as a vehicle for secret political activities and subversion (most recently observed in Italy in the 1980s). Freemasonry has also been accused of being the equivalent of a "gateway drug" for individuals drawn to the occult, who then go on to "harder" pursuits; Aleister Crowley, the most famous black magician of the twentieth century, incorporated what he regarded as Masonic insights into his occultism. Oddball English civil servant, Freemason, and "hereditary witch" Gerald Gardner essentially created the modern Wiccan movement from scratch in the mid-twentieth century, based partly on Masonic concepts.

The remains of a different kind of occultist are to be found entombed in Washington, D.C., at the Scottish Rite Supreme Council's House of the Temple on 16th Street, Northwest—a grand building designed by noted architect John Russell Pope, who is best known for creating the Jefferson Memorial. The remains are those of lawyer, Confederate general, enthusiastic Masonic reformer, and prolific esotericist Albert Pike, who is sometimes wrongly accused of being a satanist. His almost unreadable magnum opus, *Morals and Dogma,* does make some references to Lucifer, but in their context it is difficult to claim he had a specifically Luciferian intent. Those seeking a more shocking image in that direction would do well to take the Austrian Airlines non-stop flight from Washington to Vienna, having booked a luxurious weekend at the Schlosshotel Rosenau in the deep countryside of Lower Austria. This secluded country-house hotel, with its fine restaurant, combines the charms of a nobleman's Baroque residence, a Catholic chapel, and an official Masonic museum of the Grand Lodge of Austria. Bizarrely, the still-functioning chapel's choir loft forms part of the exhibition space of the Masonic museum. Perhaps the most interesting—or horrifying—object on display is a contemporary piece of art from 1979, called *Baumeister aller Welten* (Architect of the Universe) by artist Rudolf Kedl. In Masonic lodges, God is normally referred to as the "Great Architect of the Universe," but this disturbing Austrian depiction of the Deity shows a massively muscular, three-faced being wearing Masonic regalia and crouching (in the style of some "Baphomet" drawings) on an orb with a menacing skull at its center. The traditional pillars, called Jachin and Boaz, on either side appear so phallic as to be almost pornographic. This image would not appear to be the best possible public relations vehicle for Austrian Freemasonry, but the Schloss Rosenau and its collection are well off the beaten path—to say the least.

Also off the beaten trail is the so-called Masonic Chapel in Pushkin, Russia, some 15 miles (24km) south of St. Petersburg. Pushkin was formerly called Tsarskoe Selo (Royal Village) in imperial times, and it served as a summer residence of the czars. Freemasonry was once highly fashionable among Russian officers and intellectuals, and even Tolstoy's *War and Peace* gives some snippets of dialogue to the Swedish Rite members then active in elevated circles. By 1830, Freemasonry had become illegal, which it remained until the end of the Romanov Empire. The somewhat run-down, Gothic-style "Masonic" chapel is said to have a bronze statue of Christ gesturing in a Masonic greeting, and the third-floor inner sanctum is only accessible by a rope ladder, where clandestine lodge meetings were supposedly held. According to an article published in a mainstream, large-circulation Masonic magazine (later reprinted elsewhere), the chapel was the site of meetings that finalized the abolition of the monarchy and sealed the fate of the imperial family. If this is accurate, the chapel is a very significant place indeed. Russian Freemasonry has been reestablished since the fall of the Soviet Union, although the Eastern Orthodox churches forbid membership "on pain of excommunication"—at least in principle, if not always in practice. Exiled Russian princes and nobility in New York, including the debonair Prince Serge Obolensky, tended to join Holland Lodge No. 8 in Manhattan, and some still belong. Exiled King George II of Greece became master of his lodge in London. Most curiously of all, a recent photo in one of Britain's two leading Masonic magazines shows a traditionalist Greek Orthodox bishop—Bishop Evlogios of Milan—wearing his grand lodge regalia on top of his clerical garb.

Gnosticism Today

A New Zealand–born, UK-based Freemason, Michael Baigent, was the man who sparked the contemporary revival in Gnostic ideas with his 1980s bestseller *The Holy Blood and the Holy Grail*—in many ways a key precursor to *The Da Vinci Code* (see Chapter 1). In fact, he later unsuccessfully sued Dan Brown's publisher in a London courtroom, for what he claimed was a form of plagiarism. Baigent's style and that of his two coauthors has been described as ". . . anti-History, in which myth, speculation and rumour are given equal weight with hard evidence and in which their own highly suspect interpretations are treated as conclusive." Their misinterpretation of the innocuous church inscription *Terribilis est locus iste,* already noted in Chapter 1, was typical of that tendency.

In matters Gnostic, it is worth recalling the words of the late scholar and Dominican friar, Victor White, as repeated and augmented by contemporary Oxbridge academic and Dominican friar Aidan Nichols:

> While gnosticism has no room for faith, faith has room indeed for gnosis. Gnosis cannot be a substitute for faith, but the possession of gnosis is part and parcel of the gifts to the faithful Ecclesia. In the body of Christ are many members, each with their several functions, and those of the gnostic are among the most honourable. Without the intuitive understanding of what in faith she believes, the Church itself would be incomplete—uncatholic. But it is gnosis in faith, not despite of faith; and it is for the benefit of the whole body and not only for the individual member . . . Once these principles are recognised, the Church can have her own contemplatives and mystics, and even "her alchemists and cabbalists"—but always on the condition that none claim by these titles a perfection superior to the *plebs sancta*, the common people of God.

Chapter 4

GOTHIC NIGHTMARE

Wewelsburg Castle, Westphalia, Germany

*I*t is one of the most evil places on earth. Wewelsburg Castle, near Paderborn in Westphalia, Germany, was the satanic Camelot created by Heinrich Himmler as the mystical headquarters for his Nazi perversion of the medieval ideal of chivalry—a knightly Order of SS murderers. Blown up at his command in 1945 to prevent it from falling into the hands of advancing U.S. troops, the castle has been restored as a monument to Nazi depravity. It is the only castle in Germany built on a triangular plan. Today it grimly dominates the attractive Alme Valley, a massive structure on a wooded height, its three towers rearing menacingly above the skyline. It seems unreal: a Dark-Age lair whose looming bulk conjures the music of Richard Wagner, proclaiming the Twilight of the Gods.

The evil that haunts Wewelsburg is of a different character from that of Auschwitz or Bergen-Belsen. Mass murder was committed here, too, but on a much smaller scale: It is estimated that 1,341 prisoners died, not in the castle itself but in the adjacent Niederhagen concentration camp, the smallest camp in the Nazi gulag, set up to provide labor for work on the castle. By Nazi standards, this was a modest death toll; but it is not chiefly the memory of those victims—tragic though it is—that invests Wewelsburg with a particular horror. It is more the fact that Wewelsburg was the center of the quasi-religious cult established by Himmler to provide a spiritual dimension to the aberrations of the Third Reich. Wewelsburg was a kind of "Black Vatican"—the headquarters of a theology of death that brought grotesque suffering and extermination to millions. Visitors to Auschwitz and other death camps have often been moved to ask the question: How could they do it? The answer lies in Wewelsburg. There, with the help of ancient Nordic pagan mythology and the extravagant theories of twentieth-century esoteric philosophers and downright cranks, Himmler manufactured a pseudoreligion designed to take the place of Christian morality, to give his SS units an alternative "spirituality" that would steel them to commit mass murder under the banner of a Germanic mysticism at once old and new. That is the most chilling aspect of Wewelsburg: Without its dark inspiration, the killing of millions of innocent people would have lacked the impetus of a mystical zeal, perhaps even faltered in the light of more conventional morality.

The massive castle took six years to build, from 1603 to 1609, being intended as a residence for the Prince-Bishop of Paderborn, one of the many ecclesiastical rulers presiding over the 360 small states of the Holy Roman Empire. Its architecture is impressive, in the Renaissance style, but the fortress had a bloodstained reputation even in its early years, as the place of execution of many women convicted in seventeenth-century witchcraft trials in the Westphalia region of Germany. That, however, was not what brought it to the attention of SS Reichsführer Heinrich Himmler in the twentieth century: Wewelsburg stood on a site that had enormous resonance with the pagan mystics who advised him. Close by was the Teutoburg Forest, where the Germanic tribes defeated the Roman legions under Varus, halting the advance of the conquering Roman Empire—a significant triumph of German nationalism much relished by the Nazis. Also nearby was Externsteine, a rock formation that had been the site of pre-Christian religious rites. Most important, the castle stood at the intersection of certain "ley" lines, lending supposed authority to Himmler's declaration that Wewelsburg was the "Center of the World."

By the time the Nazis came to power in Germany in 1933, Himmler had already resolved to turn his black-uniformed bodyguard, the Schutzstaffel (SS), into a pagan order of "knights," its organization partly modeled on the Catholic religious military orders such as the

Teutonic Knights and on the Arthurian Round Table, but drawing its main inspiration from Nordic mythology and occult theories. After the first few months spent in setting up the police state that would be the power base of the Third Reich, Himmler had time to turn his attention to his pet project. He was resolved that only a classic German fortress-type castle, or Burg, could provide a fitting home for his knightly Order, so he indulged in a macabre house-hunting expedition. He found two castles that had possibilities, but finally, on November 3, 1933 he visited Wewelsburg and recognized immediately that this was the ideal site for his Nazi Camelot.

The man who aroused Himmler's interest in Wewelsburg and first took him there was Karl Maria Wiligut, also known as Hitler's "Lord of the Runes" and as "Himmler's Rasputin," so strong was his influence on the SS leader. Wiligut had been an officer in the Austrian Imperial Army, with an impeccable service record during the First World War. Subsequently, however, he became mentally unstable, convinced that he was descended from a secret line of German kingship. Inspired by this delusion, he became involved with an organization called the *Ordo Novi Templi* (the Order of the New Temple), which intensified his obsession with the occult. In 1924 he was diagnosed as suffering from schizophrenia and megalomania and, at the request of his wife, confined to a mental asylum from which he was released after three years. By now he was immersed in occult theology, at first influenced by Guido von List, who preached the renewed worship of the Nordic god Wotan; but discipleship could not long satisfy an egotist like Wiligut and he broke away and formed his own religion of Irminism. In 1932 he moved from Austria to Germany—an individual who was now in the full throes of schizophrenia, paranoia, and megalomania fitted in perfectly well in the upper echelons of the emergent Third Reich. The following year he was introduced to Himmler and became his esoteric guru. Wiligut was enrolled into the SS under the pseudonym of "Karl Maria Weisthor" and his promotion within its ranks was meteoric; by September 1936 he had attained the high position of Brigadeführer (the SS equivalent of Brigadier-General).

Reichsführer SS Heinrich Himmler, whose "spiritual" adviser Wiligut now became, had a mind fully as unbalanced as his tutor's. Though not clinically insane—Himmler was bad rather than mad—he exhibited a degree of eccentricity regarding the occult that even Hitler found unsettling. When Wiligut showed Wewelsburg to Himmler, he instantly decided to acquire it; but even when ambitiously creating the mystical Nazi Center of the World, the Reichsführer retained a sensible caution regarding money. In 1934 the SS took out a hundred-year lease on the castle from the district of Büren, for a peppercorn rent of one Reichsmark annually. The local authority did not think it wise to haggle with so formidable a tenant. Otherwise, Himmler was not parsimonious: The proposed budget for converting Wewelsburg into an extended fortress-city was an astronomical 250 million Reichsmarks (roughly $1.3 billion in today's money). Wiligut then drew up elaborate plans for the development of Wewelsburg and managed to win Himmler's enthusiastic support. Even before the architectural plans were completed, Wiligut began to perform pagan religious services at the castle, including weddings of SS officers. He devised the *Totenkopf* (death's-head) ring, which Himmler presented to favored SS officers. All this was only a preliminary to the major development of Wewelsburg as the religious capital of the New Order.

Despite his overblown opinion of himself and his talents, Wiligut could not claim to have architectural skills, so the design was assigned to the SS architect Hermann Bartels. Three years of labor was expended on the castle—much of it involving restoration work and the rest focusing on interior alterations—so the building as it stands today is still substantially that of the Prince-Bishop of Paderborn. It is built of yellowish stone, with a decorative ridge running between each story, in classic Renaissance style. The building is triangular, enclosing a courtyard. An arched stone bridge leads to the entrance; most of the main structure is two or three stories high, rising to five stories in the towers. Two towers are topped by cupolas in the fashion of Eastern European castles and the third and largest—the North Tower—is sturdier, with a greater diameter, and more squat, having no cupola on top. With Himmler's approval, Bartels decided that the focal point of the castle must be the North Tower.

Its basement level was to become a vault for the commemoration of fallen SS heroes. Today, entry to the vault is prevented by a barred cage within the locked door of the tower, but special permission can be obtained to view it if the custodians are satisfied that the inquirer is not a neo-Nazi visiting in a spirit of homage. There is a pit in the middle of the floor with a cuplike declivity in its center, which some people have speculated could have been the scene of animal or even human sacrifice. While there is absolutely no evidence of this, the Nazis' notorious indifference to human life and the ready supply of victims at the adjacent concentration camp makes the theory at least plausible. The official function of this pit was the burning of the coats of arms of deceased members of the elite Twelve (Himmler's senior knights), the ashes of which would thenceforth be reverenced—an uncharacteristically tame ritual by SS standards, which may have concealed darker purposes. There is a swastika carved into the domed vault ceiling. The room is now known as the Himmler Crypt, since he intended to be buried there; but it was formally dedicated to the Saxon King Heinrich I (Henry the Fowler), with whose ghost Himmler held conversations and of whom he possibly believed himself to be the reincarnation (Wiligut was not the only Nazi with delusions of royal descent). Despite the crypt's official name, however, it is almost certain that it was designed for a more exalted purpose, at least from July 12, 1940. On that date Hitler gave Himmler permission to demolish a nearby church in order to enlarge Wewelsburg; it is believed that this was because, as a reward for Himmler's acceptance of the assignment to carry out the Final Solution—the extermination of the Jews—Hitler had privately agreed to honor him by appointing the Wewelsburg crypt as his own future burial place, with the SS Reichsführer as guardian of the tomb and mystical successor.

On the floor above is the Hall of Supreme Leaders. This is the most significant place in the castle, containing the mysterious *Schwarze Sonne* (black sun) emblem. The large mosaic is inlaid in green and black on the gray marble floor, representing a disk with twelve crooked arms, like those of a swastika, radiating from the center. It is the spot that the Nazis regarded as the center of the world. The black sun emblem is similar to ancient German or Merovingian designs; it has been suggested that the twelve arms represent the months of the year, which the sun passes through. What is not known is whether this mosaic already existed in the floor of the castle or whether Himmler had it installed. The design was perfect for his purposes, since the cult celebrated within the castle was to be presided over by the "Twelve Knights" (SS officers of Gruppenführer status) appointed by Himmler. Each of them had a room in the castle assigned to him and named after a German hero, with appropriate furnishings: Henry the Lion, King Arthur (an honorary German?), and, of course, for Himmler, Henry the Fowler. These officers were his Round Table and their special ceremonial meeting place was to be in the Hall of Supreme Leaders. A great circular table made of oak was installed there in Himmler's time, with a dozen chairs set round it, each with its owner's name inscribed on a silver plate. Around the walls were hung shields bearing the coats of arms of the twelve senior SS officers, invented for them by the Ahnenerbe, the arm of the SS created to deal with mystical matters, since these recently manufactured "knights" were mostly of commoner descent. The only recorded full meeting in the hall took place in March 1941, when Himmler briefed his immediate subordinates on the planned invasion of Russia. He also made a speech to SS officers in the castle before the invasion of Poland, steeling them to the task of eliminating the Jews: that was the central tenet of the "spirituality" cultivated at Wewelsburg.

The castle guardhouse, a two-story building open to the public, has been turned into a museum. Here are displayed the architect's plans for the uncompleted development, and grisly SS memorabilia, including a prisoner's characteristic striped uniform from the adjoining concentration camp. Although undoubtedly educational, it is not a comfortable place. What remains obscure, since any records there may have been were destroyed, is the precise nature, scale, and frequency of the Nazi rituals within Wewelsburg. There were pagan celebrations of the winter and summer solstices, as well as anniversaries significant in Nazi lore, with torchlight processions and sacred fires. The notorious Reinhard Heydrich, later assassinated while Protector of Bohemia, is known to have attended an Irminist "baptism" ceremony there for the son of Karl Wolff, Himmler's chief adjutant, in January 1937 and civil marriages of SS officers were celebrated with pagan rites. It was certainly well established as the ideological center of SS mythology long before the end of World War II. On the other hand, the elaborate development plans envisioned by Himmler were not fully implemented. He had intended to construct a semicircular wall, with a diameter of one kilometer, around the castle, creating a larger settlement, but this was never done. Construction work on the main castle, which needed much restoration, only began in 1939 and ended in 1943. It was this endeavor, rather than any rites that took place in Wewelsburg, that caused the greatest suffering and loss of life. Until that is taken into account, the superstitious posturings of the SS leaders might almost be dismissed as an immature fantasy—a kind of Halloween all year round for credulous racists—but for some thousands of people Wewelsburg was hell on earth.

Labor was supplied by the Niederhagen concentration camp, immediately to the east of the castle. Initially it housed just 480 prisoners: It was the camp allocated to receive Jehovah's Witnesses. It was a peculiarity of the camp, perhaps because it was not officially an extermination center, that very few of the prisoners were Jewish. In the course of its existence, from 1940 to 1943, there were 3,900 inmates at Niederhagen, of whom 56 were executed and 1,285 died of starvation, overwork, or beatings. The closure of the camp in 1943 was no consolation to the survivors, since they were transferred to Buchenwald, apart from a small number who were moved into the castle to perform menial tasks. A memorial to those who died there was erected in 2000. They represented the human cost of Himmler's grotesque ambition to create a pseudoreligion in the service of Aryan supremacy.

The weird cult of which Wewelsburg was the basilica is a potent

testament to the infantile nature of Nazi beliefs. For decades before
the Nazis seized power, Germany had been a center for many eccentric neopagan cults, united in glorifying the mythological origins of
the German race. Organizations such as the Thule Society and the
cult of theosophy were early precursors of Nazi mysticism. Closer
still was Guido von List, with his Nordic cult of Odinism, from which
Wiligut diverged. The extravagance of some Nazi theories was downright embarrassing; for example, the notion that the Aryan race had
originated on the star Aldebaran or that there were originally two
suns—this was a theosophical notion—which did battle with each
other 330,000 years ago, leaving the black sun (of Wiligut's lore)
burned out, but representing an opposing force. Even if Nazi rule had
been benevolent, the fact that a movement whose leaders entertained
such notions ruled most of Europe for several years is still alarming.
How far Hitler believed in it is debatable. He does seem to have been
fascinated by such trophies as the "Spear of Destiny," the lance that
pierced Christ's side and of which three competing relics survived (see
Chapter 10). Yet he had no time for the cult of Wotan, on the characteristic grounds that "Nothing dies unless it is moribund"—which
might be considered an appropriate epitaph for his own doomed
cult.

Himmler, on the other hand, was a believer. Quests for the Holy
Grail, a Nazi expedition to Tibet to prove that its native aristocracy was
racially equipped to become allies and instruments of Aryan expansion in the region, even the search for Atlantis—all of this fascinated
Himmler, a former member of the Thule Society. His special organization for pursuing this interest was the SS Ahnenerbe (Ancestral
Heritage Research and Teaching Society), founded by Himmler in
1935. Naturally, the Ahnenerbe became closely involved in the development of the Wewelsburg project. This led to the marginalization of
Wiligut. By this time he had persuaded Himmler to send the leaders
of competing esoteric cults to concentration camps, but before the
outbreak of the war his own star was on the wane. The successive
heads of the Ahnenerbe were hostile to him, repelled by his chaotic

personality and addiction to drink. In 1939 Karl Wolff found out about Wiligut's earlier incarceration in a mental asylum, which he reported to Himmler, and his "resignation" was instantly accepted. There was no shortage of lunatics in SS circles, but the embarrassing thing about Wiligut was that he had the paperwork to prove it. This dismissal into obscurity just before the outbreak of hostilities probably saved Wiligut from a war crimes trial after Germany's defeat. He died in 1946.

During the war, Wewelsburg continued to serve as the mystical center of the SS, with an accompanying death toll among slave laborers until 1943. Thereafter, as Germany began to lose the war, Himmler had increasingly less time to devote to esoteric pursuits. The end came for Wewelsburg on March 31, 1945. On that day Himmler sent an SS commando, led by Sturmbannführer Heinz Macher of the Waffen-SS Panzer Division Das Reich, to blow up the castle, to prevent it from falling into the hands of the Allies. The castle was already surrounded by U.S. armor, but the sixteen-man task force managed to penetrate the American lines. Macher did not have sufficient dynamite, but he set the charge in the southeast tower and relied on the fire spreading, having warned the local fire brigade not to put it out. Much damage was done, but the notorious North Tower remained virtually unscathed, reinforcing rumors of its mystical power. Two days later troops of the U.S. Third Infantry Division took Wewelsburg and liberated the surviving slave laborers—just forty-two of them. The Gothic nightmare was over.

Yet even today Wewelsburg preserves one last mystery. Like many other secret sanctuaries, it is credited with a hidden treasure. The *Totenkopf* (death's-head) rings, devised by Wiligut and which Himmler presented as a bravery award to SS officers, were required to be returned to Wewelsburg on their owner's deaths. For understandable reasons, many such deaths had lately occurred and more than nine thousand rings were stored in a shrine in the castle by the end of the war. As the Allies advanced, Himmler ordered the rings to be taken to a cave close to the castle and the entrance sealed. This hoard has never been found. The rings were made of silver and today are prized by collectors. Each one's estimated value could be as high as $10,000, making the hidden collection worth anything up to $90 million. Unfortunately, treasure-hunting experts have pointed out that, since their current value is based on their rarity, if nine thousand of them flooded the market at once, it would make the price plummet. On the other hand, it could be that the complete collection, if preserved as a unit, would retain its huge value, cornering the market in Nazi memorabilia. The problem is academic, since there is no clue as to this treasure's location. The likeliest hypothesis is that Sturmbannführer Macher removed the rings before he blew up the castle. If so, he took his secret with him to the grave in 2001.

The grave is now the repository of most of those—murderers and victims—who participated in the grotesque history that was Wewelsburg. Today the castle still rears up over the wooded Westphalian landscape, a looming Wagnerian fantasy steeped in an evil that can hardly be exorcised. Wewelsburg is the Gothic nightmare that turned into the Valhalla of the Third Reich.

The Goetheanum, Dornach, Switzerland

Another Central European site, which in no way replicates the sinister elements of Wewelsburg Castle but is of considerable mystical significance, is the Goetheanum at Dornach, six miles (10km) south of Basel in Switzerland. This structure is the world center of the Anthroposophical movement and was conceived by Rudolf Steiner, who erected the original Goetheanum here between 1908 and 1925. Although many of its purposes were straightforward, others were esoteric and are still largely a matter for speculation.

The overt uses of the building were to stage performances of Steiner's Mystery Plays, to provide a venue for "eurythmical" dance, and to act as a conference center for lectures attended by the senior members of the Anthroposophical Society. Some investigators, however, believe more mystical rites were also enacted here. Helmut Zander, of the Humboldt University in Berlin, believes that the original structure, no longer in existence, was built to house quasi-Masonic ceremonies of the Esoteric School. To unravel the layers of mystical significance is complex because not only have there been two different buildings on this site, but they have had two different names. Before considering the character of the building, it is necessary to understand the meaning and history of the Anthroposophical movement.

The term *anthroposophy* means "wisdom of man." The movement's founder, Rudolf Steiner (1861–1925), defined it thus: "Anthroposophy is a path of knowledge that would guide what is spiritual in man to the spiritual in the universe." Steiner, the son of an Austrian stationmaster, graduated from the Vienna Institute of Technology and became an expert on the scientific writings of Goethe. Throughout his life, Steiner's interests were very varied, though the eccentricity of his spiritual beliefs gained him the most notoriety. He involved himself in philosophy, literature, art, education—his Waldorf School movement remains active in many countries—and even the agricultural activity that was the forerunner of modern organic farming. The Anthroposophical movement was originally part of the Theosophical Society, founded in New York in 1875 by Helena Petrovna Blavatsky and Henry Steel Olcott. Steeped in Indian mysticism, their aims were to cultivate the occult, promote universal brotherhood, and revive Oriental philosophy. In 1902 Steiner became general secretary of the German branch; but in 1912, following differences with Annie Besant, the society's president, he formed a breakaway Anthroposophical Society. Although the Theosophical movement had already cultivated some elements of Freemasonry, Steiner's group was much more intensively involved in Masonic ritual. Steiner introduced the rite of Memphis-Misraim, incorporating nine degrees of Masonic hierarchy, as well as Rosicrucian influences.

By the time Steiner broke with mainstream theosophy, he was already intending to build an esoteric headquarters for his followers. Having been refused planning permission in Munich, he moved the site across the border to Dornach, where the foundation stone was laid in a secret ceremony in 1913. The building was originally named the Johannesbau, in reference to the St. John lodges, or Craft lodges, of Freemasonry. E. A. Karl Stockmeyer, who helped plan the structure, observed: "The First Goetheanum . . . was planned in a way that a greater circle of people under the great cupola could have the experience of the cult, celebrated under the small cupola . . ." The cult was that of the three altars and two columns, the latter being the Masonic columns Jachin and Boaz. In 1918 the more overtly Masonic name of the Johannesbau was changed to the more discreet title of Goetheanum, in honor of the great German writer Goethe whose works Steiner had helped to edit.

The First Goetheanum was one of seventeen buildings designed by Steiner; it was built principally of wood between 1913 and 1919. It incorporated stained-glass windows and ceiling paintings portraying human evolution. There were huge columns and a peculiar, bulbous double dome set on a curved concrete base. It was burned down in an act of arson on New Year's Eve 1922. Right-wing nationalists had frequently threatened Steiner—Hitler himself had denounced him the previous year—but the destruction of the Goetheanum was probably committed by a disgruntled anthroposophist. It had a disastrous effect on Steiner's health, aggravated by a punishing routine of lectures. He went into rapid decline and died in March 1925.

Nevertheless, despite his health problems, the year after the fire Steiner designed a replacement building known as the Second Goetheanum, which is the present structure. Any danger of its suffering the same fate as its predecessor was mitigated by building it entirely in cast concrete. Construction took place between 1924 and 1928. Because of its early use of unmasked concrete, it has been declared a Swiss national monument. Its concrete fabric gives it the appearance of having been hewn rather roughly out of rock. The structure is irregular and it rises in places to five stories. Its focus is an auditorium seating a thousand people, which has been remodeled twice: once in the 1950s and again in the early years of the twenty-first century. The ceiling paintings and the large columns are replicas of those in the First Goetheanum and the stained-glass windows date from Steiner's day.

Steiner had made much of his claim that the First Goetheanum had largely been intended for theatrical and dance performances. In reality, it was mainly designed for the celebration of esoteric rites derived partly from Freemasonry. This emerged plainly in the 1950s when the Anthroposophical Society's membership had to come to a decision regarding the interior decoration of the great hall of the Second Goetheanum. Although Steiner had apparently abandoned cultish celebrations in 1914 and therefore never used the earlier building for that purpose, one of his associates, E. A. Karl Stockmeyer, revealed in 1957 that Steiner had told him after the end of the First World War that he intended to resume the practice of rituals. Since Steiner died in 1925, while the new building was still under construction, he never performed rites within it; but it was designed for that purpose. Some anthroposophists were initiated into the second or third class of what was known as the Esoteric School and were sworn to Masonic-style secrecy. Steiner had begun a course of lectures to instruct them in the rituals only a few months before he died, though it has been questioned whether all of them understood the quasi-Masonic nature of the school. In any case, Steiner's death rendered the project stillborn and the hostility of the Nazis, who set about destroying all esoteric cults except their own from 1937 onward meant that anthroposophy gained little impetus from Germany, where it had formerly been strongest. So the Goetheanum was regarded as a cultural rather than an esoteric phenomenon. But the significance of this curious building can only be properly appreciated if one recognizes the occult purposes for which it was designed.

Bollingen Tower, Lake Zurich, Switzerland

A much more elegant structure than the Goetheanum, but also sited in Switzerland and designed to express certain mystical concepts, stands on the water's edge at the northern end of the Lake of Zurich. This is the Bollingen Tower, the rural retreat of Carl Jung (1875–1961), the father of analytical psychology. Jung did not confine his interest to psychology: He studied a wide range of subjects, including alchemy and astrology. His city home was in a suburb of Zurich, but he created the Bollingen Tower as a place to retreat for meditation in the country. It is situated near the village of Bollingen, twenty-five miles (40km) east of Zurich, in the canton of St. Gallen. In 1922 Jung bought a parcel of land by the lakeside on which he decided to build a modest residence—in effect, a hermitage.

Although some writers have referred to the building as an expression of turrophilia (love of towers), the first impression a visitor gets is that the tower is not very tall—just two stories—and its significance is further diminished by the buildings to which it is attached. The appearance is that of a bijou castle. This complex, however, took shape very slowly, over the period from 1922 to 1955, as Jung added more buildings to the basic structure. At the beginning there was only the tower, which he built himself. Jung bought stones from a nearby quarry and hired two stonemasons, who instructed him in the arts of splitting and dressing the stones and the correct method of erecting the structure. The hearth, as in traditional folklore, was the centerpiece of the modest dwelling, which amounted to little more than a hut and lacked all modern amenities on its completion in 1923; Jung added an upper story four years later, converting it into a tower. Here he lived a very simple life, cultivating the kind of existence that is often sought by environmentalists today, glimpses of which can be gleaned from his book *Memories, Dreams, Reflections*: "I have done without electricity, and tend the fireplace and stove myself. Evenings, I light the old lamps. There is no running water, and I pump the water from the well. I chop the wood and cook the food. These simple acts make man simple; and how difficult it is to be simple!"

Jung ascribed all sorts of mystical and emotional attributes to this original tower. It "represented for me the maternal heart," he claimed. He described it as a "representation in stone of my innermost thoughts and of the knowledge I had acquired . . . a confession of faith in stone." In 1931 he added an annex containing a "retiring room." This had been suggested to him by what he had seen in houses in

India. "I wanted a room in this tower where I could exist for myself alone," he explained. "I had in mind what I had seen in Indian houses, in which there is usually an area—though it may be only a corner of a room separated off by a curtain—to which the residents can withdraw." They would meditate in that space for up to half an hour and Jung wanted to imitate this example. So he built what is now the central part of the building with his very secret private room. There he would not only meditate, but paint murals, write his magician's log, and transport himself into a state of timelessness.

Jung's priority was to commune with his ancestors. He believed this was facilitated by the simplicity of his way of life at Bollingen and the absence of contemporary distractions: "There is nothing to disturb the dead, neither electric light nor telephone. Moreover, my ancestors' souls are sustained by the atmosphere of the house, since I answer for them the questions that their lives once left behind. I carve out rough answers as best I can. I have even drawn them on the walls. It is as if a silent, greater family, stretching down the centuries, were peopling the house."

In 1935 Jung decided on a further expansion and built a courtyard and loggia, with pillared arches and another hearth, whose enclosing wall brought the increasingly fortresslike edifice right down to the edge of the lake. By this stage the house was taking on the appearance of an elegant lakeside villa, such as a prosperous professional man might have built for himself—until it was subjected to closer inspection. Not only had Jung decorated the interior walls with pictures of his ancestors and other mystical and visionary concepts, but he had also carved the external stonework in a dramatic way. Human figures can be discerned, carved in relief, in the stonework, among other symbols. One lintel-like stone has images of the sun and the moon, above what looks like a Christian eucharistic representation of a chalice surmounted by a communion host bearing a cross. Overall, the imagery at Bollingen is derived from a wide variety of religious and cultural traditions.

The most celebrated carving is on a stone in the grounds, close to the lake. Its history is well documented. When a delivery of stone to provide materials for the encircling wall of the courtyard arrived from the local quarry, it mistakenly included one large cubelike block that was completely unsuitable. Instead of returning it, Jung placed it in the ground and carved a number of alchemical mottoes on it. One was in esoteric verse:

Here stands a mean, ungainly stone,
It's very low in price!
The more it is disdained by clowns,
The more loved by the wise.

On the front face of this stone Jung carved an eye and a homunculus, with a Greek inscription celebrating Telesphoros, "who ranges throughout the dark parts of the cosmos . . ." On another face of the stone Jung engraved more Latin alchemical inscriptions: "I am an orphan, solitary; yet I am to be found everywhere. I am one, but in conflict with myself." Jung, of course, had studied alchemy during his periods of solitude at Bollingen.

It would be unfair to judge a man by his choice of garden furniture, his poetic fancy, or his interest in studying ancient sciences as a matter perhaps of academic curiosity. Yet the cumulative impression created by the chaotic esotericism evinced by Jung in his life at Bollingen, as well as in his prolific writings, is that his is one of the great scholarly reputations of the twentieth century that may well be revisited by critical commentators in the twenty-first.

Although Jung had hailed the four stages of development of the tower, at four-yearly intervals, as a "quaternity," representing psychic wholeness, after the death of his wife he added an upper story to the more recent part of the house in 1955. That completed the building as it stands today and, by this stage, the originally Spartan conditions had been modified by the introduction of electricity. The house (by now the original tower was complemented by another turret of similar height) was still differentiated from more commonplace lakeside villas by the smallness of its narrow, arched, and mullioned windows. The overall effect is of a small medieval castle. Its interior today is much more comfortable and elegant than in those early years when Jung lived the life of a peasant within its unpretentious walls. The paneled library and the polished wooden flooring give it something of the appearance of a stately home in miniature.

Yet the enlargement of the property has so reduced the significance of the original feature that the name *Tower* is almost misleading. Jung, however, even as he added to his property, still thought of it as the Tower and it was in the original part of the house that the essential spirit of the enterprise resided, as far as he was concerned. "There is nothing in the Tower that has not grown into its own form over the decades, nothing with which I am not linked," he wrote. "Here everything has its history, and mine; here is space for the spaceless kingdom of the world's and the psyche's hinterland." In Bollingen Tower, Jung certainly gave voluble expression to his own psyche. Today the picturesque little castle is owned by the Jung family trust; it is not open to visitors.

In this chapter we have explored three very different buildings, one in Germany and two in Switzerland, ranging from the Gothic nightmare of Wewelsburg Castle, to the spiritual center of anthroposophy and the private retreat of the man who made the study of the human psyche his primary interest, but who also studied such esoteric subjects as alchemy and astrology. While it would be grossly inappropriate to link the Nazi grotesquerie of Wewelsburg with the other two sites in any other respect, they do have one factor in common: All three buildings were dedicated to the study of mysticism, whether in a barbaric or holistic form. In that sense, all three sites described here are of interest to students of the esoteric, the occult, and the arcane.

Chapter 5

CITADELS OF CHIVALRY

ewelsburg, as we saw in the preceding chapter, was an example of how the great ideals of Christian medieval knighthood could be perverted from their true aims of serving God and humanity—especially its weakest members—and some of the empty trappings appropriated to serve the most evil ends. As an antidote, we shall now look at how three of the surviving great military-religious orders of knighthood still pursue their charitable vocations today, often operating out of historic buildings that have great spiritual and aesthetic significance—true sanctuaries or citadels of chivalry. The doyen of all religious orders of knighthood is the Sovereign Military Hospitaller Order of St. John of Jerusalem, of Rhodes, and of Malta. That lengthy title is in itself a record of its adventurous history, an itinerary of the successive bases from which it strove to uphold its crusading ideal and defend Christendom. The Knights of St. John were famous builders. During their time in the Holy Land they hugely enlarged the fortifications of the castle they occupied at Le Crac des Chevaliers, located in present-day Syria, constructing concentric defenses that made it virtually impregnable. It was only finally captured by the Saracens in 1271 by a ruse, sending in a carrier pigeon with a forged message from the master ordering surrender. Even then, the garrison was in trouble simply because it numbered only two hundred men, when two thousand were required to man the castle's extensive defenses. So massive is the stonework at Crac that it is more or less intact even today. Lawrence of Arabia called it "probably the most wholly admirable castle in the world."

With such a heritage of military architecture it is unsurprising that when the Knights Hospitaller of St. John later ruled Rhodes, they built fortifications there that were also regarded as impregnable, many of which can still be seen today. They repeated the same exercise on Malta, which enabled them to withstand the frenzied Turkish siege of 1565. All these locations are familiar to international tourists; but more interesting, in the context of sanctuaries, are those private but picturesque premises from which the Knights of Malta conduct their vocation today.

The Knights of Malta, Rome

The Order of Malta is not easy to explain—or to understand—given its three most important characteristics, shared by no other institution in the world. First, it is one of the oldest religious orders; according to some commentators, *the* oldest (since earlier ones like the Benedictines were really then just independent abbeys based on a common rule). The core of the Order has always been its Knights in religious vows, and this remains no less true today. Second, it is the world's oldest continuously existing order of knighthood. Third, it is a sovereign entity, and recognized as such by a majority of the world's countries and international bodies, with its own (miniature) legal and court system. All this history and its resultant appurtenances are dedicated to the service of the sick, the poor, and refugees around the world— from the Order's leprosy clinics and rehabilitation centers in Thailand and Cambodia to Bethlehem, where it runs the only advanced maternity and neonatal hospital serving Muslim women and babies in the Palestinian territories. Despite (or perhaps because of) its crusading heritage, it enjoys good relations with Islamic countries. As historian H.J.A. Sire expresses it: "The vast charitable works . . . have shown the viability of an ancient chivalric ideal in the modern world. The peculiar achievement of the Knights of Malta is the conjuring trick by which they turn titles and ceremonies into hospitals, ambulances, medical supplies, transport of goods for the needy and services of all kinds—a conjuring trick the more singular because its ingredients are fantasy and its product substance." The Order's dignitaries gently twist the arms of CEOs of major pharmaceutical, food, and shipping companies to donate goods and services, which typically arrive duty-free (or via diplomatic pouch) thanks to the Order's special sovereign status and prestige. The Knights regularly outwit or circumvent local warlords, and sometimes ingeniously find ways to reuse material that's been discarded; for example, a derelict former hospital train has been refurbished by the Order as a night shelter for some thirty thousand homeless people in Budapest.

Some may regard the Order of Malta as a highly effective anachronism, but what also makes it unique is that it remains in possession of a number of architecturally and culturally important buildings and properties across Europe. Foremost among these is the Order's world headquarters and official seat, the Magistral Palace, located at Via dei Condotti, 68 in the heart of Rome within sight of (and a few paces from) the glorious Spanish Steps; the structure, occupying a large part of a city block, is sometimes also referred to as the Palazzo Malta. The Via Condotti (Street of the Water Pipes) is today Rome's most glamorous shopping destination, lined with the boutiques of Gucci, Bulgari, Ferragamo, Prada, Armani, and other high-fashion Italian couturiers with an international (and recently quite heavily Russian) clientele. However, both shoppers and window-shoppers have a tendency to stop at the gated entrance to the Magistral Palace, to peer into the courtyard with its Maltese cross fountain and cars displaying a mix of diplomatic and *SMOM* license plates (the Order, as a sovereign entity, has the right to issue its own car license plates). Overhead, from the balcony on the Via Condotti side, fly the two main flags of the Order: the state flag with a white Latin cross on a red field (reminiscent of the Danish flag) and the flag of the works of the Order—a white, eight-pointed Maltese cross on a red field. Brass plates on three sides of the palace display the Order's state arms and give notice that it is an extraterritorial property.

Although an impressive building, the Magistral Palace was once merely the Order's Embassy to the Vatican, and only became its headquarters after the loss of Malta. The interior includes various reception rooms, rich with silk-lined walls and gilded frames enclosing portraits of past grand masters, where visiting chiefs of state, heads of government, ambassadors, cardinals, and other dignitaries can be worthily entertained. There are also offices and meeting rooms, apartments for the grand master and those professed knights who live there, and a fine, small chapel. The chapel entrance includes a plaque commemorating the christening there of the baby Juan Carlos de Borbón, who is now King Juan Carlos I of Spain—born in Rome in 1938; during his family's exile from Spain, the Order provided hospitality to the Bourbons. Other "footnotes to history" within the house (as its resident knights call it) include several items relating to the brief, bizarre episode when Czar Paul I of Russia became de facto grand master of the Order, 1799–1801, in the chaotic period following Napoleon's expulsion of the Knights from Malta. Hanging on a wall in the palace is a curious portrait of the czar simultaneously wearing his imperial Russian regalia with the insignia of the grand master of the Order. Although canonically ineligible (he was, after all, not even Catholic), Czar Paul had a great affection for the Knights and their history, and irregularly assumed the headship in an effort to save the Order from extinction. In St. Petersburg, the Order's two palaces from that period (the Vorontzov Palace and the Prioral Palace) stand as beautiful reminders of Czar Paul's obsession; even today, the Knights of Malta constitute the only Roman Catholic institution for which Russians (and the Russian Orthodox Church) have an instinctive, passionate affection.

At the side of the Magistral Palace, at Via Bocca di Leone, 68, are two other interesting places, both of which can be visited without an invitation or appointment. One is the Order's main Roman medical clinic, which provides poor or homeless patients with free diagnostic and therapeutic care of a high caliber. Located at the same side entrance is the Order's Magistral Post Office, with its red post office boxes, where anyone can drop mail—provided they've bought stamps there issued by the Order and are sending letters or postcards to one of the countries with which the Order has a bilateral postal treaty. Some sixty nations have signed individual postal treaties with the Knights, although some nuisance is caused by the misunderstanding that still persists about the nature of the Order's sovereignty. Although the Order maintains full diplomatic relations with over one hundred countries and has permanent observer status at the UN, it has not yet been able to join the Universal Postal Union in Berne, Switzerland, the multilateral agency for the world's postal services. Still, the Order's stamps are beautifully designed, and are prized by collectors, whose purchases provide additional income to support the Order's various medical and charitable works around the world. While the stamps have been denominated in euros since 2005, the Order's handsome coins are still minted in gold, silver, and bronze for collectors in its traditional currency—the scudo. Like the similar nondecimal Roman-origin monetary units— shillings, for example—used by the UK (until 1971), Australia (until 1966), and New Zealand (until 1967), the Order's scudo (plural *scudi*) is divided into twelve tari, with each taro representing twenty grani. The Order's nondecimal coinage is probably the last such currency in the world. Definitely not available for purchase by collectors are the Order's diplomatic (red) and official service (blue) passports. These were formerly made in fine morocco leather (with their own leather slipcases), but bogus "Orders" and criminals frequently tried to forge them and pass themselves off as ambassadors or high officials of the Order at airports and border crossings around the world. Today, the Order's new high-tech biometric passports are produced by the Austrian State Printing house in Vienna, which is renowned globally for the precision and quality of its passport and banknote printing.

At the Magistral Palace, liveried footmen still wear rose-colored tailcoats and white gloves, but the normal attire for the busy knights inside is dark business suits, worn as they move from meeting to conference call and then back to e-mail, overseeing major medical and charitable projects in more than 120 countries. On the most formal state and diplomatic occasions (for example, some visits by presidents and prime ministers), they still don the ceremonial dress of the Order, a nineteenth-century military uniform of red tunic, gold-fringed epaulets, cocked hat, and sword. For solemn religious services, they put on a distinctive religious habit, a black choir-mantle whose design varies with the rank and status of the knight. Yet as they make their way by car to one of the Order's two other major properties in Rome, they are invariably in *abito scuro* (dark suit) with a discreet rosette in their lapel buttonhole.

Knights based at the Via Condotti regularly attend to other business at the substantially more ancient Casa di Rodi, occupied by the Order since the twelfth century at the Forum of Augustus, with its wealth of atmospheric imperial ruins. The Casa di Rodi, located at Piazza del Grillo, 1, is the seat of the Association of Italian Knights of the Order, numerically the largest in membership of the national associations existing today from Scandinavia to Singapore. However, the glory of the Order's sites in Rome is without doubt the Magistral Villa—or Villa Malta—located on its hilltop site at the Piazza dei Cavalieri di Malta, 4, on the Aventine, with the Tiber River below. Often referred to simply as "the Aventino," this private extraterritorial compound has stunning gardens and views of Rome, including via the famous keyhole in the front gate mentioned in nearly every tourist guide: By looking through it one can see the dome of St. Peter's Basilica framed by the garden hedges on either side of the main pathway inside the property. Arguably, it is the only place on earth where, in a single view, you can take in three sovereign entities: Looking through the Order's compound one can see the Vatican City State, with the Italian Republic in between. The Magistral Villa's priory church and exterior wall are also famous to art historians, as they were magnificently designed by artist and etcher Giovanni Battista Piranesi (in fact, they are the only architectural designs of his ever executed). The Aventino buildings and grounds perform several functions today, including serving as the Order's embassy to Italy as well as the seat of the Order's Grand Priory of Rome.

Even though the Order lost the vast majority of its European properties in the upheavals of the last few centuries (the Reformation,

French Revolution, and Napoleonic Wars), it has also retained (or in some cases recovered) other important parts of its nearly thousand-year-old patrimony. In Venice, for example, the attractive Palazzo Malta, at Castello 3253, remains, as it always has been, the seat of the Grand Priory of Lombardy and Venice. In Prague, the Czech Republic returned the splendid Baroque palace and Gothic priory church confiscated by both the Nazis and the communists; so the Grand Priory of Bohemia is back at its old address in the Mala Strana. The Grand Priory of Naples and Sicily is at Via del Priorato, 17 in Naples, and the Grand Priory of Austria remains substantially lodged at Johannesgasse, 2 in Vienna, with its nearby small, jewel-box-like priory church—the Malteserkirche—always a favorite with tourists. In Vienna, *New York Times* travel writers have occasionally recommended the four-star Hotel Mailberger-Hof at Annagasse 7, a family-run (if somewhat plain) hotel based in one of the Order's buildings, which promotes itself based on its knightly connection. The Mailberger-Hof was originally built to provide a Viennese base for the Order's ancient Commandery of Mailberg in Lower Austria. Rounding out some of the Order's other remaining European properties are the grand master's summer residences of the Villa La Pagana in Rapallo, on the Riviera-like Ligurian coast of Italy, and the Castello di Magione, an old Umbrian castle that also remains one of the Knights' three working wineries. (The Villa La Pagana was previously owned by the Spinola family of Genoa, who had the foresight to become early backers of an obscure seafarer we now know as Columbus.)

Wine sales do help fund the Order's hospitaller activities around the world, and in Italy the Knights also produce excellent grappa, honey, and olive oil—all sold ostentatiously marked with the Maltese cross and other appropriate heraldic flourishes. The decent red wines from the Castello di Magione and from Rocca Bernarda in Ipplis, in Udine (near Slovenia, in Italy's Friuli wine region) are now marketed in North America. The latter agricultural property and its castle were bequeathed to the Order in 1977 on the death of the Duke of Udine. At the earlier-mentioned Commandery of Mailberg in Austria, a fine schloss and small museum are at the heart of its vineyards, which produce a very drinkable white Grüner Veltliner as well as Sekt, the sparkling wine that is the Austrian and German version of champagne—also now exported widely.

The Knights are back, too, in Malta, more than two centuries after their loss of their island state. The 1802 Treaty of Amiens committed the European powers to return Malta to the Order, but in the end the British government (which had captured it from Napoleon) found it too strategic a Mediterranean naval base to comply—treaty or no treaty. Today the Order has returned, not as a ruler, but in its historic hospitaller, spiritual, and cultural role. The Order's flag flies over its fortress-turned-embassy at St. John's Cavalier, on Ordnance Street, in the capital city of Valletta, and also over the headquarters of its Maltese Association at Casa Lanfreducci, 2, Victory Square. Even more significant is the Order's presence once more at Fort Sant' Angelo in Birgu, the most important of the Order's fortresses, where it had planned (if necessary) a heroic last stand during the siege of Malta in 1565. In the 1990s, the Order and the Republic of Malta entered into intensive negotiations about the possibility of the Order's return to the fortress, which is now used as a training and retreat center as well as a venue for museum-quality exhibitions. The republic had at one point considered ceding the fortress and the land it stood on to the Order as sovereign territory in perpetuity, which would have been a welcome gesture. Even though the Order is able to assert its nonterritorial sovereignty, with the majority of the world's countries and multilateral institutions recognizing it, in some sense it would have been simpler for it to possess a portion of sovereign territory, no matter how small. After the fall of Malta, the king of Sweden briefly offered the Baltic island of Gotland, while others hypothetically suggested Elba or Ibiza, among other possible territories. In the mid-twentieth century, a sympathetic President Charles de Gaulle weighed in with some notions of his own. From 1933 to the departure of British forces in 1979, Fort Sant' Angelo had served as the Royal Navy shore establishment HMS St. Angelo, after which the place became an empty shell in need of a loving tenant. In the end, the Republic of Malta offered the Order a ninety-nine-year, extraterritorial lease, roughly on the model of the status of the New Territories in the former Crown colony of Hong Kong. In December 1998, on the basis of a new ninety-nine-year treaty, the Knights of Malta formally took repossession of the fortress, with all its history and a truly commanding view of Valletta's Grand Harbour—one of the world's great deep-water ports. As their history shows, they had paid a heavy price for it in blood more than four centuries earlier.

The Tuscan Order of St. Stephen Pope and Martyr, Pisa

If imitation is the sincerest form of flattery, then the founder of the smaller, but also highly militarily effective, knightly Order of St. Stephen paid the Order of Malta a high compliment. The Sacred Military Order of St. Stephen Pope and Martyr was the last crusading order of knighthood to be founded—as late as 1562. It was not thought a propitious time: The Knights Hospitaller of St. John had lost Rhodes in 1522 and were now reduced to the barren rock of Malta; in the same year that the Order of St. Stephen was founded, the Teutonic Order lost the last remnant of its once-mighty Baltic empire. Yet the creator of the Knights of St. Stephen, Cosimo de' Medici, first grand duke of Tuscany, was known as a realist rather than a romantic, so it was assumed that he had good reason for his action. Indeed he had: Under the hereditary grand mastership of his dynasty, he forged an important naval fighting machine, closely modeled on the Order of Malta—its red, eight-pointed cross on a white background was a straightforward reversal of the Maltese insignia. It also imitated the Knights of Malta in waging seagoing warfare.

Today the Order of St. Stephen is recognized as the predecessor organization of the Italian Navy. The Knights of St. Stephen waged unremitting war against the Turkish and Barbary corsairs who infested the Mediterranean, sacking entire cities in Sicily and on the Italian mainland, massacring or enslaving their citizens. In fact, Cosimo I's timing proved uncannily good: Three years after he founded his Order, the Knights of Malta successfully defended their island against a massive Turkish force, killing thirty thousand of the besiegers, and six years after that the great Christian naval victory at the Battle of Lepanto, in 1571, neutralized Turkish sea power for the remaining centuries of the Ottoman Empire. Suddenly, with the Christians winning, the crusade no longer seemed passé and the Order of St. Stephen had no shortage of recruits.

In the course of its crusade, between 1563 and 1775, when it fought its last action by participating in a Spanish attack on Algiers, the Order of St. Stephen is known to have sunk 44 Ottoman and allied vessels and captured 270, taken 14,870 prisoners, freed 4,840 Christians from slavery, and carried off 350 enemy flags. Since the records are incomplete, that must be regarded as an underestimate. Clearly, these latecomers to crusading were serious players. The Order lost its connection with the state when the Grand Duchy of Tuscany (by then under Habsburg rule) was absorbed into the unitary kingdom of Italy in 1859, but it still exists today. The fascinating legacy it has left to the civilized world is its conventual church and the administrative buildings that surround it in the Piazza dei Cavalieri in Pisa, the city where the Order had its headquarters.

This square, which is Pisa's most important concentration of architecture, was the concept of the artist and architect Giorgio Vasari, who also built the Uffizi in Florence. On the site of the old Church of St. Sebastian, Vasari began construction of the Conventual Church of St. Stephen on April 17, 1565; it was consecrated on December 21, 1569. The entire frontage of the church is decorated in marble installed between 1594 and 1606. Inside, the church is divided into a central nave and two side aisles, all richly decorated with military trophies relating to the Knights' battles. The high altar, which depicts Pope St. Stephen I in glory, is made of marble from Luni, jasper from Barga and Sicily, and bronze gilt. It incorporates a marble papal throne and the body of Pope St. Stephen (the Order's patron, martyred in 257), brought here with great ceremony in 1682. On either side of the high altar are two historic organs, the one on the right, by Onofrio Zeffirini, dating from 1567, the one on the left, by Azzolino Bernardino della Ciaia, dating from 1732. The church also contains four side altars ornamented with laurel leaves and ribbons carved in white Carrara and yellow Siena marble. Various paintings in the church illustrate episodes from the life of St. Stephen, of which *The Martyrdom of St. Stephen, Pope* is attributed to Vasari himself.

The church's crowning artistic glories, however, are to be found on the ceiling, where painted panels record the history of the Order, with scenes such as *The Robing of Cosimo I as Grand Master* by Ludovico Cardi ("Il Cigoli"); *The Return of the Fleet of the Order After the Battle of Lepanto,* by Jacopo Ligozzi; and *Maria de' Medici Embarking on her Journey to Wed Henri IV, King of France,* by Cristofano Allori, all executed in 1604. The same theme of the Order's military glory is emphasized by fragments of its state galleys, which decorate the walls of the church; these are richly carved with representations of Turkish slaves and military trophies. What gives the visitor the sensation of brushing against history is the display of flags captured from the Turks and Barbary corsairs over more than two centuries of crusade. The most important is the great battle flag of the Kapudan Pasha—Ali Pasha, the commander-in-chief of the Turkish fleet—captured by the Knights of St. Stephen at the decisive moment in the Battle of Lepanto, October 7, 1571. It hangs to the left of the marble pulpit. There were originally 117 banners hanging in the church, of which 92 survive today. Their preservation was due to the dedication of an Irishwoman named Sarah Butler Staunton Handcock who, in the nineteenth century, undertook conservation work on them as a labor of love, including the standard of the Kapudan Pasha and the next most significant trophy, the large pennant taken from the flagship of the corsair fleet of Biserta (a pirate port of the Barbary corsairs) by Camillo Guidi, admiral of the Order, on July 19, 1675. The Conventual Church of St. Stephen maintains its connection with the Order and it was here, on Sunday, June 11, 1994, that its present head, the Grand Duke Sigismund of Tuscany, was solemnly enthroned as seventeenth grand master of the Order.

Adjoining the church is the very impressive Palazzo dei Cavalieri Carovanisti or Palazzo della Carovana (Palace of the "Caravan")—the term *caravan* was used to describe the periods that knights spent on service at sea, which counted toward their eventual promotion to a commandery. This was the principal residence of the Knights and its splendor reflected the high birth and military renown of its occupants. Here the young knights spent three years studying courses in geography, cosmography, mathematics, nautical science, and naval and land strategy. Vasari began work on this building at the same time as the church. Behind its uniform façade he was actually incorporating the existing buildings, of irregular design, of the old Palace of the Elders, as a cost-saving measure. He worked so fast that, within two years, the Knights were able to move in. Work continued, however, until 1567, and was resumed on the kitchen and service areas from 1577 to 1580. The internal decoration was subdued, except in the two public saloons: the Weapons Room (now the *Sala Azzurra*) and the Fencing Room (now the *Salone degli Stemmi*), which were given decorative paneled ceilings.

But if austerity reigned inside this dwelling for warrior monks, the opposite applied with regard to the external façade of the palace. Here Vasari made everything as grand and symmetrical as possible. The ornate arms of the Medici, incorporating the cross of the Order of St. Stephen, surmount the entrance, repeated at each end of the frontage; on the same level, six niches contain imposing portrait busts of Medici grand dukes of Tuscany who were also grand masters of the Order. Yet what really gives the façade an impression of overwhelming grandeur is the carefully worked *sgraffito* that covers every available panel of stonework. This art form originated in Germany, its technique consisting of applying layers of plaster tinted in contrasting colors to the moistened wall surface and then scratching on it to produce outline drawings. When applied consistently over so large a wall surface as the entire frontage of the Palazzo della Carovana, the overall impression is sumptuous, though it was probably a relatively inexpensive art form, compatible with Vasari's restricted budget. The decorations were executed by Tommaso di Battista del Verrocchio and Alessandro Forzori di Arezzo. In later times marble was introduced into the balcony and the front doorframe. The statue of Cosimo I, with its fountain, which stands in front of the palace, was commissioned by Grand Duke Ferdinand I (who reigned from 1587 to 1609); the elegant external staircase leading up to the front entrance was redesigned in neoclassical style in 1821. The Order of St. Stephen lost this building, along with the rest of its property, in 1859; five years later it became the seat of an academic institution, Pisa's Scuola Normale Superiore.

When Vasari embarked on his enterprise of transforming the old city square that became the Piazza dei Cavalieri, he envisioned turning it into a unified complex dedicated to the Order of St. Stephen. So he also allocated a site on the south side of the piazza to the Canonica, more grandly known as the Palazzo dei Cavalieri Sacerdoti, the residence of the chaplains of the Order. The building, based on Vasari's concept, was constructed by Davide Fortini, who had also been director of works for the Conventual Church, in 1566. It is sober in style, built of reddish-brown stone, and clearly delineates the inferior status of the chaplains compared with the military knights in their grandiose Palazzo della Carovana. The remaining Stefanian buildings in the Piazza dei Cavalieri include the Palazzo dell' Orologio, known to the knights as the Palazzo del Buon Uomo (meaning, the Infirmary), since the Order's Grand Hospitaller was known as the Buonomo dell'Infermeria. This palazzo was created by merging two medieval towers—the Torre delle Sette Vie (this was the original name of the square, since seven roads led into it, until the creation of the new complex reduced them to four) and the Torre dei Gualandi. The latter was also more ominously known as the Tower of Hunger because, in the thirteenth century, Count Ugolino della Gherardesca, the chief magistrate of Pisa who had Guelph sympathies, was imprisoned there by the rival Ghibelline Party, along with his children and grandchildren, to die of starvation. The episode is mentioned in Dante's *Inferno,* Canto XXXIII. The clock from which the palazzo now takes its name was removed from the bell tower of the Conventual Church and installed here in 1696.

The remaining building of interest is the Palazzo del Consiglio dei Dodici (Palace of the Council of Twelve—referring to the dozen high officers of the Order of St. Stephen). This palace was renovated in late-Renaissance style in 1603 by Pietro Francavilla, who also made the statue of Cosimo I that stands in front of the Palazzo della Carovana, to make it harmonize with the other buildings in the square. Only as late as 1691 was it fully absorbed into the Order's administrative machinery. It has many ornamental features and houses several significant works of art. It was in this palace, just after his enthronement in the Conventual Church, that the present grand master of the Order of St. Stephen gave an address in which he rededicated the Order to its charitable works and saluted Tuscany, of which "completely without any personal merit, but for historical reasons, I am today the living symbol, the incarnation of her Tradition."

The Teutonic Order

The Teutonic Order of St. Mary in Jerusalem was the junior partner of the two earlier-established knighthoods of the Temple and the Hospital. Its membership was drawn from the lands within the Holy Roman Empire and its unique feature was that, besides fighting like the other crusaders in the Holy Land, it also conducted a crusade of its own, on the Baltic coast, against the heathen Prussians and other savage tribes of northeastern Europe. After the fall of the Latin kingdom of Jerusalem, the Teutonic Knights established a temporary headquarters in Venice. Then came the suppression of the Templars, which filled the other military orders with foreboding. These fears were well founded, in the case of the Teutonic Knights: In 1308 they learned that the Archbishop of Riga, jealous of their power on the Baltic, had demanded the suppression of their Order on the basis of extravagant allegations similar to those that had brought the Templars to ruin. Unlike the Templars, the Teutonic Knights had a base to which they could retreat, beyond the reach of papal and inquisitorial power. In 1309, therefore, the Grand Master Siegfried von Feuchtwangen moved his court from Venice to the castle of Marienburg in East Prussia, outside the boundaries of the Holy Roman Empire, where he and his successors could reign in unchallenged sovereignty.

From Marienburg, on the east bank of the River Nogat in Poland (it is now known as Malbork), the grand masters ruled a vast empire, stretching from the River Oder to the River Narva on the Gulf of Finland. Marienburg (the "Castle of Mary," in honor of the Mother of God) was the largest Gothic fortress in Europe, continuously being expanded over 230 years, from 1274. After the Knights' serious defeat by the Polish king at Tannenberg in 1410, which marked the beginning of the Order's decline, Marienburg successfully resisted a siege. It was never conquered, but was pawned by the bankrupt Order in 1457 to mercenary soldiers who sold it to the Poles. In 1945 it was more than half destroyed by artillery fire, but today has been entirely restored, apart from the church.

Marienburg is a symphony in red brick and gray stone. It is a maze of steep, red-tiled roofs, dormers, towers, mullioned windows, arches, and cobbled courtyards. From the main enclosure, with its grassy lawns, it looks as if some Oxford college had somehow grown to massive proportions. The visitor cannot help but be overwhelmed by so much fortified masonry: It covers fifty-two acres (21ha)—four times the area of the great Windsor Castle in England. This is the epitome of medieval Gothic Catholic crusading ideals—hard praying and hard fighting—the genuine version of what Himmler tastelessly parodied at Wewelsburg: This is the genuine article. It is divided into three main fortifications: the High, Middle, and Low castles. Among the statues on display is one of Siegfried von Feuchtwangen, the first grand master to reign from here; the statue is in perfect condition except that, almost symbolically, the grand master's right hand is broken off. The most striking and realistic statue is that of Winrich von Kniprode, one of the greatest of the Order's grand masters who presided over an era of expansion in the fourteenth century: He is buried in the mausoleum beneath the Chapel of St. Anne. Marienburg also has a museum with both permanent exhibitions relating to its history and specially themed ones on a regular basis. Restoration work has begun on the church, but is expected to be lengthy and expensive, if it is to be faithfully returned to its original Gothic style. When seeking directions from Polish locals, visitors are well advised to ask for "Malbork"—its Polish name—and not "Marienburg," as historical and cultural sensitivities run deep.

At the Reformation, when its apostate grand master Albrecht von Hohenzollern embraced Lutheranism, secularized the Teutonic Order's remaining Prussian lands in 1525, and laid the foundations for Hohenzollern Germany, the remaining Catholic Knights established their headquarters at Mergentheim in Franconia, situated today in the state of Baden-Württemberg. The circumstances were not auspicious: Mergentheim had been sacked in 1526 during the Peasants' Revolt, but the surviving Knights assembled there the following year and elected a new grand master, Walther von Cronberg. From 1527 to 1809, the grand master ruled as a prince of the Holy Roman Empire from the Deutschordenschloss (Castle of the Teutonic Order) in Mergentheim. The sovereign state surrounding it—a typical Holy Roman Empire principality—extended to forty square miles (104km²) within which the grand master ruled over 200,000 subjects. Cronberg began the expansion of the Schloss, the work being continued by his successors, until the various buildings in the inner courtyard were joined into a single white Renaissance-style complex dominated by twin towers topped by pinnacles, typical of Middle European castle architecture. A famous spiral staircase between the west and north wings, designed by the principal architect, Blasius Berwart, was built in 1574. The main feature is the church, built in the Baroque style in 1730. Its interior, in the more lush rococo style, is crowned by ornate ceiling frescoes by Nikolaus Gottfried Stuber, illustrating such themes as *The Defense of the Faith* and *The Emperor Constantine's Vision of the Cross.* The grand masters enjoyed a congenial lifestyle here throughout the seventeenth and eighteenth centuries, in the typical manner of a small German court, though their military force (apart from the formidable Hoch- und Deutschmeister Regiment stationed in distant Vienna, of which the grand master was ex officio colonel) was reduced to a small corps of elegant Life Guards in ornamental white uniforms. This agreeable existence was terminated in 1809 by Napoleon, who drove the Knights out of Germany. The rococo chapel became Protestant and remains so today. The Schloss is open to the public and includes a museum dedicated to the Order, as well as elegant state rooms renovated in the 1990s.

Having been dislodged from Mergentheim in 1809, the Teutonic Order moved to its final, and current, seat at Singerstrasse 7 in Vienna. Far from its origins in the Middle East and from its lost outposts on the Baltic, the Order regenerated itself in the cozy, coffee-flavored embrace of the Habsburg imperial capital, opening up hospitals and other charitable facilities. Under the dynamic grand mastership of Archduke Eugene (d. 1954), an Austrian career army officer (later field marshal) who took religious vows as a Teutonic knight, the renewed Order flourished. So did its crack infantry regiment, the Hoch- and Deutschmeister, which also had an excellent military band. However, after the loss of the First World War and the breakup of the empire, Archduke Eugene stepped down and agreed to the Order's transformation into a clerical (rather than knightly) order, so as to maximize the chance of its survival. Today, the Singerstrasse head-quarters is the base for an approximately one-thousand-strong order of priests, brothers, sisters, nursing volunteers, donors, and a small handful of honorary knights working not only in Austria, but also in neighboring Italy, Slovenia, Slovakia, the Czech Republic, Germany, and other parts of Central Europe. Mozart lodged at the Order's Singerstrasse residence for a few weeks in 1781, and the Knights' church there remains a rare Gothic survival in a part of Europe where everything tended to be absorbed by the Baroque—if not the rococo. On its walls hangs an outstanding collection of heraldic shields of professed knights who took their vows until the fateful year of 1914, when the last new knight—Baron Georg Skrbensky von Hrzistie—was solemnly invested. The Treasury (or *Schatzkammer*) is the Order's museum, open to visitors, which includes not only precious art objects, but also nearly a thousand years' worth of flotsam and jetsam from the peregrinations of the Knights, including unremarkable bits of Baltic amber and a curious "Viper Tongue Credenza"—a device that was said to detect poison in food and render it harmless. In Vienna, admittedly, such curiosities hardly count as unusual, given the contents of the city's Funeral Museum, Pathological-Anatomy Museum, Tobacco Museum, and Freud Museum.

As a consequence of the firestorms and compromises that followed in the wake of the Reformation, the Teutonic Order became—for a time—a triconfessional order, with Catholic, Lutheran, and Calvinist leadership positions allocated by the Treaty of Westphalia in 1648. The unique survival from this period is the Dutch Bailiwick of Utrecht of the Teutonic Knights, still located at its elegant Duitse Huis at Springweg 25, in the city of Utrecht in the Netherlands. Since the main Catholic Order was transformed into a clerical body of priests and brothers in 1929, one might claim that the Dutch members of the Utrecht Bailiwick are the last traditional-style Teutonic Knights in existence (though the main Order still creates a limited number of Knights of Honor). The Bailiwick has a relatively small but distinguished membership of Dutch noblemen of the Reformed faith, who are admired by the public for the charitable projects they pursue in Holland. The Duitse Huis has a number of impressive rooms, including the meeting room for the Bailiwick's officers; on the walls hang portraits of every *Landcommandeur,* living and dead. Until recently, each head of the Bailiwick was painted wearing armor with a white Teutonic mantle draped on his shoulders. In view of the large size of the Bailiwick's property in central Utrecht, the Knights decided to redevelop some of the unused buildings and grounds of the Duitse Huis as a hotel. This is now the Grand Hotel Karel V, a five-star hostelry that opened in 1999 with a restaurant that has been awarded a Michelin star.

Chapter 6

GROTTOES AND GROTESQUES

*H*hat is it that drives us to seek sanctuary under-ground? Does our distant cave-dwelling past prompt some kind of genetic memory to trigger our troglo-dyte instincts? Or is it, more practically, the simple fact that when people are engaged in some nefarious enterprise, intent on evading authority, their deeds are best transacted in a subterranean hideaway? Whatever the motivation, it is a matter of historical record that con-spirators and fugitives have notoriously sought protection in caverns and grottoes, natural or human-made. The early Christians' sojourn in the Catacombs was just the best-known example. In this chapter we shall consider the ancient secret passageway in Rome known as the Passetto di Borgo (made famous in Dan Brown's novel *Angels and Demons*); the Magic Door, situated in the same city (not actually under-ground but worthy of inclusion because of its geographical proximity and its weird history); the Grotto of the Beati Paoli in Sicily; and the many priest holes in England that sheltered fugitive Catholic clergy being hunted by the Protestant authorities in the sixteenth and sev-enteenth centuries.

The Passetto di Borgo, Rome

Friday, May 6, 1527 dawned foggy in the city of Rome, capital of the Papal States and of the Catholic Church. Before sunset that day, the Holy City would suffer the cruelest depredation inflicted on it since the Barbarian invasions a thousand years earlier. For advancing through the fog to the north of the city walls was an army of crazed mutineers, nominally under the authority of the Holy Roman Emperor Charles V, but by now a murderous rabble bent on slaughter, pillage, and rape. The Imperial Army, waging war in the north of Italy against the French and other members of the alliance known as the League of Cognac—which included the pope, Clement VII—had not been paid, so it had forced its nominal commander, an exiled French prince, Charles III, Duc de Bourbon, known as the Constable de Bourbon, to march south to Rome. The Eternal City would offer rich booty, but there was a further motive involved: Of the 22,000 mutinous troops, the majority were German Lutheran mercenaries who loathed the Catholic Church and wanted to destroy the Vatican. At the same time, the minority of Spanish Catholic regular troops in this nightmare army did not conduct themselves with any more restraint. The pope knew that his enemies were at the gates. None of his own troops were in the city, apart from his Swiss Guard, a small unit that could not hope to hold off the many thousands of merce-naries descending like wolves on his capital. A few hundred Roman citizens manned the walls, but they too represented a forlorn hope.

Clement VII had brought this crisis upon himself, due to his weakness, duplicity, and diplomatic blundering. He was the second pope elected from the wealthy Medici family of Florence. His father, Giuliano de' Medici, had been murdered a few months before the future pope's birth and he had been brought up by his uncle, Lorenzo the Magnificent. He had entered the Church, becoming a cardinal under the patronage of his cousin Pope Leo X. In 1523 he was elected pope and began to engage in diplomatic maneuvers to free himself from the dominance of the Holy Roman Emperor Charles V. The emperor's power became even more oppressive in 1525 when the king of France, Francis I, was defeated and captured by the Imperial Army at the Battle of Pavia. To counteract this, an alliance was formed known as the League of Cognac, in which the pope foolishly joined forces with France, England, Florence, Venice, and Milan against the emperor. Charles V was furious with the pope for what he regarded as his treachery in joining the League and made no serious effort to prevent his troops—by now, in any case, totally out of control—from marching on Rome, though he came to regret the tragic consequences.

That misty May morning, the pope deliberated about whether to receive the invaders defiantly, seated on his throne and surrounded by his court, as Pope Boniface VIII had done in the face of another invasion two centuries earlier, or as Leo the Great had confronted Attila the Hun in 452; but this notion was quickly dismissed as unrealistic. The Lutherans would have killed him, precipitating a religious war across Europe. Instead, the pope went to pray in St. Peter's Basilica, protected by the Swiss Guard. This unit, which had been formed only twenty-one years earlier, consisted of just 189 soldiers, commanded by Kaspar Roist. These troops came from Zurich, where the Reformation was already under way, so the authorities had summoned them home. Roist and his men, however, had refused to break their oath of loyalty to the pope, a chivalrous gesture that was to cost them dearly this day. As the invaders swarmed into the city, the pope had to cut short his prayers and seek refuge. The only possible refuge lay in the mighty fortress of Castel Sant'Angelo and although the imperial troops were already pouring into the Borgo, the residential area that lay between the Vatican and the castle, Clement VII knew of a secret route to safety. There was not a minute to lose. The enemy had just stormed into the Hospital of the Santo Spirito, where they slaughtered all the patients, whose screams first alerted the Romans to the full savagery of the horror that was descending upon them. Even the pope could expect no mercy in the face of such bloodlust. So he was urged to make his escape through one of the most ancient secret passages in Europe: the Passetto di Borgo.

Roist and most of his gallant Swiss volunteered to hold off the invaders as long as they could, to buy time for the pope to make his way to Castel Sant'Angelo. The remainder, forty-two guardsmen led by Hercules Göldli, surrounded the pontiff to protect him during his flight via the Passetto to the castle. Unlike most secret passages, which are underground, the Passetto is high up inside an ancient wall, at the height of a third story. The history of the wall that hides the passageway goes back to very early times. The first wall running along this site was built around 550 by Totila, a king of the Ostrogoths who conquered much of Italy. Even today a few stone blocks still survive from that original wall. Pope Leo IV was determined to rebuild the wall, and on June 27, 852 he ceremonially inaugurated the project by walking barefoot around the circuit of the proposed structure which ran for 1.3 miles (2km) and was reinforced by forty-four towers. The wall ran around the Vatican and the adjoining area, now enclosed by the fortifications, was named after this pope: the Leonine City. It had a separate administration from the rest of Rome and the pope populated it with Corsican settlers. Later, in 1277, Pope Nicholas III created the Passetto, running along the interior of the wall, high up, for a distance of 875 yards (800m), to form an enclosed and secret passageway between the Vatican and the impregnable fortress of Castel Sant'Angelo, which had originally been the mausoleum of the Emperor Hadrian.

Initially, this private escape route was known as the Corridore di Borgo (Corridor of the Borgo district)—*Borgo* being the name of the quarter within the Leonine City next to the Vatican, whose houses and vegetable gardens occupied the area between the Basilica of St. Peter and Castel Sant'Angelo. Finally, in 1492, Alexander VI completed the structure by building a battlemented footway along the top of the wall. This had the effect of further camouflaging the Passetto: To the casual observer, it appeared to be a thick defensive wall with machicolations on top where defenders would be posted in time of war. What looked like defensive loopholes immediately below the battlements were actually narrow windows illuminating and ventilating the Passetto. For further security, at the point where the wall finally connected with the Castel Sant'Angelo, it passed over the moat of the fortress above a row of windowless archways, disguised as an aqueduct serving the castle. Just two years later Alexander VI had recourse to the Passetto, to escape into Castel Sant'Angelo when Charles VIII of France and his army marched into Rome.

The interior of the Passetto is narrow and claustrophobic, the ceiling forming a rounded arch along its length. On this morning in 1527, Pope Clement VII only just made it into the safety of this escape route: One chronicler remarked that if he had waited long enough to say the Credo three times he would have been captured. Behind him, Kaspar Roist and his 146 gallant, doomed Swiss Guards fought like lions to buy time for the fleeing pontiff. They were cut down by swarms of German mercenaries close to the spot where the obelisk stands in St. Peter's Square. Clement VII was indecisive, but he was no coward. Yet the inhuman sounds of the Holy City being put to the sword unnerved him and everyone in his entourage. The pope had an olivine complexion, well-defined dark eyebrows, and a long graying beard, forked in the center. His most prominent feature was his nose, very long and straight, unlike the acquiline version usually associated with Italian nobles; as he aged, it had grown more pronounced. Clement had thrown the long red silk cloak and train—the *cappa del papa*—that popes wore in those days over his nightshirt. One of the cardinals running, panting, beside him along the narrow Passetto, where only two men at a time could walk abreast—with difficulty—bundled up the voluminous silk train over his arms to help the pope move more freely. As they passed the windows, they could hear the German soldiers below shouting derisively in praise of "Pope Luther." Convinced that the murderers might glimpse the pope through one of the windows—actually very unlikely—the cardinal threw the red mantle over the pope's head to conceal his face. In this manner, stumbling blindly along the narrow tunnel, Clement VII reached the safety of Castel Sant'Angelo.

The castle was filled with refugees of lesser rank and those able-bodied men who were willing to offer resistance to the invaders. The carnage in the city below was appalling. Clement stood on the battlements of Castel Sant'Angelo, raised his tear-filled eyes to heaven, and quoted the biblical words of Job the afflicted: "Wherefore, then, hast thou brought me forth out of the womb? Oh, that I had died and no eye had seen me!" A more robust response came from the most prominent among the defenders of Castel Sant'Angelo—Benvenuto Cellini, complete man of the Renaissance, genius, artist, and thug par excellence. The only thing Cellini enjoyed more than crafting exquisite statuettes in gold or silver was uninhibited violence (he was credited with killing four men in the course of his life). In the first attempt by the invaders to storm Castel Sant'Angelo, the constable of Bourbon, at the head of his troops, was killed—apparently by Cellini. The leadership of the rabble then devolved upon Philibert, prince of Orange, Frustrated in their attempt to take the great castle, the invaders indulged in an eight-day orgy of murder, rape, and plunder. Churches were ransacked, prelates humiliated and tortured. Some of the unfortunates tortured by the imperialists were driven to seek refuge in suicide. There were striking instances of enterprise as well: A cardinal found refuge in Sant'Angelo by having himself hauled up the walls in a basket suspended from ropes, on the model of the scriptural account of St. Paul, except that the situation was reversed, with the fugitive seeking entrance instead of egress.

By the end of those eight days of mayhem and the less concentrated terror that continued afterwards, the population of Rome had fallen from 55,000 to 10,000, though it is impossible to determine what proportion of the missing citizens were dead and how many had fled the city. The pope held out in Castel Sant'Angelo until he eventually surrendered on terms. The brave Kaspar Roist, though severely wounded, survived the battle in St. Peter's Square; later, however, Spanish soldiers stormed into his quarters and butchered him in front of his wife. That day earned the Papal Swiss Guard as much honor as it brought disgrace to the imperialists: To this day, new recruits are solemnly sworn into the Swiss Guard on May 6, to commemorate the heroism of the unit, whose only survivors were the small contingent that had escorted the pope through the Passetto.

As recently as the early twentieth century, it was still customary for an NCO of the Swiss Guard to keep custody of the entrance to the Passetto, in case the pontiff should ever again need to make his escape through it. Today it is closed up and in a state of some disrepair, though it is still occasionally possible to make special arrangements to enter it. The Passetto also regained fame when it was featured in Dan Brown's novel *Angels and Demons,* though the author imaginatively altered the real geography of the secret passage by relocating its entrance to the pope's library. The Passetto di Borgo is a badly kept secret, insofar as most Romans know of its existence and history, yet very few have ever been inside it. More than seven centuries old, embedded in a wall more than 1,100 years old, it remains one of the eeriest and most atmospheric places in a city that has more than its share of secrets.

The Magic Door, Rome

Still in Rome, there is another curiosity which, because it stands aboveground, can hardly be classed as a grotto, but most certainly belongs in the category of the grotesque. This is the Magic Door, in the Piazza Vittorio Emmanuele. It is a white doorway that leads to nowhere, guarded by two large and outlandish statues, set in a wall and bricked up. Above the door is a large disk bearing the six-pointed star emblem of King Solomon and the archway is decorated with cabalistic signs and inscriptions in Latin. This is all that remains of the Villa Palombara, the meeting place for an active group of alchemists in Rome in the seventeenth century.

The wall in which this door is set originally belonged to the nearby Church of Sant'Eusebio and adjoins the remains of the third-century "nymphaeum" of Alexander Severus, once a decorative fountain complex. Both it and the Magic Door are situated in a garden in the center of the busy city square, Piazza Vittorio. In the seventeenth century, the whole area of the square was occupied by the Villa Palombara, the magnificent town house of Massimiliano Palombara, marquis of Pietraforte (1614–1680). The marquis, like others of his credulous generation, was obsessed with alchemy and the search for the Philosopher's Stone that would turn base metals into gold. Beside his villa he had an outhouse that he used as a laboratory; the peculiar door with its esoteric symbols is all that remains of that summerhouse laboratory. Palombara was rich and moved in the highest social circles. One of the amateur alchemists who belonged to the Villa Palombara group was the exiled Queen Christina of Sweden, who had an elaborately equipped laboratory of her own in what is now the Palazzo Corsini, under the supervision of Pietro Antonio Bandiera. Palombara was said to be a member of the Rosicrucians, the esoteric secret society that was arguably a forerunner of modern Freemasonry, and his companions were as exotic as that affiliation would suggest. Even the most colorful of them were outdone, however, by an adventurer who suddenly appeared in their midst: Giuseppe Francesco Borri, whose memorial is the Magic Door.

Borri, an alchemist and messianic prophet, was born in Milan and entered a Jesuit seminary in Rome in 1644. There he was taught by the Jesuit scholar Athanasius Kircher, an eclectic genius who was the first to understand the origins of the plague and how to contain it and who, in a spirit of scientific inquiry, once had himself lowered into the volcanic cone of Mount Vesuvius shortly before an eruption. Kircher was a genuine, if sometimes misguided, scholar (he appears in Umberto Eco's novel *The Island of the Day Before*). He was also the founder of the study of Egyptology and spent much of his life trying unsuccessfully to decipher Egyptian hieroglyphics. That was the aspect of his teaching that had the greatest effect on his pupil Borri, who soon abandoned the conventional vocation of the Church for a career as an itinerant alchemist. His life was necessarily nomadic, as he was frequently just one step ahead of the Inquisition and other authorities that took a dim view of his occultism.

The legend of the Magic Door runs as follows. One morning in 1657 the servants of the marquis caught somebody gathering herbs in his garden. The intruder, who turned out to be Borri, told Palombara that he was aware of his alchemical experiments and he proposed a mutual exchange of research information, claiming he had knowledge of how to transmute base metal into gold. After some animated conversation, Borri began an experiment in the laboratory belonging to Palombara. He asked to stay in the villa overnight and begged for the keys to the laboratory so that he could look in from time to time to see how his experiment was developing. The marquis agreed; but when he went to the laboratory the following morning Borri had disappeared, leaving behind him an upturned crucible, streaks of gold on the floor, and some papers covered with hermetic symbols.

The flaw in this dramatic account is that Borri had almost certainly known Palombara for years (he was already acquainted with Queen Christina), so the notion of him being found by the servants in the garden, as a stranger, is absurd. On the other hand, on the basis of an existing friendship with Palombara, he might well have conducted an "experiment" in his laboratory and decamped unceremoniously, leaving behind carefully contrived traces intended to persuade this rich patron that he had succeeded in transmuting base metal into gold during the night. In any case, Palombara was convinced that the incomprehensible notes contained the secret of turning metal into gold and, to prevent them from being lost or destroyed, he had their contents engraved on the doorposts of his villa. The surviving door is reputed to be the one that led into the laboratory and the inscriptions are numerous and deeply cabalistic.

Along the top of the doorframe is the Hebrew inscription: *Ruah Elohim* (Holy Spirit). Beneath that is a longer inscription in Latin, referring to the legend of Jason and the Golden Fleece, beginning "The dragon of the Hesperides guards the entrance to the magic garden . . ." The reference to the search for the Golden Fleece is just the first coded allusion to a metal. The uprights of the frame on either side each bear the symbols of three planets that also represent metals: Saturn (lead), Mars (iron), and Mercury (mercury) on the left side; Jupiter (tin), Venus (copper), and the Sun (gold) on the right. Each symbol is accompanied by a Latin motto; for example, Saturn, "When in your house black crows shall beget white doves, then you will be called wise." The other five mottoes are equally esoteric, being couched in the allegorical language of alchemy. Along the bottom of the doorframe is a further inscription flanking a symbol of the monad (the emblem for God, or the first being, or the totality of being), which reads: "It is the secret task of the truly wise man to open the earth so that it may propagate salvation for the people." On the step there is a Latin motto that can equally be read forward or backward: *Si sedes non is* ("If you sit you do not go forward"); or *Si non sedes is* ("If you do not sit you go forward").

Above the doorframe, also set into the wall, is a large disk-shaped plaque with a Latin motto encircling the star of Solomon, which reads: "There are three wonders: God and man, mother and virgin, one and three." This appears to bear more of a relation to Christian theology than the pagan and cabalistic mottoes on the doorframe. The bottom half of the star is partly obscured by a circle surmounted by a cross, containing a triangle and a circle, a Rosicrucian symbol, with the motto: "The center is in the triangle of the center." Apart from the obviously Judeo-Christian derivation of most of the symbolism and the larger inscription on this disk, its meaning is as elusive as the carvings on the doorframe. The disk is identical to the frontispiece illustration in the 1677 edition of an allegorical book *Aureum Seculum Redivivum* ("The Golden Age Reborn") by Henricus Madatanus, the pseudonym of Adrian von Mynsicht, a Rosicrucian alchemist. An ex-libris, or bookplate, bearing this identical symbol was allegedly found among the papers of Bérenger Saunière, the priest of Rennes-le-Château (see Chapter 1), whose secretive career inspired the controversy over Templar treasure and other issues provoked by the book *The Holy Blood and the Holy Grail*.

The two large, grotesque statues set into the wall on either side of the Magic Door are straightforward to interpret. They have no connection with the door, having been moved to this site in 1888 from the Quirinal Hill where, in pre-Christian times, there stood a temple of the Egyptian deity Isis, whose cult had a following in Rome. The two extremely ugly statues, with stunted bodies and demonic, bearded faces, represent the god Bes, patron of the home and babies in ancient Egypt. Even though they have no historical link with the Magic Door, they add an extra touch of drama to its appearance: The

Romans showed good taste when they recognized the affinity of these ancient deities from the Nile with the alchemical laboratory door and its bizarre hieroglyphics.

Palombara never discovered how to transmute base metals into gold—and neither did anybody else. Borri, the unheeded (except by the authorities) messianic prophet and alchemist led a hunted life, wandering through Switzerland, Austria, and Denmark. Finally, he was arrested in Moravia and extradited to Rome where he was imprisoned. For all his alchemical charlatanry, Borri was a good doctor of medicine, so he was eventually released from prison in 1678 to tend to a French nobleman, whom he cured. Thereafter, though under loose confinement in Castel Sant'Angelo, he was allowed out into the city, where he resumed his friendship with Palombara. The accession of a less tolerant pope, however, saw him finally imprisoned within the fortress where he died of fever in 1695. The striking memorial to his tumultuous and futile life is the Magic Door—which the Romans more accurately call the Alchemical Door—that still exudes the cabalistic atmosphere of those strange days when Rosicrucians and other occultists vainly strove to capture the elusive secret of the Philosopher's Stone.

The Grotto of the Beati Paoli, Palermo, Sicily

Back underground, but still in Italy, there is a menacingly sinister grotto beneath the streets of Palermo, the Sicilian capital, that was once the headquarters of a ruthless secret society of black-robed and hooded murderers known as the Beati Paoli. The Mafia claims descent from this lethal cult, but there is little evidence to prove the link: In any case, the Beati Paoli were sinister enough in their own right, even without the addition of the Mafia brand. Of all secret societies, this was one of the most obscure: No records of any kind were kept and its history depended entirely on folk memory. For that reason, even the historical period in which it operated cannot be determined with certainty. Some historians have asserted that it was a medieval sect that existed during the fourteenth and fifteenth centuries; the more widely held opinion is that it came into being later than that. The situation has been further complicated by the fact that its modern fame is due to the success of a popular novel written in the early twentieth century, which set the Beati Paoli in the context of the late seventeenth–early eighteenth century, and that image has remained in the public imagination even though it is based only on a work of fiction and there is every possibility that it may have had more ancient origins.

The Grotto of the Beati Paoli lies beneath the Capo district of Palermo. It is part of a large underground complex originally gouged out by the River Papireto and later artificially modified by Arab and Norman engineers. In the fourth and fifth centuries, this subterranean labyrinth was the site of very extensive Christian catacombs. Access to the cave can be gained from the Alley of the Orphans, in the Capo district, beside the Church of St. Maruzza. An entrance off the alley leads to a flight of stone steps running down into the cavern. There is a further entrance via a neighboring house. The grotto is paved with small square cobbles and the curved walls show the artificiality of its construction, betokening human occupation. Staples for iron fetters have also been found in the walls. There is no doubt that this was the headquarters of the fearsome secret society that inflicted only one punishment on its enemies: death.

Who were the Beati Paoli? Originally, they appear to have been a benevolent confraternity devoted to piety and good works, probably dedicated to St. Francis de Paola—hence their name. This religious character was also the likely origin of their black, monkish robes and cowls—a common enough costume for penitential brother-hoods in ancient Italy. Later, however, both the confraternity and its habit acquired a much more sinister significance. The two most powerful institutions in Sicily in historical times were the Crown and the Inquisition. The Beati Paoli appear to have set themselves up in opposition to both, and the resourcefulness and audacity with which they mounted their challenge suggests that they may have been drawn from the nobility, or at least had an aristocratic leadership. What remains in dispute to this day is their motivation. In Sicilian legend they have sometimes been represented as fulfilling a Robin Hood role—championing the poor and oppressed against church and state. In reality, however, they were almost certainly pursuing a selfish agenda: carrying out vendettas for personal revenge, committing murder for motives of gain, or simply reveling in the exercise of power through secrecy and violence.

There does seem to have been some resemblance between the Beati Paoli and the Sacred Vehmgericht in Germany, in that, like their German counterparts the Sicilian conspirators appear to have placed their victims on trial, even if in absentia, and to have arrogated to themselves the authority of a tribunal. They operated exclusively at night, making their way up from their subterranean hiding place into the narrow, unlit alleyways of Palermo, camouflaged in their black robes and hoods, to come upon their victims by surprise and strangle or stab them to death. The balance of opinion among historians is that the sect did actually exist even if, for obvious reasons, the only record of its activities was oral.

What brought the Beati Paoli out of folklore and into print was their discovery by a succession of writers in the early nineteenth century. In the 1830s Gabriele Quattromani and Vincenzo Linares mentioned the organization in their writing. In 1848, the year when Europe erupted in rebellions against entrenched authority, Carmelo Piola wrote a book about the Beati Paoli, which prevented their memory from fading into oblivion. But what turned this obscure secret society into a household name in Italy was the fiction of Luigi Natoli. In 1909, under the pen name of William Galt, he contributed an adventure serial to an Italian newspaper, titled *I Beati Paoli* and featuring a secret society of black-robed avengers in Palermo between 1698 and 1719, seeking justice for ordinary people in the Robin Hood tradition. It was a success and in 1921 the story was published in book form and became a best seller— *The Da Vinci Code* of its day. From that moment on, the cult of the Beati Paoli was established in the public mind. The theme of a secret society defying the government and punishing its officials did not find favor with Mussolini's fascist government, so further reprints were not issued. After the fall of fascism, however, a film based on Natoli's novel, called *The Black Masked Knights,* was made in 1947 and proved so popular that the novel was reissued in 1949.

From then on, the Beati Paoli had so firm a grip on the Italian, and especially the Sicilian, imagination that the Mafia tried to claim descent from them. Such a claim, if believed, would have burnished the Mafia's image in two ways: It would have given that image a centuries-old pedigree and it would have credited the Mafia with disinterestedly championing the poor and weak, rather than pursuing criminal activity. Historians have remained skeptical. They have also remained baffled in their attempts to discover more about this very shadowy secret society, whose reality only becomes chillingly apparent on visiting the Grotto of the Beati Paoli beneath the Alley of the Orphans in Palermo's Capo district. Aboveground, a street, a square, and a restaurant all bear the name of this once dreaded confraternity.

Priest Holes in England

Unlike in Germany and Switzerland, the Reformation in England was imposed upon the country by the king, from the top down, rather than occurring as a result of large-scale conversion of the population to Protestantism. So desperate was King Henry VIII to divorce his wife, Catherine of Aragon, and marry Anne Boleyn, that in 1534 he had Parliament pass the Act of Supremacy, appointing him head of the church in England and breaking with Rome. So, under Henry, his son Edward VI, and his daughter Elizabeth I, much of the population remained Catholic in belief, but the old religion was prohibited. Priests caught celebrating Mass and those who harbored them were sentenced to death.

Under these grim conditions, Catholics resorted to elaborate secrecy to escape detection. The surviving oases of Catholicism were the manor houses of the many families of the landed gentry who had remained loyal to the Catholic faith—known as "recusants" for their refusal to attend Protestant services—which became centers of devotion and resistance. In these country houses, visiting priests were concealed and said Mass for trustworthy people from the surrounding neighborhood. At first the Catholics relied on fairly makeshift hiding places for priests, Mass furnishings, and vestments. A favorite place for hearing illicit Masses was in the attic area under the rafters of large houses, where there was sufficient space to accommodate large numbers of worshippers and time to rush the priest into hiding if the royal troops were heard approaching. As the situation worsened, however, rough-and-ready hiding places were no longer adequate. The searchers had become extremely professional.

So had the Catholic clergy. During the early period of the Reformation, Mass had been said clandestinely by priests of various types surviving from the brief reign of Henry VIII's Catholic daughter, Mary (1553–1558). After Elizabeth I restored Protestantism and resumed the persecution of Catholics, a much stronger resistance developed from 1580, when the first Jesuit missionary priests landed in England and began their underground ministry. The Jesuits were a new Order, dedicated to promoting the Counter-Reformation, and to them martyrdom was their natural destiny. Few of them expected to leave England alive; but if their presence was to be effective, it was also their duty to defer discovery and arrest as long as they could, in order to say as many Masses, hear as many confessions, and minister to as many souls as possible. So they needed really ingenious hiding places and they received into their ranks, as a humble lay brother (technically a "temporal coadjutor"), the man who was to become the best constructor of so-called "priest holes" in England.

Nicholas Owen was not a physically attractive specimen. He was only slightly larger than a dwarf; he was afflicted with a large hernia and in later life he was maimed by an accident in which a packhorse rolled on top of him. Yet this little man had the sweetest, most generous spirit and the heart of a lion. He was born in Oxfordshire in about 1550, so that his childhood was spent in the openly Catholic atmosphere of Queen Mary's reign. His father was a carpenter; two of his brothers were priests, a third was a printer of underground Catholic literature. Nicholas went abroad and joined the Society of Jesus (the Jesuits) around 1577, when he was received as a lay brother. By trade he was a carpenter and mason. In 1588 he returned to England with Father John Gerard and soon put his skills to use constructing priest holes to conceal Jesuits.

These were no ordinary priest holes, like the earlier clumsy hiding places. Owen used tricks of trompe l'oeil and meticulous craftsmanship to create secret chambers that defeated the priest hunters, or "pursuivants" as they were called, even though they brought professional carpenters and masons with them to measure every wall and investigate every cranny in suspect houses. Searches of Catholic recusant houses could last for days, with entire walls and floors being demolished in the hunt for priests. Owen even devised an ingenious system of feeding tubes, embedded in the mortar between stones or bricks, through which water and liquid sustenance could be passed to the fugitives.

Owen operated under a variety of aliases. He was most frequently known as "Little John," but he also went under the names of "Little Michael," Andrewes, and Draper. His life was extremely hard. To establish his bona fides, he would work in a house all day, in front of servants and visitors, carrying out some ordinary carpentry or masonry work. Then, at night, he would descend into the bowels of the mansion and labor secretly on his real project, a hidden chamber. He invariably worked alone, which was one of the reasons he avoided betrayal or detection for so long. It was a harsh, lonely existence, the work made all the more difficult by his hernia, and he must certainly have suffered from sleep deprivation. "Little John's" consolation came, however, when, with a small congregation of faithful Catholics, he knelt and listened to the priest murmuring the timeless Latin prayers of the Mass, in a place of covert worship made secure by his dedication.

Little John built more than a hundred priest holes in locations across central England between 1588 and 1605. In 1594 he was arrested and imprisoned in the Tower of London but, thanks to the many aliases he had employed, the authorities were uncertain of his identity, assumed he was of little importance, and allowed a kindly Catholic to purchase his liberty. Three years later, Nicholas Owen is believed to have arranged the escape from the tower of his superior Father John Gerard. Both Jesuits then resumed their perilous careers. What brought things to a head was the Gunpowder Plot in 1605, when a band of Catholic conspirators, led by Guy Fawkes, maddened by generations of persecution, plotted to blow up James I at the formal opening of Parliament. The plot was discovered and it provoked a ferocious witch hunt against Catholics that lasted for months.

On January 20, 1606, Owen, who had had nothing to do with the Gunpowder Plot, was at Hindlip Hall in Worcestershire with two priests, Father Henry Garnet and Father Edward Oldcorne, and his apprentice Ralph Ashley, whose appropriate pseudonym was "Chambers," when Sir Henry Bromley, the local Puritan magistrate, arrived with more than one hundred armed men to search for priests. If the fugitives had to be trapped in a house, Hindlip was the best location, since Owen had constructed no fewer than eleven hiding places there. The priests hid in one, Owen and Chambers in another. The priests' place of concealment had an iron feeding tube through which broth was passed; but Owen and his apprentice had no such amenity and were starving, with just one apple between them. On the morning of January 23, Owen and his companion gave themselves up. Owen apparently tried to pass himself off as Father Garnet, in the hope that the searchers would abandon their efforts to find him. Instead, they continued their hunt for a week until the two priests also gave themselves up. These clerics were subsequently hanged, drawn, and quartered. It is significant that even a week's intensive search had failed to discover Owen's ingenious priest holes.

Robert Cecil, first Earl of Salisbury, James I's chief minister, wrote: "It is incredible how great was the joy caused by his arrest ... knowing the great skill of Owen in constructing hiding places, and the innumerable quantity of dark holes which he had schemed for hiding priests all through England." Nicholas Owen was taken again to the Tower of London and interrogated, but rejected the offer of his life if he would betray the priests in his hiding places. Under the law it was forbidden to torture him because of his maimed condition; but Wade, the torturer, a ferocious anti-Catholic, illegally subjected him to appalling torments on the Topcliffe rack, hanging in iron manacles from a wall with his wrists shackled in iron rings and heavy weights on his feet. He died as a result of this torture, without betraying any of his secrets. Knowing that the torture had been illegal, the governor of the tower laconically recorded: "The man is dead—he died in our hands." A more factual account stated, "They tortured him with such inhuman ferocity that his stomach burst open and his intestines gushed out."

The near-dwarf, disfigured and maimed, had gone to his eternal reward. More than three hundred years later, on October 25, 1970, at a solemn ceremony in Rome, Pope Paul VI proclaimed that Nicholas Owen had "ascended the altars" and canonized him as St. Nicholas, one of the Forty Martyrs of England and Wales.

Many of Owen's priest holes still survive; so cleverly were they constructed that some have yet to be discovered. His earliest work was at Oxburgh Hall, in Norfolk; Braddocks, in Essex; and Sawston, near Cambridge. Oxburgh, a moated country house, is today in the hands of the National Trust and open to the public. The priest hole built by St. Nicholas Owen is under a trapdoor, undetectable in the tiled floor; visitors are allowed to enter it. At Braddocks, which belonged to the Wiseman family, from which Nicholas Cardinal Wiseman descended, the "cubbyhole" in the chimney was opened in the 1930s and found to be in as good condition as when Owen crafted it. Sawston was sold by the Huddleston family in the 1980s and at present is the subject of a major controversy, with Catholic heritage groups trying to save it from developers. The priest hole made by Owen is in a dilapidated condition. It is on the top landing of the staircase and the entrance slants imperceptibly into the masonry of a tower. A floorboard in the landing is the secret key to a tunnel leading down to a concealed chamber that could accommodate up to six people. The carpentry that gives an illusion of solidity to the hollow area is of great ingenuity, as might be expected of Owen.

Hindlip Hall, where he was captured and which contained eleven hiding places, was demolished in 1820 and replaced by a modern mansion. Other priest holes survive, however, at Ufton Court, in West Berkshire, Towneley Hall in Lancashire (of a later generation than Owen) and many other places. The greatest surviving monument to the skills of St. Nicholas Owen, however, is Harvington Hall, near Kidderminster in Worcestershire, another grand, moated manor house. Here a series of four priest holes attributed to Owen can be seen, all situated around the great staircase. The house belongs to the Catholic Archdiocese of Birmingham and visitors are welcome.

One of the fascinating features of priest holes is that, since they were so cleverly made and hard to detect, over the centuries the knowledge of them has often been lost, so that they may be stumbled upon accidentally. The majestic old house of Compton Winyates, near Banbury in Warwickshire, gained modern celebrity when the film *Candleshoe*, starring David Niven and Jodie Foster, was made there in 1977. In earlier times, however, it was a Catholic recusant house where Mass was illicitly celebrated in a chapel high up in the roof space. Its present owner is probably Britain's most famous Buddhist convert—Spencer Compton, the five-times-married seventh Marquess of Northampton and heir to a fortune of some £70 million ($103.5 million). The marquess is noted for his intense interest in matters esoteric and hermetic, and served for many years as pro–grand master of English Freemasonry. Just over one hundred years ago a bricked-up chamber in the house was discovered containing a skeleton—a piquant experience more likely to fascinate than distress its inheritor.

In the early nineteenth century, at the Elizabethan manor house of Bourton-on-the-Water in Gloucestershire, when some wallpaper was stripped off, the entrance to a secret room eight feet square ($0.7m^2$) was discovered. It contained a table and chair, over the back of which a priest's cassock was draped; on the table stood an ancient teapot, cup, and silver spoon, while the tea leaves in the pot had turned to dust. That discovery explained why two adjacent rooms had been known as "the chapel" and "the priest's room." This time capsule enshrined the memory of the days when Catholicism in England lived underground, served by priests and laymen whose courage unto death must be marveled at.

Chapter 7

MODERN-DAY BOLT-HOLES

*J*he sanctuaries we have so far been looking at belong to past centuries, to periods of history redolent of secret passages, masked and caped conspirators wearing swords, and all the atmospheric romance of the days when horses were the means of transport and Machiavellian princes plotted dynastic coups. But the need for secrecy, evasion, and survival remains as paramount to those in government in the twenty-first century as in the days of swashbuckling adventure. We now examine some sanctuaries of the present day, hideouts made doubly secure by all the resources of modern technology, state-of-the-art refuges designed to shelter the Great and the Good in the event of war or natural catastrophe.

Mount Weather Emergency Operations Center, Bluemont, Virginia

Where was U.S. Vice President Dick Cheney spirited off to, amid the chaos and panic of September 11, 2001? At the time it was a jealously guarded state secret, but it is now widely believed that the vice president was taken to near "Journey's End." That peaceful-sounding name, which might belong to a rest home for senior citizens or some similarly tranquil haven, appears on a house sign close to the concealed entrance of the federal government facility officially—though very restrictedly—known as Mount Weather Emergency Operations Center. It is situated seventy-five miles (121km) from Washington, in Bluemont, Virginia. Mount Weather is the senior of all the U.S. government's underground or heavily defended installations created for purposes of national security. Dating back to the 1950s and the cold war risk of imminent nuclear devastation, these underground bolt-holes are the secret sanctuaries of the modern age, turning the most powerful men and women on earth into potential cave-dwellers.

If you stumbled into Mount Weather (an impossibility, due to the high level of security surrounding it), you might think you had entered a parallel universe, like Alice in Wonderland falling down the rabbit hole. For here, according to insiders, is a complete replica of the federal government, even including an underground wing called the "White House," with an official playing the role of president, to keep the machinery of power well-oiled until the moment when the real president, or the senior surviving member of the government in time of disaster, arrives to take charge. Duplicates of various federal departments are there, as well as other major institutions, even independent government bodies such as the Federal Reserve. The duplicate heads of department are treated as if they actually held Cabinet rank and are addressed as "Mr. Secretary" or "Madam Secretary." Apparently, the underground complex itself has a vast infrastructure, which includes streets, hospitals, private accommodations, dormitories for two thousand people, restaurants, a freshwater lake filled by underground springs, a battery-powered subway, and secure computer and television systems. Aboveground, behind massive perimeter security, there are buildings housing further communications equipment, tanks holding up to half a million gallons (2.2 million liters) of water, a sewage treatment plant, and helicopter pads. But the real nerve center of Mount Weather is belowground, where the U.S. backup government is in waiting: The Situation Room there would replace the Oval Office in the event of war.

The site is west of Washington, reached by Route 66, Highway 50 and, after a fifty-mile (80km) drive, Route 601, otherwise known as Blue Ridge Mountain Road. This road is deliberately kept as a modest two-lane country access route, as part of the low-profile strategy for Mount Weather. The surrounding community supplies useful cover. But, on September 11, 2001, a procession of government limousines with police escorts roared along Route 601 to Mount Weather. Among the high officials whom the authorities virtually admitted had been rushed to safety there while the Twin Towers blazed were the Speaker of the House of Representatives and other senior Members of Congress. But the belief persists that Dick Cheney was also taken there, which would make sense, considering the government facilities available on-site and the targeting of the White House by the terrorists, even though Cheney is known to have been at Site R (Raven Rock), another secure facility, during the days following the attack.

For less exalted and uninvited visitors to Mount Weather, the reception is more inhospitable. Because of the deliberate policy of maintaining a façade of normality and the need to allow the surrounding community to go about its everyday business, it is possible to drive close up to the facility. Motorists and hikers on the Appalachian Trail, casually exploring a nondescript rural road winding up onto a ridge, have often been startled to find themselves confronted by two ten-foot (3m) high fences made of razor wire and signs reading: *US Property. No Trespassing.* A longer notice spells it out more baldly: *All persons and vehicles entering hereon are liable to search. Photographing, making notes, drawings, maps or graphic representations of this area or its activities are prohibited.* It is easy to deduce that something more significant than chicken farming is going on behind the razor-wire perimeter. The visible structures, out of a total of around sixty-five main buildings, are a dozen large metal sheds that are clearly not in the running for any architectural awards; but, as has been said, the real heart of Mount Weather is underground. Nevertheless, sightseers will quickly find themselves under surveillance by police or security guards; cameras and even sketch pads are liable to be confiscated.

Such government bolt-holes are by no means peculiar to America: Similar installations exist in other Western countries, in the former Soviet Union and its ex-satellites, and in nations across the globe. But Mount Weather, quite literally, is the granddaddy of them all. As its name suggests, it was originally owned by the National Weather

Bureau. In 1902 Herbert and Mavin Allen sold 94 acres (38ha) on Paris Mountain to the U.S. government for $1,373.50; today the complex extends over 561 acres (224ha) of the Blue Ridge. In 1907 the world altitude record for a meteorological kite was set there. President Calvin Coolidge contemplated constructing a summer White House at Mount Weather—an uncharacteristically extravagant project for a fiscal conservative—but this scheme was never realized. On March 19, 1929 his successor, President Herbert Hoover, told a press conference:

> I do not propose to do anything, at the moment at least, about rebuilding Mount Weather. I rather prefer the more rustic and intimate type of a log cabin than a more formal place, like at Mount Weather with all its encumbrances of servants, et cetera. That is not to say that Mount Weather might not yet be available, but in any event for the present I am entirely satisfied with the arrangements which the director of the [Shenandoah] park is making for my entertainment for a day or two during the summer.

This referred to the fact that the director of the Shenandoah Park, knowing that Hoover "was cognisant of the fishing facilities of the upper Rapidan [river] from previous experience," had offered to build some roads, trails, and a fishing cabin for the president at the headwaters of the Rapidan River, about nine miles (14km) from Madison, Virginia. So the new president's fondness for fishing left Mount Weather on the back burner. But it is startling to see Hoover claiming more modest and rustic tastes than Coolidge, who was himself famous for his primitive domesticity—he had been sworn in as president by his attorney father under a kerosene lamp in his family's home, which was still unequipped with electricity.

For the time being, therefore, high-level politics passed Mount Weather by and it served more humbly as a work camp for down-and-outs during the Depression, until the site was acquired by the Bureau of Mines, which conducted various tunneling operations there. In 1954 the U.S. Army took over the tunneling project which, by now, was designed to be security-related. By 1959 the basic under-ground complex had been completed, at a cost of more than $1 bil-lion in today's dollars. Mount Weather had assumed its new identity as a federal bolt-hole facility. On October 2, 1962, in the immediate run-up to the Cuban Missile Crisis, President John F. Kennedy signed Executive Order 11051, which stated that "National preparedness must be achieved as may be required to deal with increases in international tension, with limited war, or with general war including attack upon the United States." That was, in effect, Mount Weather's founding charter. Strangely, despite the timing of this executive order, Mount Weather insiders are adamant that the facility was not activated during the Cuban crisis, although a state of increased alertness was imposed. On the other hand, the installation was pressed into service at the time of Kennedy's assassination.

Seven years after the Cuban Missile Crisis, in October 1969, Presi-dent Richard Nixon signed Executive Order 11490, which made no specific mention of war but employed what was to become the key strategic terminology "to assure continuity of government . . . in any national emergency." That marked a significant policy change, implying that Mount Weather and similar federal facilities could start functioning even in peacetime, if the government declared a state of emergency. Civil libertarians were concerned about the implications. So was J. Edgar Hoover who, throughout his career, regarded the con-stitutional provisions for a total takeover of power by the executive as far too limiting and believed large-scale civil rights demonstrations should have been sufficient to trigger such a suspension of the normal democratic process.

In fact, the weird "shadow" government in Mount Weather is not as sinister as it sounds. The personnel there are only maintaining dummy portfolios and, in the event of a real emergency, would instantly surrender their posts to the proper incumbents. Even in the event of the death or incapacity of both the president and vice president, there is a fully constitutional provision for the govern-mental succession, provided for in the Presidential Succession Act of

1947 and its amendments, which specify the line of succession after the vice president: the Speaker of the House of Representatives, followed by the President *pro tempore* of the Senate and the Cabinet secretaries, according to seniority. So, in that respect, there is nothing unconstitutional about the setup at Mount Weather. Other aspects of the facility, however, are more controversial. The area was almost completely unknown to the American public until it received some unwelcome publicity in December 1974, when TWA Flight 514 crashed into Mount Weather. The crash cut the underground line leading to the Emergency Broadcast System, so that teletype machines in media centers across America temporarily transmitted gibberish (no change there, cynics claimed). The following year a Senate subcommittee elicited the information that dossiers on at least 100,000 American citizens were held at Mount Weather and the committee concluded that the establishment's databases "operate with few, if any, safeguards or guidelines." In the wake of this investigation, Senator John Tunney, a California Democrat, claimed the computers at Mount Weather could absorb millions of items of additional data on the lives of citizens simply by tapping into the information stored at ninety-six other federal relocation centers. That put a whole new perspective on the Mount Weather phenomenon. It had, from the first, functioned under executive authority, with no congressional oversight whatsoever. That had seemed acceptable, in light of its mandate to secure "continuity of government" in a national emergency. But the revelation that it was also acting as a computerized mega-policeman, storing information about private citizens without their knowledge or consent, aroused public misgivings.

Another feature of Mount Weather's disaster scenario that was bound to generate controversy in a democracy is the priority list of individuals who would be granted sanctuary there in the event of, say, a nuclear war. Precisely whose names are on the list for admission to this latter-day Ark is a tightly guarded secret. The irreverent might speculate that, in the era of JFK, Marilyn Monroe must surely have been on the coveted list. At the 1975 Senate hearings, General Leslie

Bray, director of the Federal Preparedness Agency, which at that time ran Mount Weather, told senators that there were 6,500 names on the list. Obviously, these would include all those in the line of government succession. It is also generally supposed that senior officials of the federal agencies represented within the facility would be admitted. Bray acknowledged that the list encompassed telecommunications technicians and there are macabre rumors that there are also a number of construction workers who would be charged with excavating mass graves in the aftermath of a nuclear strike. It is claimed that Earl Warren, when serving as chief justice of the Supreme Court, declined to be put on the list when he discovered that his wife would not be allowed to accompany him. Spouses are emphatically not included. So inflexible is this rule that officials contacting listed persons, in an emergency, to summon them to the sanctuary of Mount Weather, are instructed not to inform any family member answering the telephone about the nature of the call. That would seem to put a question mark over the future procreation of the American elite in the wake of a nuclear holocaust.

In the event of some national disaster, the Mount Weather list would surely supplant the Social Register and all previous categorizations of top people, to become the most coveted elitist passport of all. The ID card issued to the lucky few carries each one's photograph and the lofty instruction: *The person described on this card has essential emergency duties with the Federal Government. Request full assistance and unrestricted movement be afforded the person to whom this card is issued.* Just how readily members of the public, in the panic provoked by a four-minute warning of nuclear attack, would be willing to suspend efforts to secure their own safety in order to lend disinterested assistance to a privileged candidate for assured survival can only be surmised.

Today Mount Weather is run by the Federal Emergency Management Agency (FEMA), under the Department of Homeland Security. The facility's recent executive administrator has the unfortunately Dr. Strangelovian name of James B. Looney. Under his leadership, Mount Weather has acquired a new lease on life, due to the terrorist attacks of September 11, 2001 and the subsequent war on terror. After the end of the cold war, the facility had taken on a sleepy, dormitory atmosphere—but no more. In 2002, FEMA determined to buy a further 178 acres (71ha) of land to divert Route 601 and create a more secure entrance. Defenses were built to prevent unauthorized motor vehicles from coming too close. There are now up to 2,500 personnel working there, at least sporadically, including around 670 FEMA employees. Black sheeting has been attached to the perimeter fence to block the helipads from external view. Locals claim to have sighted Dick Cheney and Donald Rumsfeld in a neighborhood bar; significantly, nobody claims to have been engaged in conversation by them. More implausibly, a local woman has been quoted as insisting that she saw Air Force One, on September 11, 2001, fly inside the mountain, which opened up before it and closed behind it. It is generally accepted that that kind of James Bond technology does not exist at Mount Weather: The main entrance is a blastproof door ten feet (3m) high by twenty feet (6m) wide, five feet (1.5m) thick and weighing thirty-four tons (30,844kg). Demonstrably, those dimensions would not permit the entry of Air Force One.

Historically, the federal government has been more successful at concealing Mount Weather from the American public than from its foreign enemies. The Soviet Union was well aware of the existence of the facility from its earliest days and was presumed to have intercontinental ballistic missiles targeted on it. The Russians, with the chutzpah that always characterized the Soviet Union, actually attempted to purchase an estate right next to Mount Weather, supposedly to serve as a rest and recreation center for its embassy officials. The State Department vetoed the sale: "Nice try, Ivan," was the dismissive reaction.

Inevitably, Mount Weather has also found its way into thriller fiction. Most famously, very early in its existence, the facility was featured, under the thin guise of "Mount Thunder," in the best-selling spy novel *Seven Days in May*, by Fletcher Knebel and Charles W. Bailey II, published in 1962. The authors even described the drive from

Washington to the secret bunker, altering the route slightly in the later stages of the journey to avoid directing the whole world to Mount Weather. The disguise, however, was wafer-thin. The bunker was mentioned by name in the 2000 film *Thirteen Days,* about the Cuban Missile Crisis. It was also the fictitious venue for the final episode of the highly successful television series *The X-Files.* The appeal of the facility to authors and screenwriters has endured over four decades: The 2002 film *The Sum of All Fears,* based on the novel by Tom Clancy, featured a U.S. president being escorted to an imaginary bunker inside Sugarloaf Mountain in Maryland, to simulate conditions in the event of a nuclear attack. Again, Mount Weather was clearly the inspiration for this scenario.

The Federal Relocation Arc

Disaster drills are routinely practiced at Mount Weather. Twice monthly there are exercises and once a year a major simulation is carried out, attended by members of the real government from Washington. Although Mount Weather may be regarded as the doyen of such security installations in the United States, it is by no means unique. On the contrary, it is part of a vast complex of secure facilities located within three hundred miles (483km) of Washington, known as the Federal Relocation Arc. Altogether, at one time or another, this area encompassed some ninety-six federal relocation centers. The arc curves through North Carolina, Virginia, West Virginia, Maryland, and Pennsylvania. One of the most important subordinate relocation centers is Site R—Raven Rock, near Fort Ritchie in Pennsylvania, which is the alternative Pentagon. Vice President Cheney spent several days there in the aftermath of the September 11 attacks, probably after first relocating to Mount Weather.

A secret bunker beneath the Greenbrier Hotel in White Sulphur Springs, West Virginia was designed to shelter Congress in an emergency. Construction began in 1959, with concrete walls two feet (61cm) thick and reinforced with steel. It was custom-built, with separate chambers for the House of Representatives and the Senate, as well as a large hall for joint meetings of both houses. Since contractors could not be told the true purpose of the building, some fairly feeble fictions were invented. One contractor, told that he was building an exhibit hall, retorted: "We've got 110 urinals we just installed. What in the hell are you going to exhibit?" Former House Speaker Thomas P. "Tip" O'Neill frankly described the Greenbrier evacuation plan as "far-fetched." There was always a surreal aspect to the facility, in that it existed cheek by jowl with the luxury hotel, whose guests can now enjoy privileged tours of the former congressional bolt-hole, which is no longer in use.

The federal arc also encompassed an underground location for the Federal Reserve in Culpeper, Virginia and a base for emergency air defense at Cheyenne Mountain, Colorado. But all such sites, defunct or operational, have always been mere satellites to Mount Weather. There is nothing defunct about this parent facility: On the contrary, since the 9/11 massacre, it has come to life more than at any time since the Eisenhower presidency, with its acreage enlarged and its personnel more than doubled. Any notion that such sites have exhausted their shelf life is contradicted by the geopolitical realities of the world, the threat to the United States, and the war on terror. As a further testament to this reality, although the cold war is over, Russia began construction of an installation similar to Mount Weather in the mid-1990s, inside Yamantau Mountain in the Beloretsk region of the southern Urals. Terrorism, mutual suspicion among nations, and the appalling destructive potential of nuclear, chemical, and biological weaponry all conspire to turn even twenty-first-century elites into possible troglodytes. In a climate of distrust, there is still a role for Mount Weather.

Area 51: The Facility That Does Not Exist, Nevada

Despite the secrecy and speculation surrounding Mount Weather, at least it remains firmly anchored in reality. The same cannot be said of another U.S. government base that has attracted more fantasizing than sober assessment—frequently being associated with claims of an extraterrestrial presence, or at least involvement in developing technology learned from aliens. This is Area 51, the popular name for the base known internally to the U.S. military as Air Force Flight Test Center (Detachment 3) and externally not known at all, since officially it does not exist. Its other nicknames have ranged from "Dreamland" to "Paradise Ranch" to "Honey Airport."

Area 51 is situated ninety miles (145km) due north of Las Vegas, in Nevada, within the wider area of the Nevada Test Site, where 739 nuclear tests have been conducted by the U.S. government. It is on the southern shore of Groom Lake, a dry lakebed, but this most secretive military base in the world does not appear on maps. The installation dates back to 1955 when Lockheed selected it as a suitable site for testing the new U-2 spy plane, the first of which flew there in August 1955. Work at Groom Lake was sometimes disrupted by the atmospheric nuclear tests being conducted nearby. During the following decades, a succession of military aircraft was tested at Groom Lake, including the A-12 Blackbird and the F-117 stealth fighter. The base expanded correspondingly and is now believed to have seven runways, the longest extending to 23,270 feet (7,093m). That kind of information about Area 51 is easier to obtain, because of modern commercial satellite surveillance, than any facts relating to operational activities there. To say that Area 51 guards its privacy would be an understatement.

The perimeter is tightly patrolled by security guards employed by EG&G's (Edgerton, Germeshausen, and Grier, Inc.) subcontractor Wackenhut. Dressed in desert camouflage uniforms, they patrol in 4x4 pickups, armed with M16s. These are the notorious "Cammo Dudes," so-called because of their uniforms, their mirrored shades, and their intensely proactive attitude. Theoretically, a shoot-to-kill policy is enforced if an intruder ignores their order to halt. In practice, the Dudes shadow visitors on the outside of the perimeter and call in the Lincoln County Sheriff's Department to usher them off. The local law is not enamored of this extra duty and has complained about the cost, charging the base around $50,000 annually for its services. The security guards are automatically alerted to vehicles approaching by sensors placed on all the neighboring roads. Security is reinforced from the air by Blackhawk helicopters ready to track any intruders. Despite the signs proclaiming *Use of deadly force authorized,* the Cammo Dudes are under strict orders to avoid direct contact with the public, leaving the sheriff's department to make interceptions, and nobody has been hurt, though it must be supposed that the M16s are not purely decorative and that, in the event of a terrorist attack, the Dudes would shoot to kill in defense of the secrets of Area 51.

Just what those secrets are is the million-dollar question. Under normal circumstances, Area 51, as a part of the more extensive Nellis Range Complex controlled by the U.S. Air Force, would have come under the critical scrutiny of radicals, those who think the security operations of the United States should be conducted under unrealistic conditions of transparency, and pacifists of various stripes. However, such people now represent a minority of Area 51 watchers today. Most of those who obsess about the base at this point, whether in cyberspace or crouching with binoculars on the summit of Tikaboo Peak—the nearest place from which Area 51 can be seen—are not political dissidents, but every variety of UFO buff and extraterrestrial conspiracy theorist. Area 51 had long been a focus of speculation among such people, but in 1989 vague theorizings gave way to solid facts—provided one was prepared to lend credence to the evidence of a former employee at the base who went public that year with some extraordinary claims.

Bob Lazar, of Las Vegas, said he had worked on a U.S. government flying saucer, based on alien technology, at a site close to Area 51 that he called "S-4." His job had been to help in the "reverse engineering" process, to create an American flying saucer from an alien template. Disappointingly, he had not seen any aliens. But he knew a man who had. According to the legend, his closest workmate, Barry Castillio (unfortunately all we know about him is that he was "a heavyset man") told the story of how the aliens who originally worked at the base quarreled with the human staff, then killed one scientist and forty-four guards before storming out, telling the survivors they would return at a date given unhelpfully as "1625xx." Happily, they left much of their technology behind, on which Uncle Sam has reportedly been capitalizing ever since.

These aliens, apparently, came from the Zeta Retuculi 1 & 2 star system—specifically the planet Reticulum 4—which is thirty-seven light-years distant, and had been monitoring earth for ten thousand years, intervening sixty-five times to influence the evolution of humanity. They are of standard alien appearance: three to four feet (1–1.2m) tall, gray-skinned, weighing twenty-five to fifty pounds (11–23kg), having childlike torsos and large heads, with almond-shaped eyes and no hair. Lazar gleaned information about them from a "blue folder" he was given as briefing material, but emphasized that he could not vouch for the truth of any of it, as the Reticulans might have lied. Such a hardheaded, skeptical approach is refreshing to find among people reporting alien contacts.

Scientists have heaped scorn on Lazar's claims, including his assertion that he worked on flying saucer propulsion using the atomic element 115 as a nuclear fuel. They have also discredited his accounts of his own academic background and qualifications. But Lazar's story was tame compared to the statement made in 2002 by Bill Uhouse, a mechanical engineer, who claimed to have worked at the S-4 facility, under the direction of an alien known as J-Rod, a Reticulan, whose saucer had crashed near Kingman, Arizona in 1952—bad luck after successfully negotiating a trip of thirty-seven light-years. Uhouse claimed to have seen J-Rod at conferences attended by Edward Teller, father of Ronald Reagan's Star Wars program. It is also claimed that Dr. Dan Burisch (originally named Dan Crain) worked on tissue regeneration for J-Rod. According to one interpretation, the Reticulans were originally humans who developed time travel, enabling them to migrate to their distant planet; they are now in a degenerative state and require our help, through DNA and the science associated with the human genome ("J-Rod phone home"?). America has made a secret treaty with them, allowing them to take specimens, which would explain the epidemic of alien abduction of humans in recent decades. Some conspiracy theorists assert that, under a deal known as Project Serpo, twelve U.S. military personnel have been sent on an exchange mission to Reticulum 4. However, another school of thought insists that J-Rod actually hailed from the planet Gleise 675-c, which is only fifteen light-years away, further confusing the whole issue.

No matter how fiercely contested the rival theories may be, the controversy has generated huge interest among UFO buffs. Year after year, many of them have congregated at the "black mailbox" (now painted white) of a local rancher, close to Route 375, to watch lights in the sky above the distant air base. Rather than experimental flying saucers, most likely what they were seeing were test flights relating either to the semimythical Aurora Project, the alleged construction of a hypersonic stealth aircraft capable of flying Mach 6, or activity arising from various projects to develop supersonic aircraft, now known as Project Falcon.

Only on July 14, 2003 did the U.S. government finally admit the existence of Area 51, while revealing no more than the fact that the air force has an "operating location" in the vicinity. The facility has also been targeted by a lawsuit over its bad environmental and health practices in burning toxic chemicals in open trenches, with the widows of deceased contractors alleging negligence by the air force, but the curtain of privileged secrecy veiling Area 51 prevented the complainants from getting very far. Despite its barren surroundings, Area 51 has managed to generate a modest tourist industry, with reporters and UFO enthusiasts patronizing the motel in the nearby village of Rachel, which advertises *Earthlings Welcome*. It is ironic that the UFO claims, extraterrestrial chatter, and conspiracy theorizing have probably obscured some brilliant technological successes created by the genius of American innovators. But that is how Area 51 and the federal government like things to be: obscure. Yet if J-Rod is still ensconced at S-4, it is a pity if a bureaucratic obsession with secrecy is preventing him from meeting a wider cross section of Americans, or cutting a swath through Washington society, perhaps even appearing on the guest list at the State of the Union address or the Academy Awards ceremony—presumably at Steven Spielberg's side.

RAF Menwith Hill, Yorkshire, England

America's military reach spreads far beyond the United States, so other secret sites are to be found thousands of miles from the homeland. The most jealously guarded of all is the listening post known as RAF Menwith Hill in Yorkshire, in the north of England. Menwith Hill is situated eight miles (13km) west of Harrogate, on high ground on the edge of the Yorkshire Dales, surrounded by fields where sheep graze. Despite its Royal Air Force prefix, the "completely civilian" base has been controlled since 1966 by America's National Security Agency (NSA), with the U.S. Army 421st Air Base Group servicing around 4,500 military and civilian personnel. Menwith Hill covers an area of 560 acres (224ha) and presents an extraordinary sight to the traveler who comes upon it unexpectedly. The eerie, sci-fi atmosphere is chiefly created by more than twenty huge white spheres, like giant golf balls, that dominate the landscape. These are radomes, each containing a satellite dish. This indicates the main purpose for which Menwith Hill has historically been used: interception of communications. In official jargon, it is the principal NATO theater ground segment node for high-altitude signals intelligence (SIGINT) satellites. Less formally it is known as the "Big Ear."

The site is surrounded by a wire-mesh fence more than nine feet (2.75m) high, containing sensor wire that can detect noise, with cameras situated around every tenth fence post and topped by razor wire. The radome area is additionally protected with infrared cameras mounted on twenty-five-foot (8m) high posts. British Ministry of Defence Police (MDP) with dogs patrol the perimeter and the interior antenna fields. Up to forty MDP officers patrol the area and surrounding roads by car every hour. They have powers of arrest, but the American security officers who assist them in the internal site area only have authority to detain American personnel on the base. Internally, Menwith Hill is a self-sufficient community, organized like a small town. Besides two large operations buildings, where the work of the base is carried out, there are houses, shops, schools, a sports center, and a chapel. In 1995, with so many families by then living on the base, concern was expressed about inadequate child-care facilities (at that time there were 289 children under the age of four and their numbers were expected to increase). The station even has its own baseball team, the Menwith Hill Patriots, which plays in the National Northern League Championships.

What we have here is the world's biggest and most state-of-the-art listening post. The PUSHER High Frequency Direction Finding (HF-DF) system monitors radio transmissions in the high-frequency ranges from 3MHz to 30MHz, including military, diplomatic, and civilian traffic. As long ago as 1996, its digital optical fiber cables had the capability to carry more than 100,000 simultaneous telephone calls. The station has the ability to perform two million intercepts per hour. This includes both commercial and private telecommunications traffic. So an innocuous British citizen making a joke about Osama bin Laden on his telephone may be blissfully unaware that this trigger word has brought his conversation to the attention of some very unamused folks within the U.S. intelligence community. Some data is shared with Britain's Government Communications Headquarters (GCHQ) intelligence listening station, mostly material of mutual interest relating to the war on terror or international drug trafficking.

Menwith Hill's critics, however, maintain that its catchall interception of communications includes confidential commercial information that may be used to the advantage of U.S. firms at the expense of European—and even British—companies. It is especially distrusted by the Parliament of the European Union. A report by the Civil Liberties Committee of the European Parliament claimed:

> Within Europe all e-mail, telephone and fax communications
> are routinely intercepted by the United States National Security
> Agency, transferring all target information from the European
> mainland via the strategic hub of London, then by satellite to Fort
> Meade in Maryland, via the crucial hub at Menwith Hill in the
> North York Moors of the UK.

The report went on to describe a project known as ECHELON, allegedly targeting most of the satellite communications around the world,
with sites based at Sugar Grove and Yakima in the United States, at
Waihopai in New Zealand, at Geraldton in Australia, in Hong Kong
(then still British), and at Morwenstow in the UK. According to the
report, ECHELON targets nonmilitary communications, with information shared among five nations—the United States, as senior partner,
the UK, Canada, Australia, and New Zealand. The report claimed this
is part of the UKUSA system. UKUSA is the most top secret of all treaties, signed in 1947; its existence remains unacknowledged by all the
contracting parties. Under it, the five nations agreed to harmonize and
share SIGINT, and it is generally believed still to be in operation today.

There is another kind of hostility directed against Menwith Hill. It
has repeatedly been invaded by Greenpeace and Campaign for Nuclear
Disarmament (CND) protesters. Women demonstrators have been
occupying a "peace camp" close to the site for several years. Since it
is a fair assumption they are not concerned about possible interfer-
ence with commercial contract tenders, their opposition focuses on
the more military applications of the work at Menwith Hill, which
in recent years has become more evident and cutting edge. In 2007
the British defence secretary announced that Menwith Hill was to
be upgraded to furnish early warning of incoming missile attacks as
a contribution to the U.S. missile defense system. British opponents
argue that this arrangement would make Britain a target, since any
aggressor would want to take out the warning system when attacking
America. The obvious objection to that claim is that, in a global situation in which long-range missiles were targeting the United States, it

would be unrealistic to imagine that Britain would enjoy immunity while its closest ally was bombed, with or without tracking devices at Menwith Hill. Better to enjoy the protection of the U.S. umbrella is the response of British conservatives. In any case, Britain, while benefiting from the extra security afforded by the radar shield the United States proposes deploying in Poland and the Czech Republic, could hardly refuse to cooperate. So run the arguments. Two new radomes have been commissioned for the base to service the Space Based Infra Red System (SBIRS) as part of the "Star Wars" program.

For the moment, with neither Iran nor North Korea capable of such long-distance nuclear strikes—though North Korea carried out its most successful long-range Taepodong-2 missile test to date early in 2009—the emphasis remains on SIGINT (signals intelligence) at Menwith Hill. One peculiarity of the arrangement between the United States and the United Kingdom—which has not escaped the notice of British comedians—is the apparent flimsiness of the U.S. legal foothold over the property. The British government guaranteed American tenancy of the site for twenty-one years—but that was back in 1976. It has even been alleged that the documentation relating to ownership and tenancy has actually been lost by Her Majesty's government. This would accord with many recent mishaps experienced by the state bureaucracy in Britain, with top-secret documents being left on a train and computer disks containing highly sensitive information about millions of British citizens similarly mislaid. Since, however, neither Labour nor Conservative governments would have any wish to evict the Americans, and the property is a Crown freehold in the care of the Ministry of Defence, there would seem to be little danger of the landlord throwing his NSA tenants out onto the street.

Because Menwith Hill's intelligence-gathering role is very different from the experimentation and development of military hardware carried out at Area 51, there have been no rumors of extraterrestrial contacts at the base. But the site does have an involvement in the space race, according to the Global Network Against Weapons and Nuclear Power in Space, which has denounced the facility as "crucial

for the US Administration's plans for 'Full Spectrum Dominance.'"
This refers to the allegation that America has a secret agenda to gain
control of space, to the exclusion of all other nations, and aims eventually to maintain the capacity to monitor, or even destroy, global
communications across the entire electromagnetic spectrum. Such
an objective would be highly controversial, especially in the eyes of
states like Russia, China, and India. There is, of course, no evidence
that the United States is angling for that kind of hegemony with
the help of Menwith Hill. Although the army presence there is augmented by the U.S. Air Force 451st Information Operations Squadron,
which is heavily involved in the work of the base, there are innumerable technical roles that would justify its deployment.

All the sites we have looked at—Mount Weather, Area 51, Menwith
Hill, and their lesser counterparts—have the same alleged purpose: to
protect the United States and its citizens, even if, in the case of Mount
Weather, protection is to be extended to only 6,500 members of the
governing elite. Because of the secrecy surrounding these government
installations and bolt-holes, an informed debate about their purpose
and utility has never taken place. That has left conspiracy theorists,
fantasists, and space cadets in command of the field. In fairness to the
authorities, it is difficult to see how such facilities could function if
deprived of the veil of secrecy. But that very lack of accountability will
continue to fuel speculation, leaving Joe Q. Public asking himself the
worrying question: Are these top-secret establishments making me
safer and freer—or are they having just the opposite effect?

Chapter 8

ISLANDS OF MYSTERY

hy do islands fascinate us? There is an undeniable aura of romance that attaches to almost any piece of land, however barren or unattractive, that is surrounded by water. Most likely, it has something to do with a sense of proprietorship. Most people do not simply want to visit an island—they want to own one. An island is the most exquisite assertion of ownership; unlike a landed estate, its boundaries are self-evident, demarcated by the sea. Then there is the privacy, the exclusiveness, the feeling of inhabiting a world of one's own. For those not privileged to be owners, there is a degree of mystery about private islands that human curiosity longs to penetrate. Add to that the exoticism of tropical islands, with palm-fringed coral beaches, and the attraction becomes irresistible. There is also the traditional association with buried treasure; Robert Louis Stevenson raised the profile of even the most insignificant sea-girt rock in the public imagination, for all time, by writing his great adventure story, *Treasure Island*. In past centuries, islands were often associated with religion, either serving as oases of peace where hermits could devote themselves to prayer and meditation, or as centers of a cult and its worship.

In this chapter we visit five islands that represent a cross section of these characteristics. One is the most celebrated site of hidden treasure, still undiscovered and almost impossible to access, in the world. The next three were historic centers of very different religious or esoteric traditions. The fifth has a future rather than a past, being the secure storehouse of seeds of all the species of plants on earth, kept refrigerated in Arctic conditions against the eventuality of a plane-tary disaster that might wipe out the global food chain, threatening humanity with extinction.

Montecristo: The Forbidden Island, Off the Italian Coast

We begin with an island that is not particularly remote geographically, but which is jealously guarded by a government exclusion zone. Thanks to the imaginative genius of a great nineteenth-century novelist, it is also a household name: Montecristo, the Forbidden Island. One of the most restricted places in Europe, the island of Montecristo in the Tuscan Archipelago, set in the Tyrrhenian Sea, as that part of the Mediterranean off the west coast of Italy is known, is forbidden to visitors without special permission from the Italian government. This is seldom given and only to scientists (the island is a nature reserve); the waiting list for permission is said to be five years. The waters around the island are patrolled to prevent boats from sailing close; even fishing is forbidden. The island is uninhabited apart from two "guardians" and a couple of forestry officers.

Why does even an important nature reserve require such privacy? Because of the fabulous treasure said to be concealed there: The Italian government is afraid that treasure hunters will tear the island apart. They have already done so for centuries, beginning with Cosimo de' Medici, grand duke of Tuscany, in the sixteenth century. But what has turned the Montecristo treasure into a global legend for generations is the famous novel *The Count of Monte Cristo,* by Alexandre Dumas. (There's no denying that the name *Montecristo* has a ring to it, further reinforced by the luxury cigar brand and the frankly less memorable 1970s culinary concoction known as the Montecristo sandwich.) If that book had never been written, Montecristo Island would not have required the elaborate protection it now enjoys. Dumas was the grandson of a French marquis and an African slave girl; despite his genius, he was often subjected to racist abuse, which made him all the more determined to succeed. In 1842 the famous novelist discovered Montecristo by chance. He was traveling in Italy with Prince Napoleon

Bonaparte, nephew of the Emperor Napoleon, and the two tourists decided to visit Elba, scene of Napoleon's first exile. Bored by Elba, they moved on to the very flat island of Pianosa nearby, intending to shoot game. But Pianosa offered only rabbits and partridges, so they had themselves rowed in a fishing boat to another island in the archipelago, which they were told was heavily populated by wild goats. "It was the first time, and in this fashion," Dumas later recalled, "that the name of Montecristo sounded in my ears." In any event, Dumas and his traveling companions did not land on the island (there is only one landing place), but contented themselves with sailing around it, before heading back to the Italian mainland.

However, the dramatic appearance of the island had made a strong impression on Dumas, then at the height of his powers and about to write his most famous novels. Two years later, in 1844, he gained worldwide fame with the publication of *The Three Musketeers*. The following year he wrote *The Count of Monte Cristo,* the story of a young French sailor, Edmond Dantès, who loses his fiancée and his freedom when some jealous friends falsely accuse him of treason. Imprisoned for fourteen years in the dungeons of the Château d'If near Marseilles, Dantès is befriended by a fellow prisoner, an old Italian priest, who lets him into the secret of a great treasure buried on the island of Montecristo. The priest dies and Dantès escapes, eventually making his way to the island and recovering the treasure. He then buys the island, becomes the Count of Monte Cristo and, in this guise, returns to France as a billionaire (in today's terms) and wreaks terrible vengeance on all those who had wronged him. It is the most famous revenge story ever written.

Dumas usually based his novels on true events and this was no exception. It was inspired by the real-life story of a Frenchman named Pierre Picaud who was falsely denounced by supposed friends and imprisoned for years, during which an old Italian priest told him the whereabouts of a treasure. After his release, Picaud found the treasure (in Milan, not on Montecristo) and used it to pursue and kill his persecutors, only to be murdered himself by the last of those who survived. Since this real-life treasure was found in Milan, it might be supposed that Dumas transferred it to Montecristo simply because it was a more exotic location. But there was more to it than that. Montecristo had been rumored for centuries to conceal a fabulous hoard of treasure—and with good reason. To understand the circumstances that gave birth to this legend, it is necessary to explore the topography and history of the island.

Montecristo is located some twenty-four miles (38.5km) south of Elba and twenty-nine miles (46.5km) west of the island of Giglio, halfway between Corsica and Argentario on the Tuscan coastline. It is an extinct volcano, now a mass of gray-pink granite usually shrouded in mist, rising in three peaks to a maximum height of 2,116 feet (645m) above sea level at Fortress Mount, where a ruined stronghold stands. Montecristo is six square miles (15.5km²) in area and its coastal circumference is ten miles (16km). The island was known to the ancient Greeks as Artemisia and to the Romans as Oglasa, as recorded by the classical writer Pliny, or Mons Jovis—Mount Jove: There was a temple to Jove on the island. In the year 455, St. Mamiliano, Archbishop of Palermo, took refuge there from the Vandals. According to legend, he slew the dragon that guarded the island, changed its name to Montecristo, and established a hermitage in a grotto. Pilgrims flocked to visit the saintly bishop and to seek his blessing. When he died, his relics were jealously appropriated by the inhabitants of the nearby island of Giglio. Other hermits followed until, about 600, Pope St. Gregory the Great approved the establishment of a regular community under the Rule of St. Benedict, whose monks built a monastery there. In 1216 Camaldolese monks took over and built a new monastery dedicated to St. Mamiliano. This became an important house with possessions in Corsica, Sardinia, Piombino, and the neighboring islands of Elba, Giglio, and Pianosa.

With the rise of Islam, the Mediterranean became a battleground between Christians and Muslim corsairs, based on the Barbary coast of north Africa, who raided and plundered every coastline and island, including Montecristo. Despite intermittent threats, the monks of Montecristo remained a small but thriving spiritual community until the middle of the sixteenth century. But it all ended in tragedy in 1553, when Dragut Rais, the Turkish pirate, devastated the Tuscan archipelago, slaughtered the inhabitants of Montecristo, and carried the monks off into slavery. It is from this sanguinary episode that the legend of the treasure of Montecristo dates. To understand its complex ramifications, we need to understand the career of Dragut the corsair, who destroyed the peaceful life of this remote island by fire and sword.

Dragut Rais (a *rais* was a Muslim ship's commander) was the most formidable and feared Islamic sailor of the sixteenth century. Today his name would be more correctly rendered as Turgut Reis. He was born in 1485 in the village of Charabalac, today named Turgutreis in his honor, on the Bodrum peninsula in Anatolia, in Asia Minor. When he was twelve years old, he was talent-spotted by a Turkish officer who took him to Egypt and enrolled him in the Mamelukes military unit as a cannoneer, specializing in siege artillery. From the beginning, he showed an uncanny talent for accurate artillery fire, in an age when this science was in its infancy. Such a talent would have the greatest opportunity to flourish at sea, so he joined the corsairs and eventually owned and commanded his own galliot, which he armed with the most sophisticated guns then available and devastated Christian shipping. In 1520 he went to serve under the famous admiral, Barbarossa, and was soon promoted to second-in-command. Thereafter, his exploits became ever more audacious and spectacular, attacking coastal settlements around the Mediterranean, as well as ships. His career came to an abrupt halt in 1540 when he was taken by surprise while repairing his ships on the coast of Corsica and captured. He served as a galley slave for four years before being imprisoned in Genoa. His chief, Barbarossa, laid siege to Genoa with a massive fleet until the Genoese agreed to ransom Dragut for 3,500 gold ducats.

This proved to be a disaster for Christian towns and cities in the Mediterranean. Dragut resumed his campaign with even greater ferocity and, after Barbarossa died in 1545, was universally acknowledged as his successor and the sultan, Suleiman the Magnificent, appointed him commander-in-chief of Ottoman naval forces throughout the Mediterranean. In 1548 he became bey of Algiers and in 1551, when he captured Tripoli from the Knights of St. John, he became bey of that territory also. The following year the sultan made him beylerbey (chief regional governor) of the Mediterranean. His coreligionists awarded him the title the "Drawn Sword of Islam." That was the career he had enjoyed and the rank he had attained when, in 1553, he raided the island of Montecristo. For Dragut, this small island was a very minor and insignificant target. It was barely habitable and, after he had annihilated the population, the very modest prize he gained was the captured monks as slaves. That year he had already sacked most of Sicily, captured three towns on Elba and another three on Corsica (in the name of France, with which he was disgracefully allied), and the island of Pianosa. So it was hardly worth the time and effort of the beylerbey to gobble up so small a morsel as Montecristo.

He probably did so for two reasons: To Dragut, any place on earth where the cross of Christ was venerated was worth laying waste; and he may have wanted to use the island's sheltered anchorage to effect ship repairs after an intensive campaign. As has been said, it was this raid, which left Montecristo depopulated and ended civilized life there, that gave rise to the story of the treasure. The most common version is that the monks hid their treasure from Dragut before he landed. This tale has some plausibility: It would certainly have been routine procedure for a religious house threatened with depredation to bury its sacred vessels to avoid desecration. These would have been made of precious metals and, along with furnishings, such as candlesticks, would have been of some value. The monastery strongbox, too, perhaps containing donations saved over the years (what was there for the monks to spend money on?) could have contained a respectable sum, considering that the monastery had possessions in Corsica and Sardinia, as well as the other islands of the Tuscan archipelago. But, at the most generous estimate, the amount of resources this modest settlement could have commanded, in an area that was far from wealthy and constantly plundered by pirates, could not have amounted to much. To Dragut, it would have been small change. By no stretch of the imagination could the assets of the Monastery of San Mamiliano conceivably have been rated as a fabulous treasure. Yet the legend persisted: That was clearly what induced Dumas to make Montecristo the focal point of his famous novel, even though the treasure in the real-life story he used as a skeleton for his plot had been found on the Italian mainland. But there is an alternative explanation and one that makes perfect sense.

Having reviewed all the evidence available, we (the authors of this book) have come to a different conclusion from the commonly accepted version, which, as we have just demonstrated, does not square with the facts. We believe there is indeed a fabulous hoard of treasure still concealed on Montecristo, but it never belonged to the good monks. So far from being concealed from Dragut, it is our contention that *it was Dragut himself* who brought the treasure to the island and buried it there. Consider the circumstances. By the time Dragut landed on Montecristo in 1553, he had already sacked or held up for ransom more than forty cities, towns, and islands. The proceeds from any one of those raids would have amounted to a fortune. In the years between 1553 and his death in 1565, he plundered as many cities again. Then there were the proceeds from his piracy at sea: One galley alone that he captured from the Knights of St. John netted him seventy thousand gold ducats. His piracy lasted for a period of forty-five years; in every one of those years he took an immense booty. Even if portions of it had been allotted to his crews, the mighty rais would always get the lion's share. Among the rich cities he plundered were Rapallo, Sorrento, and Tripoli, the whole Italian Riviera and the Ligurian coast (several times), the coast of Spain—in short, just about every settlement accessible from the waters of the Mediterranean. As both a Turkish admiral and the greatest corsair of his age, it is likely that he was the richest man in Europe and Asia Minor—in modern terms, a billionaire.

As with all rich men, the question would inevitably present itself:

How could he keep his fortune safe? No doubt, as befitted his position, he would have remitted some of it to Constantinople, where he enjoyed the favor and protection of the sultan. But Ottoman favor was notoriously fickle: Dragut must have known that, in the event of his falling out with the sultan, he would be extremely vulnerable if all his wealth were within his master's reach. As governor of both Algiers and Tripoli, no doubt he also had nest eggs salted away in those cities. But the political situation on the Barbary coast was volatile, to say the least. Like all pirates, Dragut's instinct must have been to conceal much of his fortune in some isolated place, unfrequented and known only to him, and a pirate's favorite resort has always been to bury his treasure. Montecristo—that inhospitable, barren, remote rock—was the ideal site for that purpose. Since he had massacred the population, it was uninhabited and free from prying eyes. Dragut is known to have put in there from time to time, using it as a base for repairs or a place of ambush from which he could sally forth to attack Christian shipping. Montecristo has only one possible landing point, the sheltered Cala Maestra (Master Cove, formerly King's Cove) on the western coast of the island. There, secure from surprise, he would have had complete privacy to off-load bullion, coins, jewels, plate, precious objects—the rich fruits of his marauding—with the help of a few trusted crew members who would have known the penalties of betrayal.

That scenario, rather than the notion of a few sacred vessels and pious offerings buried by monks, would justify the legend of a phenomenal treasure. The fact that this island was frequented by the richest pirate of all time, a man who lived his life surrounded by treachery and violence, who must surely have looked around for a secure repository for his stupendous wealth, suggests more than a strong likelihood that he deposited a significant portion of it on Montecristo. His own depredations had returned it to its desert island state. When one assembles the facts, the question becomes, not so much, Is it likely that Dragut hid a treasure trove there? Rather, is it credible that he did not? As for the emergence of the legend, even the wildest places generate gossip; Dragut's own crew must occasionally have speculated in whispers; and local fishermen are an astute breed.

But there is more than mere speculation and logic to support the existence of the treasure. The first man to launch a search for it was that supreme realist Grand Duke Cosimo I of Tuscany. He would never have undertaken such an enterprise unless he had solid grounds for believing in the existence of the treasure. As recounted above (in Chapter 5), Cosimo was the first Medici grand duke of Tuscany and founding grand master of the Order of St. Stephen, which existed to fight the Muslim corsairs. As such, he had good intelligence about the movements of Dragut. Contemporaries supposed he was searching for treasure hidden by the monks; but Cosimo, unlike many other rulers, had always zealously respected the rights of the Church and was head of a canonically established military-religious order. He knew perfectly well that if he had unearthed the monks' sacred vessels he would have been compelled by public and ecclesiastical opinion to restore them to the Camaldolese Order, whose brothers had been enslaved by Dragut, in which case his search would have been profitless. Dragut's treasure would have been a totally different matter, and we conclude that this is what he was searching for. Since Cosimo died in 1574, the search must have been conducted before then—possibly shortly after Dragut was killed in 1565.

Another treasure hunter is reputed to have been Alessandro d'Appiani, prince of Piombino, spurred on by his wife Elisabetta. Again, this must have happened while Dragut was still a recent memory, since d'Appiani was assassinated in 1589. These early treasure hunters have been blamed for the destruction of most of what was left of the monastery church, ransacked in the quest for gold. But the worst damage was probably done later. Unfortunately, an ancient book was discovered, which advised treasure seekers to dig under the altar, with disastrous consequences for the structure; but no treasure has ever been found. Dragut, the owner of this putative treasure, met his death at the age of eighty while taking part in the Great Siege of Malta in 1565. Since he and the other Turkish commanders disdained to take cover from the fire of the Knights of St. John, he was easily identified and a well-aimed cannon shot fatally wounded him: As a renowned artilleryman, presumably he would have appreciated the accuracy of the shot.

Whatever the truth behind the legend, all treasure hunting has now been banned. The island had a succession of different rulers, eventually passing in 1814 into the jurisdiction of the Habsburg grand dukes of Tuscany until 1859. From then until 1945 it was part of the territory of the kings of Italy. An English botanist, George Watson-Taylor, owned Montecristo from 1850 to 1860 and built the Villa Watson-Taylor at Cala Maestra. It was renovated by a later owner, the Marquis Ginori, and subsequently renamed the Villa Reale (Villa Royal) because King Victor Emmanuel III used it as a hunting lodge and spent his honeymoon there. When Montecristo's twentieth-century owners proposed to turn it into a country club for the ultra-rich in 1970, the Italian government intervened and declared it a nature reserve. A book, *Prisoners of Paradise,* describes the experience of a series of married couples who acted as lonely guardians of the island since 1956. At first their conditions were extremely primitive and there was a crisis when a seriously ill child had to be evacuated to a hospital on the mainland. On another occasion, one of the guardians was responsible for saving the lives of two parachutists he spotted in the sea through a telescope.

The present regime on Montecristo consists of two caretakers who live in a house next to the villa, for whose upkeep they are responsible. The villa includes a small botanical and geological museum and the garden. There are also two forestry officers who are relieved every fifteen days. The island is under the administration of the Tuscan Archipelago Parks Commission. The restrictions are severe: Nobody can land on the island without special permission, boats may not anchor offshore, fishing and swimming in its waters are prohibited. In March 2008 the commission announced an extension in the number of visitors who would be allowed to land each year; but they will only be able to do so after attending a daylong course of environmental education and as members of a party organized and conducted onshore by government officials. So there will still be no possibility of indulging in any treasure hunting. The wildness of the island, covered in Mediterranean scrub and populated by wild goats and rabbits—there is even a species of viper unique to Montecristo—makes it an unspoiled environmental gem. The Italian government is determined to keep it that way. Quite simply, the authorities are afraid that treasure hunters could tear the island to pieces. The island's unique ecology is the true treasure, claim environmentalists. However, that is unlikely to dissuade those who remain convinced that a fabulous treasure remains hidden on Montecristo. As we have shown, that belief is well founded.

But there is pressure from another source for increased access to the island: the Catholic Church. Montecristo also qualifies as a shrine because of the veneration of St. Mamiliano, strong in the Mediterranean, focused on the grotto dedicated to him at the Cove of the Saint and probably established centuries ago by Benedictines. Monsignor Comastri, Bishop of Marine-Piombino, celebrated Mass there in July 1991 and the Church authorities would like to have regular services at the grotto. They would also like to preserve the artistic treasures of the place and to stabilize the crumbling monastery of San Mamiliano, wrecked by pirates and treasure hunters and used for target practice by the German Navy during the Second World War. But even bishops have difficulty landing on what is one of the most jealously guarded islands in the world, so there is little prospect at present of unearthing the priceless treasure that may well be hidden there.

Easter Island: Mysterious Graven Images

Easter Island is one of the most remote places on earth. It is located in the South Pacific, 2,237 miles (3,600km) west of Chile and 1,290 miles (2,075km) east of Pitcairn Island. But it is not just its geographical situation that renders it eerie and challenging. Its name derives from its discovery by Westerners on Easter Sunday 1722. In the local language the same word is used to describe the inhabitants, their language, and the island: *Rapa Nui*. The origins of this civilization have baffled anthropologists. Some have speculated that it is the remains of a lost continent; fanciful theorists have even conjectured that the long-lost inhabitants came from an alien settlement. In fact, Easter Island, which is composed of three extinct volcanoes, giving it a triangular shape, covers sixty-three square miles (163km²) and seems to have been settled by Polynesians, possibly as late as AD 1200. It had a bloody history of tribal war and ecological disaster, as the expanding population consumed the resources of the island. The ensuing chaos and food shortages led to the adoption of cannibalism, which only ended after the natives' conversion to Christianity. Islanders were abducted to work in the Peruvian mines in the nineteenth century and the few survivors who returned brought smallpox and tuberculosis, which ravaged the population, including the last member of the royal family, who died of tuberculosis in 1867. A century ago the population had shrunk to just over 100, but today it is around 3,800.

For a few months in 1955–56 the Norwegian adventurer and ethnographer Thor Heyerdahl—most famous for his *Kon-Tiki* expedition—visited Easter Island with a team that included archaeologists. On a combination of folk tradition and archaeological evidence, he concluded that the island had originally been settled by a fair-skinned race from the South American mainland, that the Polynesians had arrived much later, perhaps as recently as the sixteenth century, and had subsequently overthrown and massacred the dominant "Long-Ears" (they were said to be able to tie their elongated earlobes together at the back of their necks) in the eighteenth century. He published his conclusions in the book *Easter Island: The Mystery Solved*. Today, however, genetic research suggests the Easter Islanders are more closely related to people in Southeast Asia than to South American Indians.

What has earned Easter Island its fame and reputation for mystery, however, is the array of massive stone sculptures, known as "Moai," found there. They were constructed in quarries, then transported to various sites around the island. Apart from their purpose and significance, the most baffling question is this: How were they transported? The Moai are statues of torsos and heads, some as tall as forty feet (12m), which were set up around the coast. But they were cast down by the islanders themselves, when they inexplicably turned iconoclasts in the early 1770s. All the statues now standing have been re-erected in recent times. The islanders' memory of the traditions associated with the statues has largely been lost, though they were apparently an expression of ancestor worship. Such cultural amnesia, in an enclosed community like an island, is very unusual and can only be attributed to the fact that the population at one point dwindled close to extinction; folk memory was lost, along with the people who formerly embodied it.

Although it can be considered tactless today to raise the topic of cannibalism on the island, whose people are now deeply embarrassed by their ancestors' politically incorrect cuisine, it is a matter of interest to anthropologists. It is generally agreed there were three motives for cannibalism: a kind of religious ritual, a means of wreaking vengeance on an enemy family, and a perverted gourmet tradition. It appears that male Easter Islanders developed a taste for human flesh, if only because there were no other large mammals to hunt. Cannibal feasts were held in isolated places, probably in caves, with women and children normally excluded, though they were usually on the menu. The *kaitangata* (man-eaters) imprisoned their victims in huts at the site of the banquets before sacrificing them to the gods. The cannibals then ate them, the fingers and toes being regarded as the greatest delicacies. If a family had one of its members abducted and eaten, this humiliation created a vendetta and revenge became a motive for further cannibalism. The notorious taunt of a man-eater to the humiliated relations of someone he had consumed was: "The flesh of your mother sticks between my teeth."

Even more tantalizing than the puzzle as to why the Rapa Nui overthrew the giant Moai images they had made in the nineteenth century is the mystery of the Rongorongo scripture, the only written language in Oceania. Apparently composed by a priestly caste, this language has baffled scholars, who have been unable to decipher it. Of the hundreds of Rongorongo tablets known to have existed, only twenty-six survive. But the islanders themselves cannot understand them, possibly because only the historic priesthood and aristocracy were ever literate, so that since 1863 (when the population was hugely reduced as islanders were abducted to serve as slaves in the Peruvian mines) nobody has been able to read the tablets. Scholars today cannot even be certain that the hieroglyphics constitute a written language. It is thought, however, that Rongorongo is an unusual example of a written language being created, in one place, from no preceding tradition. Its other peculiarity is that it is not particularly ancient. It is different from the more than four thousand Polynesian "petroglyphs" carved on stone at various sites around the island. One theory is that it was invented by the ruling class as an elite form of communication after the visit of a Spanish ship in 1770 exposed them to the concept of literature. It is a striking coincidence that the casting down of the Moai began about the same time. In the 1950s two-and-a-half lines on one tablet were successfully identified as a lunar calendar and another tablet was tentatively interpreted as recording a genealogy, but progress remains stalled. Today, despite modern expertise in cryptography, the surviving Rongorongo tablets defy all attempts to decipher them further. Easter Island jealously guards its mysteries.

Isle of Lewis, Scottish Hebrides

The nearest equivalent Europe has to Easter Island and its dramatic Moai is not Stonehenge, but rather the standing stones at Calanais, on the Isle of Lewis, off the northwest coast of Scotland. There stand more than twenty monuments between 2,500 and 4,000 years old. They are situated close to the village of Calanais (English pronunciation: "Callanish"), on a ridge of ground overlooking Loch Roag. The most famous group is known as Calanais I and consists of fifty individual stones, including an inner circle of thirteen that are between eight and thirteen feet (2.4–4m) tall, arranged around a central stone sixteen feet (5m) high. There is a stone tomb at the center of the circle, but of later date than the upright stones. The arrangement of the whole system forms a cross, but that is coincidental, since the monuments are pre-Christian. The stone circle and the lane of stones pointing north are believed to date from 2900 BC; the three other lines and the tomb are from circa 1500 BC. Despite their height and commanding appearance, during part of their history the monuments were partially submerged beneath almost six feet (1.8m) of peat that formed around them as a consequence of climate change and was only cleared away in 1857.

Although the stones are ancient, there is evidence that they were replacements for even older monuments that formerly stood on the site. The chambered cairn, believed to be a tomb, was plundered at some stage in its history, leaving no clue as to its contents. It is widely believed that the arrangement of the stones relates to the lunar cycle. Two researchers, Gerald Ponting and Margaret Curtis, reported their findings at an archeo-astronomy conference in 1980 on the relationship between the extreme southern path of the moon and its setting among the Calanais stones, and subsequently developed that research.

Besides the main site, there are two other complexes nearby. Calanais II is the smallest, consisting of just ten stones, half of which are still upright. About two hundred yards (183m) to the east there is the larger complex of Calanais III, composed of twenty stones forming a double ring. The stones are known in Gaelic as *Fir Bhreig,* "The False Men," and there is some evidence that they were historically regarded as men who had been turned into stone. According to one pious legend, St. Kieran turned them into stone for refusing to convert to Christianity. There is no doubt, however, that the stones predate the Christian era. There is a visitors' center close by, including an exhibition on the history of the stone circles. The intriguing questions are these: Who built these monuments? For what purpose? And who was important enough to merit a tomb at the center of this exceptional group of dramatic, upright stones?

Iona: St. Columba's Scottish Island Sanctuary

Also off the Scottish coast, less than a mile (1.6km) from the larger island of Mull, lies Iona, where the early Christian missionary and monk, St. Columba, founded a monastery that was to transform Scottish society. Columba was one of the most interesting personalities in sixth-century Europe. Through his father, he belonged to the royal house of O'Donnell in Ireland, being the great-great-grandson of Niall of the Nine Hostages, high king of Ireland. He trained for the priesthood at the celebrated Abbey of Clonard, in County Meath, under St. Finian. Unfortunately an argument over a copy he had made of a religious book developed into a pitched battle in which many men were killed. Filled with remorse, Columba volunteered to go into exile in Scotland and to convert as many men to Christianity as had been killed in the battle.

He sailed first to the Mull of Kintyre, where he landed in 563; but he could still see Ireland from that coastline, so he moved farther north, where he was given land on the island of Iona, just off the coast of Mull. This became the center for his missionary work among the pagan Picts and the substantial abbey he built there is his physical monument, just as the spread of Christianity in the land of the Picts was his spiritual legacy. We know so much about St. Columba because, unlike most people of his era, he had a biographer, St. Adamnan, who left a chronicle of Columba's life. The abbey he built on Iona still stands, having been restored from ruin in the twentieth century. It always had a tempestuous history, being sacked by the Vikings four times between 795 and 825. In 1200 the Lord of the Isles replaced the original structure with a more ambitious Benedictine monastery, as well as an Augustinian nunnery close by. Both buildings were further developed in the late fifteenth century. In the following century, however, they were destroyed by the Protestant Reformers in the 1560s. In the seventeenth century King Charles I attempted to turn the surviving east end of the abbey church into a Cathedral of the Isles, but this failed and the ultra-Presbyterian Covenanters, to whom monastic buildings were anathema, ousted the king. Thereafter, Iona fell into complete ruin.

Finally, in 1902, restoration work began and the nave was completed by 1910. Further restoration continued until 1965 and is now complete. The abbey is approached via the graveyard and the Chapel of St. Oran, where are buried many ancient Scottish kings. Striking stone Celtic crosses stand in the abbey grounds. Since 1938 the abbey has been occupied by the Iona Community, a Christian Socialist group, and modern sculpture has been integrated into the older structure. Although the various chapels and other buildings are now fully restored, the cloisters being especially impressive, the abbey has been reordered to accommodate Presbyterian or interdenominational worship. The original atmosphere has been lost, however, and this departure from its designated purpose has created an unsympathetic ambience. The heavy influx of visitors—140,000 a year—has also inevitably destroyed the isolated, contemplative character of the island. That said, it is still well worth a visit since, if one can wander off to an unfrequented area, it is still possible to recapture the atmosphere of what was once one of the most important sanctuaries of Christian Europe.

Svalbard: Norway's Arctic Eden

The Norwegian islands of Svalbard, in the Arctic Circle, are reminiscent in some ways of the secret government installations and bolt-holes described in Chapter 7. Svalbard is not an island, but an archipelago, situated halfway between Norway and the North Pole. It has been part of Norway since 1925. This small settlement, previously home only to a group of scientists and coal miners, is so far north it is permanently frozen. Polar night lasts from late October to mid-February. Besides reindeer, Arctic foxes and even polar bears have been known to amble through the few streets of the settlement at Longyearbyen. Of the three populated islands in the archipelago, it is Spitzbergen that has acquired a more serious, and some claim sinister, significance. In a special, refrigerated security vault built there, plans call for the storage of specimens of the seeds of all plant life on earth.

The idea is that, if some doomsday event—nuclear war, climate meltdown, asteroid strike, or whatever—brought life on earth close to extinction, all crops, cereals, fruits, and other plants could be regenerated from the seed bank in Spitzbergen's vault. The project has been jointly sponsored by the Norwegian government and the Global Crop Diversity Trust. The high-security vault, as long as a football field, will preserve the means to recultivate the earth with all foodstuffs grown from seed. Many millions of seeds will eventually be stored there and security is stronger here than at any similar facility anywhere on the planet. It has been described as "the backup for the whole world" and more than a hundred countries have supported its construction. Svalbard was chosen as the location for this storehouse for two reasons: first, because of its isolation, and second, even if the artificial refrigeration systems failed for years, it would be unlikely to matter, since the natural temperature is so low anyway. In the event of global catastrophe, this remote island could turn out to be a second Eden for humanity.

That, at any rate, is the official version. Others take a different view. Critics claim that the participation of partners like the Rockefeller Foundation, Bill Gates, and others in the "Doomsday Seed Vault" project needs to be investigated. The possibility of somebody cornering the market in world seeds and the involvement of those with an interest in genetically modified (GM) crops have aroused the suspicions of conspiracy theorists. Some have gone so far as to allege a scheme to control the future food production of the entire planet, claiming that "self-destruct" mechanisms in genetically modified hybrid seeds would compel farmers to go back to the private companies for a fresh supply when the seeds they originally purchased had become moribund. Others see the further possibility of a form of biological warfare, relating to crop supplies, being developed in the future. Commercial and political controversies are likely to make the Svalbard Doomsday Vault a subject of fierce debate for years to come.

The vault is sited 390 feet (119m) inside a sandstone mountain.

Special refrigerators keep the seeds at a temperature of −18 degrees Celsius and the vault has the capacity to store 4.5 million of them. Even if the refrigeration broke down, the temperature in the surrounding environment is so low it is estimated that little damage would occur for several weeks. The Nordic Genetic Resource Center manages the facility, which is owned by the Norwegian government. Already, however, one ill omen has attended the project. One of the reasons Svalbard was selected was its absence of tectonic activity. But just five days before the vault's official opening, on February 21, 2008, the strongest earthquake ever recorded in the history of Norway, measuring 6.2 on the Richter scale, shook the archipelago. Its epicenter was at Storfjorden, just eighty-seven miles (140km) southeast of Svalbard. The old maxim about putting all your eggs in one basket comes to mind.

Chapter 9

HOLIES OF HOLIES

pringtime, and a young man's fancy turns to . . . the Book of Revelation? Actually, some would say it's hard to be romantic or to think of procreation, given the onrush of seemingly cataclysmic events—mass terrorism, endless regional wars, predictions (correct or otherwise) of disastrous climate change, and economic doom. True, the global computer shutdown some insisted would happen on Y2K (January 1, 2000—remember?) seems positively dorky in hindsight, as do many of the more breathless millennialist claims of impending Apocalypse. As at least one economist has sensibly noted, the Stone Age didn't end because we ran out of stone; likewise, the world isn't so much likely to run out of oil and resources as it is to supersede them with more advanced technologies and energy sources. Those American survivalists who headed for the hills long ago have found themselves having to lurch from the *X-Files* 1990s (government as lying Big Brother in black helicopters), to post-9/11 national unity (Uncle Sam as proactive superhero), to late 2000s mistakes and uncertainty (government as chronic bungler).

We survived the twentieth century without nuclear oblivion, but it appears we may have arrived at our good fortune by the skin of our teeth: After the fall of the Berlin Wall, detailed plans emerged that the Soviets had contemplated a very high-speed conventional war in Europe—on the presumption that the West would not escalate. Eerily, a secret vault was found in the former East Germany with field marshal's epaulets ready to be put on the shoulders of East Germany's commander-in-chief at the beginning of World War III, and a cache of decorations to be awarded to the first East German soldiers to cross the Rhine. Happily, they were never used.

Still, it's hard not to be edgy these days, and one thing that both science and almost all religions agree on is that the world will end at some point. Atheists, too, have largely come around to the view that human beings do indeed have a natural hunger for the spiritual, including the desire to grapple with the age-old questions of humanity's place in the cosmos, the deep past, the far future—and what both theologians and physicists call "ultimate reality." Nations and societies seem to have this unalterable impulse as well, and even officially secular states have been unable to function without sacred reference points, from Lenin's Tomb on Moscow's Red Square to the French Republic's national Pantheon in Paris (with its burial crypts of Voltaire and Rousseau, the latter especially worth seeing for its macabre qualities). According to Hungarian-born philosopher Thomas Molnar, this phenomenon is both timeless and universal:

> The sacred relationship with a transcendent reality was at all times deeply embedded in the life of every community. The channels with the sacred—ruler, clergy, ritual—were supplemented in physical form by such external validations of the community's existence as architecture, music, ceremony and . . . the citizens' belief that, one way or another, their community belonged to a [higher] reality . . .

Sancta Sanctorum, Rome's Lateran Palace

If one is on the trail of a higher reality and emanations of ultimate human destiny, an obvious first port of call is the only location anywhere marked with the bold inscription *NON EST IN TOTO SANCTIOR ORBE LOCUS* ("There is no holier place in all the world"). This is the Sancta Sanctorum (Holy of Holies), a hidden chapel and strictly private papal oratory contained within the old Lateran Palace in Rome—"embellished," according to a noted art historian, "with

appropriately concentrated splendour, as if it were itself a holy reliquary turned outside-in." Hanging there, and only dimly seen from
the always-locked entrance grille, is the important but too little known
image of Christ Acheiropoeitos—a Greek expression meaning not
made by human hands. According to a fifteenth-century visitor, this
precious and numinous painting was then guarded, in relays around
the clock, by four men with iron maces. Encased with fittings of gold,
silver, and bronze, it continues to beguile scholars and to inspire the
select few visitors privileged to get up close to the image. The chapel
itself is of thirteenth-century origin, constructed in the form of a
cube twenty-five feet (8m) across, with frescoes, mosaics, cross-ribbed
vaulting, and stone inlays of a remarkable jewel-box character. The
apse reuses older columns of Egyptian porphyry, a stone once considered so valuable that its quarrying and use were only permitted by the
direct authority of the Roman emperor.

Only the pope himself may celebrate Mass in this place, and the
atmosphere remains hushed, to say the least—in the spirit of the
original *sancta sanctorum.* No one was allowed to enter the holy of holies
in the Temple of Jerusalem (destroyed in AD 70) except the high
priest on one day of the year, Yom Kippur, the Day of Atonement.
Modern rabbinical opinion has been that Jews should avoid ascending
the Temple Mount (called the Noble Sanctuary by Muslims), to prevent the accidental desecration that would result from walking on
or near the former holy of holies. However, a controversial Temple
Institute in Israel has as its long-term goal the construction of a new
(technically third) Temple there, an objective opposed by many
Orthodox and other Jewish scholars on both theological and prac-
tical grounds—not to mention the immense difficulty of finding a
young cow that meets the unusual standards required of a sacrificial
red heifer. Given that the al-Aqsa Mosque and Dome of the Rock are
now on the Temple Mount, any serious ambition to displace Islam's
third most important sanctuary would be deeply offensive to Muslims
worldwide and extremely ill-advised. With so many nuclear-tipped
countries with nerves on hair triggers, this would seem like a sure-fire
way (so to speak) to accelerate the end times.

The Pauline Chapel, The Vatican's Apostolic Palace

In the context of the last days, another thoroughly private Roman sanctuary figures in contemporary chatter of an apocalyptic nature. This is the sixteenth-century Pauline Chapel of the Vatican's Apostolic Palace, which is separated from the nearby—and much more famous—Sistine Chapel by the Sala Regia, a stately hall running about a 150 feet (46m) in length between the two chapels. The Pauline is where the cardinals gather at the beginning of each conclave, to hear a sermon about the necessity of electing a worthy successor to Peter, before processing together into the Sistine Chapel to take their solemn oaths and begin the proceedings. Unlike the much-visited Sistine Chapel, the *Capella Paolina* is never open to the public, although it has two important frescoes, painted by Michelangelo himself on the wet plaster of this momentous spot. They have been overshadowed by his works in the nearby Sistine Chapel, particularly his *Last Judgment*, but the Pauline Chapel's *Conversion of Saul* and *Crucifixion of St. Peter* are significant in size (they are both very large, each covering some 445 square feet [41m^2]) and history (they were Michelangelo's very last frescoes, completed in the 1540s).

These frescoes were recently restored, but according to the late Vaticanologist Dr. Malachi Martin, the chapel may need an exorcist much more than it needs an art restorer. Before his death in 1999, he told one of this book's coauthors that his final novel, *Windswept House,* was based solidly on fact—that is, on an actual terrifying ceremony that took place in Rome in the early 1960s. According to the book, several senior prelates, in total secrecy and apostasy, carried out a deadly serious ritual "enthronement of the Fallen Angel Lucifer" in the Pauline Chapel on June 29, 1963, in order to usher in the "Availing Time."

Martin was a fascinating, Irish-born author and former Jesuit with some sixty books to his name, a number of which were *New York Times* best sellers. Ordained a priest in 1954, he held doctorates in Semitic languages, archaeology, and Oriental history, and studied at Oxford, Louvain, and Hebrew University in Jerusalem, among other places.

With his stellar Vatican connections, he served as private secretary to Cardinal Bea in Rome during the early 1960s, but a few years later left the Jesuit order (or rather, as he said, "They left me"). He found his way to New York, where he took odd jobs (including taxi driving) to make ends meet, and was later befriended by a Greek billionaire shipping family that gave him a place to live, write, and say Mass privately (per the dispensation he received from Pope Paul VI). Until his last breath, he was slightly evasive (or perhaps careful) about the details of the Pauline Chapel narrative, saying that some facts presented in the book had to be disguised in terms of dates, places, and names, but that the essence of the events described was absolutely genuine. If so, be afraid—be very afraid.

The "Prophecies" of St. Malachy

Dr. Martin's patron saint has also been linked with some ambivalent intimations of a mystical nature. Today there is growing interest in the so-called Prophecies of St. Malachy, a list of 112 short Latin phrases said to refer to each pope, starting with Celestine II (in the twelfth century) until the final one at the end of time (or at "the end of the age"). The Church has never taken any official position on their authenticity, and many serious scholars have considered them to be a sixteenth-century fabrication. Each symbolic phrase is supposed to signify something related to that particular pontiff—his personal qualities, events of his time, or even the symbolism in the coat of arms he inherited or adopted prior to becoming pope. It turns out that this stuff is more riveting than Nostradamus, and many of the phrases "predicted" for the popes who came to office in the twentieth century seem frighteningly close to the mark. For example, the Latin phrase assigned centuries ago to the pontificate of Benedict XV (1914–1922) was *Religio Depopulata*—"religion laid waste"—a pretty good description of the self-destruction of Christian, European civilization brought about by the First World War and the Bolshevik revolution. Three popes later, the assigned phrase was *Pastor et Nauta*—"pastor and mariner"—an apparently fitting title for the pastoral pope Blessed

John XXIII, who came from the great seafaring city of Venice, where he was patriarch. On the other hand, a devil's advocate could argue that John XXIII's origins were firmly in the soil his land-based peasant ancestors tilled.

The most striking of the mottoes, however, is that applied to John Paul I, who reigned for only thirty-three days: *De medietate Lunae.* If that can be translated as "from half-moon to half-moon," meaning about the measure of a month—and it is far from incontestable that it can—it would accord startling prophetic credibility, if not to St. Malachy, at least to a sixteenth-century Venetian forger or the Jesuits (both of whom have been accused of fabricating these forecasts). You can see for yourself, and draw your own conclusions. Interestingly, there is only one Latin motto left, supposedly for the last pope at either the end of the world (or, in an alternative interpretation, at the end of the epoch). In a curious convergence, the final Latin motto could possibly be in use in 2012, the year when the intricate and accurate Mayan calendar comes to an abrupt end—provoking intense metaphysical speculation in the meantime.

The Monastery of St. Catherine of Sinai, Egypt

If your mind goes into overdrive at such thoughts, perhaps a trip into the stillness of the desert might be therapeutic. Santa Fe, New Mexico has a distinctly spiritual vibe (as befits a place still officially called the Royal City of the Holy Faith of St. Francis of Assisi); but for a more profound journey, we might recommend the sixth-century Monastery of St. Catherine of Sinai in a remote corner of Egypt, at the mouth of an inaccessible gorge at the foot of Mount Sinai—a place sacred to the three Abrahamic faiths. Getting to this UNESCO World Heritage Site used to involve a long and arduous camel journey, and even today it's not exactly easy to access. The Burning Bush, where Moses is believed to have received the Ten Commandments, is said to be a living shrub still on the property, and the monastery's codex, manuscript, and icon collection is without parallel in the world. (The word *priceless* is used pretty casually these days, but the contents of this place truly are.) Greek and Russian mystics have described icons as "windows onto heaven," and the monastery has in its possession three of the five oldest ones in existence. Especially striking are those early icons created using the encaustic technique, with paintbrush applied to hot wax. The arid Egyptian climate has helped preserve the library's irreplaceable documents, written a thousand years ago or more in Coptic, Arabic, Syriac, Armenian, Hebrew, Greek, Old Church Slavonic, Georgian, and other languages. Relations with the monastery's Muslim, mostly Bedouin, neighbors have been relatively harmonious over the centuries, and its still-existing charter of privileges guaranteeing protection from Islamic authorities is believed to have been signed by the Prophet Muhammad himself. Uniquely for a monastic complex, St. Catherine's has a small mosque within its fortified walls.

The monastery and its surrounding properties constitute the world's smallest autonomous (or possibly "autocephalous") Orthodox church—the Church of Sinai. It is headed by an abbot, who is also its archbishop, who negotiated with the Getty Center in Los Angeles prior to that fabulously rich museum's 2006 blockbuster exhibition of treasures from Sinai. The monastery's highest-profile patron and supporter is the Prince of Wales, who has involved himself with much more than casual interest in the work of the St. Catherine Foundation, which is based in London with branches in New York and Geneva. Prince Charles's paternal grandmother—"Aliki," or Princess Alice— became an Orthodox nun in widowhood, although she maintained such endearingly down-to-earth habits as card playing and chain smoking. After her death at Buckingham Palace in 1969, she was buried at Gethsemane on the Mount of Olives in Jerusalem, where she is also honored as one of the "righteous gentiles" at *Yad Vashem,* the Holocaust memorial, for her courage in saving Jews in Nazi-occupied Athens.

The Autonomous Monastic Republic of Holy Mount Athos, Greece

Of a similar spirit—but on a wholly different, vastly larger scale—is another UNESCO World Heritage Site: the Autonomous Monastic Republic of Holy Mount Athos in Greece, which takes up an entire 130-square-mile (337km²) peninsula that pierces the Aegean Sea. The Holy Mountain is denounced regularly in the European Parliament for not being an "equal-opportunity institution"—as it rigidly excludes women, whose presence is literally illegal. Media coverage also frequently claims that even female animals are not permitted on the microstate's territory, making the monks seem misogynistic in the extreme. The truth of the matter is that the whole peninsula is essentially an enclosed cloister of monks, and just as men are not allowed to enter the bounds of a female convent, the same is true here the other way around. As for animals, female cats are welcome in the "Garden of the Virgin" (another name for Mount Athos) as they keep the rodent population in check; likewise, hens are raised for eggs—both for food and for the yolks needed for icon painting. Still, much about the place makes for good copy, including the fact it is accessible only by boat, and that the waters off the coast can be rough and dangerous. Visitors are limited to a maximum of a hundred men a day (of any religion or none), who have undertaken the complicated booking procedures and have the necessary Greek government entry permit as well as a letter of recommendation from their own country's embassy or consulate. The site is physically stunning, even by the standards of Greece's many amazing islands and peninsulas, with seaside cliffs and steep slopes that rise to nearly 7,000 feet (2,134m) in some places. Mount Athos' unique and inviolable status as a self-governing monastic state within a sovereign Greece is guaranteed by both Article 105 of the Hellenic Constitution and by the 1981 Treaty of Accession of Greece to the European Communities. Secularist critics in Brussels, Strasbourg, Athens, and even London (where questions about the Holy Mountain have been raised in the House of Commons) find themselves frustrated when they realize that the ancient privileges of Mount Athos are firmly entrenched in these most modern of binding legal documents.

Athonite spirituality is not, however, based on EU law, but rather on unceasing prayer, as practiced at its twenty major monasteries organized on a structured, communal "cenobitic" principle; more than a dozen smaller "sketes," some of which follow the more informal idiorrhythmic approach, which allows each monk to devise his own spiritually fruitful rhythm; and many solitary huts for hermit monks, who are alone with sky, sea, mountain—and the Triune God. Mount Athos is a long way from the commotion of London, but as with St. Catherine of Sinai, the House of Windsor makes a regular appearance. Both Prince Charles and his father, Prince Philip, the Duke of Edinburgh, have made a significant number of very low-profile private visits and retreats to the Holy Mountain in recent years. Prince Philip, who was not notably religious as a young naval officer, formally joined the Church of England as requested shortly before his marriage to the future queen. Whether he has since quietly reentered the Orthodox Church (as some British journalists have claimed) or not, the visits have not gone unnoticed. Both father and son acknowledge their imperfections and failings, and as *The Guardian* has written, "not since the Stuarts has an heir to the throne taken such an intellectual interest in religion." This admittedly doesn't impress the chatterati, who don't particularly care either for Prince Charles's cello playing, quite good watercolor painting, or indeed any of the other civilized pursuits a gentleman used to be expected to cultivate.

As for other civilized travelers, at least one visitor to Mount Athos found striking parallels between the monasteries and a different British institution—Oxford University and its colleges, as recounted in Miles Jebb's *The Colleges of Oxford*:

> The great, many-courtyarded, rambling Great Lavra must be Christ Church; the lonely Serbian monastery of Hilandariou at the north end of the peninsula calls to mind Magdalen . . . ; the busy,

revived, cenobitic monastery of Simon Peter, an unaesthetic structure perched on a cliff, can only be Balliol; Stavronikita, with its
select group of professional monks, All Souls; and Panteleimon, a
vast barracks built by the Russians in the last century, Keble.

The Abbey of Sainte-Madeleine du Barroux, France

If Oxford and Mount Athos are some sort of parallel universes, there
is another Mediterranean sanctuary that is a kind of *Year in Provence*
with spiritual depth. In the South of France the Abbey of Sainte-
Madeleine du Barroux is renowned for both the purity of its Gregorian
plainchant and the perfection of its walnut bread (the best there is,
according to the *Food Lover's Guide to France*). The abbey is located outside the small village of Le Barroux, which is about halfway between
Carpentras and Vaison la Romaine, amid olive groves and rolling
hills, and with a distinct scent of lavender in the air. In the 1970s, a
Benedictine monk named Dom Gerard Calvet was dispirited by the
liquidation of the Church's liturgical patrimony, and decided to go
to this remote corner of the Midi with the seemingly unrealistic aim
of starting a new monastery from scratch—at a time when religious
orders were folding and beauty was regarded as a luxury, rather than
a necessary adjunct to truth. Today the abbey is a flourishing place, a
large monastic complex hand-built in stone in a simple, traditional,
sunburnt Provençal style with a panoramic view to die for—and a
waiting list of young men from both sides of the Atlantic hoping to
join the novitiate as places become available. It supports itself partly
by baking outstanding bread (sold to visitors and to local restaurants),
and by its attractive shop—the *Artisanat Monastique*—which sells what
is probably the best selection of monastic goods in Europe, from
devotional objects to some of Bavaria's tastiest small-batch craft beers
made by monks. Given the intense beauty of Le Barroux and its neighborhood, perhaps it's not surprising to spot the footprints yet again of
the aesthetically and spiritually minded Prince of Wales, who has been
a houseguest with friends in the village. (Whether he anonymously

ventured into the abbey is not known.) The current pope, Benedict XVI, has been a great admirer of the monks of Barroux, who emphasize the old ("Tridentine") rite in its full splendor.

Strangely, one of the most interesting arguments in favor of the traditional Roman rite has come from a neopagan movement leader and writer, John Michael Greer:

> As a parody and inversion of the Catholic Mass, the Black Mass depended for its effect on its contrast with the participants' memories of the grandeur of the Catholic ritual. The Second Vatican Council reforms, which banished the Latin rite, stripped away most of the mystery and power from the ceremony, and brought such dubious entertainments as folk-music masses, left little for Satanists to parody; it's hard to imagine even the most enthusiastic Satanists getting noticeable results by singing 'Kum Ba Ya' backwards.

Mr. Greer is (among other things) an archdruid, but the staunchest defenders of the old rite have more frequently been Catholic risk takers than druids and Wiccans—as you might guess. Late twentieth-century advocates of the traditional Roman liturgy have included the late philosopher Dietrich von Hildebrand, who did not shy away from threats or controversy: Hitler's ambassador to Vienna called him "public enemy number one of Nazism," and for a time he lived (serenely) in constant danger of assassination. Another such liturgical traditionalist with sangfroid was Dr. Erich Vermehren (d. 2005), also known as Eric Maria de Saventhem, who won a German Rhodes Scholarship in 1938, but was prevented from going to Oxford, and had his passport confiscated. He and his well-connected wife Elisabeth, Countess von Plettenberg, became active with various anti-Nazi circles during the war, including with friends in the Abwehr, the German intelligence service that was later found to be a key gathering place for critics of Hitler. Vermehren, a young lawyer, got himself posted in 1944 to the Abwehr's station in Istanbul, then a hotbed of espionage. When it became clear that their arrest was imminent on the order of Nazi higher-ups, the young couple faked their own kidnapping, and staged a daring defection that took them to Izmir, Aleppo, Cairo, Gibraltar, and then London. In the British capital, these courageous "guests of the Foreign Office" were debriefed by the (not yet known) traitor Kim Philby, who put them up in his mother's flat in South Kensington—before himself being transferred to Istanbul.

The Hagia Sophia, Istanbul, Turkey

Istanbul may have been chock-full of spies, but its primary interest to us is as one of the world's great spiritual nodes—known for most of its history as Constantinople, the fabled capital of Byzantium. Unlike the Roman rite alluded to above, the Byzantine liturgy used by most Orthodox and some Eastern Catholics was never denuded of its beauty. However, the holy of holies of Byzantium itself has not escaped the troubles of the last sixteen hundred years and is today used for no spiritual purposes—though it remains encrusted with various legends. This is the Hagia Sophia in Istanbul, which was formerly the Great Church of the Holy Wisdom. Built around the 530s, it became a mosque in 1453, and then was turned into a museum in 1935. One of the greatest engineering works of all time, it was the largest church in the world for about a thousand years—until the completion of the Spanish cathedral of Seville in the sixteenth century. Its dome remains literally breathtaking, and its founder, the Eastern Roman Emperor Justinian, was said to have exclaimed, "Solomon, I have out-done thee!" This was no idle boast, given the immense size of the inte-rior and its dazzling mosaics. The conquering Ottoman Turks, who turned it into a mosque, used it as an architectural model for other mosques in their empire. They added four minarets (three in white marble), a gallery for the sultan, and many other traditional Islamic features, with great care and craftsmanship.

For the Greeks, the loss of the Hagia Sophia was considered cat-astrophic, and many legends have circulated about its return to their custody in the fullness of time. Constantine XI Palaeologos—

"the Immortal Emperor"—was last seen fighting on the walls of Constantinople, but is said to be not dead, but rather sleeping, awaiting the day of his return to the imperial city. Another legend relates to a priest who was in the middle of the divine liturgy in the Hagia Sophia as the Ottomans stormed the church—but he disappeared into a wall, and will one day reemerge to complete the Byzantine rite. Still another legend held that the city would be liberated from the Ottomans by blond Slavs, and indeed the Imperial Russian government planned in 1914 to conquer what it called "Tsargrad." This is the one legend that has come true in a certain sense, as the city was wrested from the collapsing Ottoman order in the early 1920s by a blond, (part-) Slav: Mustafa Kemal Atatürk. With his gray-blue eyes and part-Slav Balkan ancestry, former army officer Kemal Atatürk created a new Republic of Turkey, and served as its first president. He was convinced that Turkey had to be reconceived as a new, European, and essentially secular country, instituting a new legal system based on the Swiss civil code, abolishing the caliphate, outlawing the wearing of the fez, and officially changing the name of Constantinople to Istanbul (which the city was called informally in Turkish). The rupture with the past was meant to be dramatic and complete, and today well-educated Turks are unable to read old Turkish books written in Arabic script (since Atatürk replaced it with the Roman). He also closed the Hagia Sophia to Islamic worship, turning it into a museum, which it remains to this day. Whatever one's views on "Kemalism" (revered by many Turks but disapproved of as too extreme in its secular modernity by many others), this sanctuary is not to be missed.

Her Majesty's Chapels Royal of the Mohawks, Ontario, Canada

All the sacred sanctuaries covered so far in this chapter are either in major cities (like Rome and Istanbul) or well off the beaten track (in relatively remote parts of Egypt, Greece, and France). We close with two closely related ones that are rural, but within easy driving range of rust-belt Buffalo, New York. It may come as a shock, but not far from the U.S. border and all the bustling modernity of American life, are two still-functioning British chapels royal, a symbol of earlier loyalties that have never been extinguished. Her Majesty's Chapels Royal of the Mohawks—one (St. Paul's) in Brandford, Ontario, Canada, the other (Christ Church) near Deseronto, Ontario—date from the late eighteenth century, and today are listed officially along-side such other chapels royal and "royal peculiars" of the British (and Canadian) Crown as St. George's, Windsor Castle; the Chapel Royal, Hampton Court; and the Chapels of St. Peter ad Vincula and St. John the Evangelist in the Tower of London. Little known, these two sites recall the intense loyalty to the Crown of the Mohawks, who to this day are remembered in the Canadian Army as the "Gurkhas of Canada" because of their fighting spirit. Not only were they instinctive monarchists, the Mohawks were deeply suspicious of "Rights of Man" firebrands in what have since become the United States; they sensed that the native peoples were more likely to get ripped off by rapacious settlers than by the representatives of the sovereign. It turns out that their instincts were correct, given how things actually unfolded over the following two centuries.

As for the two chapels, in appearance St. Paul's looks much like many typical colonial churches that were built in the "Province of New York" before the War of Independence, and, like Christ Church, it has accumulated various gifts from the present Queen and her predecessors, including silver communion plate. American Loyalist and Mohawk tribal relics are still lovingly cared for, but the most hallowed part of the fabric is the outdoor tomb of Joseph Brant, revered Mohawk leader and loyalist British Army officer. Also known by his Indian name Thayendanegea, Brant was educated at a prede-cessor institution of Dartmouth College, and was probably the best known, admired, and traveled native figure of his time. He knew both George III and George Washington personally, and his portrait was executed by many distinguished painters of the day, including Gilbert Stuart and George Romney—the former can be seen in the National Gallery of Art in Ottawa, and the latter is in the private collection of the dukes of Northumberland at Alnwick Castle in England. (A third first-rate portrait of Brant hangs in Philadelphia's Portrait Gallery on Chestnut Street, at the historic former Second Bank of the United States.) Having bravely led loyalist Mohawk troops in various Revolutionary War battles, after the war ended he helped resettle his people in Canada from their ancestral lands in what had become New York State. The other chapel royal, Christ Church, was rebuilt in a pleasant Gothic Revival style in the 1840s, and, if anything, has become even more of a Westminster Abbey shrine in miniature. Its minor treasures include a bell presented by George III, a Bible from Queen Victoria, and a new communion chalice given by Queen Elizabeth II in 1984.

While the Loyalist cause was not successful, it did originally have its strong advocates—including Benjamin Franklin. Franklin remained an ardent supporter of British imperial unity until relatively late in the game, when he concluded with some sadness that a permanent rupture couldn't be avoided. The brave young George Washington had himself painted in the proud uniform of a British colonial militia colonel in 1772. The portrait, by Charles Willson Peale, hangs in another shrine to a lost cause, the Lee Chapel at Washington and Lee University in Lexington, Virginia. (General Lee's horse, Traveler, is buried outside; children still leave apples at the gravesite for the famous steed.) Washington and Robert E. Lee were related (Lee had the further distinction, though Episcopalian, of being descended from the English Catholic martyr St. Thomas More). Less well known is the fact that Washington applied for a regular officer's commission in the British Army, a request that was turned down.

The ambition to reverse the historic decision forged at certain famous venues, from Concord to Yorktown, lingered on in some breasts where megalomania had displaced reality, even in the late nineteenth century. Cecil Rhodes, that fanatical exponent of the virtues of British colonial rule, conceived a grandiose scheme to effect, as he phrased it, "the ultimate recovery of the United States of America as an integral part of the British Empire." It is doubtful that it would have played in Peoria. In other respects, Rhodes was not a total fantasist, as his success in founding the diamond company De Beers, launching the Rhodes Scholarships, and carving out the country in Africa that once bore his name (Rhodesia—now Zimbabwe) demonstrated. But he was definitely a conspiracy freak, convinced that the Jesuits' organization offered the most effective model for exerting secret influence, as his succinct written instructions revealed in 1888: "Take Constitution Jesuits if obtainable and insert English Empire for Roman Catholic Religion."

Counterfactual History: The Eternal "What If . . . ?"

Counterfactual history is addictive with its "what ifs." What if George Washington had become a general, but on the other side? What if Adolf Hitler had been accepted into Vienna's Academy of Fine Arts, where he applied twice? Other such not-so-far-fetched possibilities are said to include Fidel Castro almost having become a professional baseball player in the United States, as, according to some sources, he was scouted for his pitching talent—but passed over—by officials from the Pittsburgh Pirates and other teams. Whether the baseball story is accurate or not, the U.S. National Archives actually has an astonishing letter in Spanglish written by a precocious young Fidel to President Franklin Roosevelt in 1940:

> If you like, give me a ten dollars bill green American . . . because never, I have not seen a ten dollars bill green american and I would like to have one of them. My address is . . . Thank you very much. Good by. Your friend, Fidel Castro.

Her Majesty's Chapels Royal of the Mohawks are themselves "counterfactual" sanctuaries, dedicated to an alternative America that never was. Close to two-and-a-half centuries after the American victory at Yorktown, the Union Jack flies over a corner of North America that is forever England—a kind of holy sanctuary of Tory and Aboriginal ideals that live on quietly, in seclusion, at the edge of the Continent—like the Last of the Mohicans.

Chapter 10

HIDDEN TOTEMS

s we have seen in the preceding chapters, the secret places of the world have a wide diversity of character and purpose. In some instances, the use for which they were originally designed is now obsolete, leaving them as empty memorials to past customs. On the other hand, many have retained their original function, which frequently is to house some kind of treasure or sacred object. Sometimes the modern location is of secondary importance to the object it protects and would not be of much interest were it not the receptacle of such a totem or talisman. It is time, therefore, to look at some treasured objects of great antiquity that are wonders in their own right, regardless of where they are housed. Many of them relate to kingship; usually there is a religious element, too, since kingship and priesthood were closely allied, a relationship that chiefly came to the fore during the ceremonies by which rulers were inaugurated, as is illustrated by many of the sacred treasures described here.

The Stone of Destiny

The best known such object in the English-speaking world is the Stone of Destiny, also known as the Stone of Scone. Despite its high profile, its origins are shrouded in mystery and controversy. The myth that attributes the greatest antiquity to it is the claim that it was the pillow on which Jacob rested his head, in the Old Testament, at Bethel when he dreamed of his famous ladder rising up to heaven: "And he took of the stones of that place, and put them for his pillows, and lay down in that place to sleep" (Genesis 28:10–12). It is then claimed that Scota, Pharaoh's daughter at the time of the Exodus, married a Greek named Gaythelus and the royal couple led the Egyptians who had survived the Red Sea engulfing Pharaoh's army to Spain, where they settled. One of their descendants, Simon Brec, migrated to Ireland, taking the Stone with him. There it was set up on the Hill of Tara, in county Meath, and was known by the Gaelic name of the *Lia Fáil* (Stone of Destiny).

The problem for Scots who accept this version of the Stone's origin is that there is still an Irish *Lia Fáil* standing on the Hill of Tara. All the high kings of Ireland were said to have been crowned on this stone (which must have been rather uncomfortable for them, considering its five-and-a-half foot [1.7m] height and phallic shape) up until Muirchertach mac Ercae, around AD 500. Somehow, another Stone of Destiny made its way from Ireland to Scotland. One theory suggests that it was taken by St. Columba to Iona (in 563, see Chapter 8), possibly as a portable altar. As Columba was said to have slept with his head on a stone, the resemblance to the story of Jacob may have created a confusion between the original Irish Stone of Destiny and St. Columba's rather Spartan pillow, which would also have been revered after his death, especially if he had used it as an altar stone on which to say Mass. There is a cross carved on the Scottish Stone of Destiny, which might support that theory.

What is known is that the Scottish Stone of Destiny was used at the inauguration of the kings of Dalriada, Gaels from Ireland who settled on the west coast of Scotland from around 500. After Dalriada was absorbed into the kingdom of Scotland, the Stone played a central role at the coronations of the kings of Scots. These took place at Scone in Perthshire. The king was inaugurated in the churchyard adjoining Scone Abbey, upon the Stone of Destiny, which was kept in the nearby Benedictine monastery. Alexander III was crowned there on July 13, 1249, as described by John of Fordun, the early chronicler of Scottish history, in his Scotichronicon: "decked with silk cloths embroidered with gold he was consecrated king, the king himself sitting, as was proper, upon the regal chair, that is the stone . . . This stone is reverently preserved in that monastery for the consecration of kings of Scotland." Alexander was killed in 1286 by a fall from his horse. His heir was his granddaughter, the Maid of Norway, who died on the voyage to Scotland to claim her rights. That left contending claimants to the throne.

Edward I of England, who claimed to be overlord of Scotland, selected John Balliol as king of Scots in 1292. Balliol was no usurper—his claim was good—but he humiliated his subjects by doing homage to Edward for Scotland, despite being crowned at Scone on the Stone of Destiny, as a sovereign. In 1296 he withdrew his allegiance from Edward, who promptly invaded Scotland and dethroned Balliol. Knowing its importance as a symbol of Scottish sovereignty, Edward took the Stone of Destiny from Scone, carried it off to England "as a sign that the kingdom had been conquered and resigned" and installed it in Westminster Abbey where it was inserted into a coronation chair specially constructed for that purpose. Since then all the kings of England and, later, of Great Britain have been crowned while seated over the Stone. In the bloody Wars of Independence that followed, culminating in the victory of King Robert the Bruce at the Battle of Bannockburn (1314), Scotland regained its national sovereignty, but not the Stone of Destiny.

In 1924, an attempt was made to pass a bill through Parliament directing that the Stone be returned to Scotland, but it was unsuccessful. Suddenly, on Christmas Day 1950, the Stone of Destiny made world headlines due to an audacious student raid. Four Scottish nationalist students broke into Westminster Abbey during the night, removed the Stone of Destiny from the coronation chair and smuggled it back north to Scotland by car. The theft (Scots called it *restitution*) of the Stone provoked a massive manhunt. The four youngsters had a series of hair-raising adventures reminiscent of Bonnie Prince Charlie's "flight through the heather" after Culloden, but their luck held and, when they reached Scotland, they had no shortage of sympathizers to help them. Unfortunately, the Stone was broken in two during the escapade, so it was handed over to a Glasgow stonemason to repair in secret. The media were agog, King George VI expressed his anxiety, the police and Special Branch detectives left no stone (so to speak) unturned in the search for the priceless relic. It was all in vain until, after a tip, the Stone was found in April 1951 on the remains of the altar in the ruined Arbroath Abbey.

Having made their point, the nationalists were content to return the Stone to the authorities. Or were they? Rumors soon began to circulate that Robert Gray, the stonemason who repaired the Stone, had also made a replica and that it was this imitation that was returned to Westminster. A rival Stone even surfaced and was solemnly housed in a Dundee parish church, even though its dimensions were different from those of the real version. In fact, there was never any doubt that the Stone returned in 1951 was the identical one that had been stolen in 1950. The clerk of works of Westminster Abbey traveled to Glasgow police headquarters to inspect the stone recovered at Arbroath Abbey. He had an unrivaled knowledge of the Stone of Destiny, gleaned ten years earlier when it had been removed from the coronation chair to be taken to a secret hiding place for safekeeping during the war. He listed six distinctive characteristics that were all present in the recovered stone, which he recognized, apart from the damage it had suffered during its recent adventure. Ian Hamilton, leader of the students who had liberated the Stone, also testified that no substitution had taken place. This was reinforced by in-depth scientific investigations carried out in 1996. So the Stone that departed on Christmas Day genuinely returned four months later.

That, however, is by no means the end of the story. When Scots suggest that the Stone of Destiny is a "fake," they do not usually mean that the students substituted a replica. On the contrary, the big question is this: Was the stone that Edward I plundered from Scotland in 1296 the genuine article? Conspiracy theorists insist that the abbot of Scone substituted a worthless stone for the true one when the English troops raided his abbey. The two strongest legends are that he hid the Stone either in a cave on nearby Moncrieff Hill, which was subsequently obscured by a landslide, or in an underground chamber farther away on Dunsinane Hill at the site known as Macbeth's Castle, recalling Shakespeare's lines:

Macbeth shall never vanquish'd be until
Great Birnam wood to high Dunsinane hill
Shall come against him.

Neither of these legends could be proved or disproved until, early in the nineteenth century, something very intriguing was reported in connection with the latter claim. Excavations were being carried out at the site of Macbeth's Castle, three miles (5km) from Scone, when two young farmhands stumbled into a fissure in the ground, down into a secret chamber. Only several years later did they report this to the landowner, Mr. Nairne of Dunsinane, who carried out further excavations. These revealed a six-by-four-foot (1.8m x 1.2m) vault in the center of which stood a large black stone weighing about five hundred pounds (227kg) and made of meteoric or metallic rock. Beside it were two metal plaques with heraldic devices and an inscription that Scottish historian Archie McKerracher translated, almost two hundred years later from an old newspaper report, as meaning: *Under your protective shadow lies the kingdom until angels carry you back to Bethel.* This episode was reported in the *London Morning Chronicle* of January 2, 1819. It claimed that the mysterious stone had been sent to London to be examined by a "scientific amateur." On the other hand, a report in a Scottish newspaper, *The Caledonian Mercury,* just five days later denounced the story as untrue.

Our natural instinct would be to dismiss the London story as an invention by a journalist short on copy, except for something that allegedly occurred a generation later. In 1857 excavations were again made at Dunsinane, when a doorway leading to a subterranean chamber was discovered, but no stone. That would have been consistent with the earlier discovery and removal to London of the concealed stone. This legend—true or false—highlights a troubling feature of the supposed Stone of Destiny that has been used at coronations in London for seven hundred years. Such limited references as we have to the ancient Stone suggest something larger than the one we know. One would also expect it to be made of marble or meteoric material. The Stone of Destiny, however, is humble sandstone (though so is the geology at biblical Bethel). It is a block of coarse-grained red sandstone measuring two feet, two inches, by one foot, four inches, by eleven inches (66cm x 41cm x 28cm). It weighs 485 pounds (220kg) and is fitted with iron staples and two carrying rings. This seems like an unlikely throne for a king. On the other hand, if it was originally a portable altar stone used by St. Columba, this would seem more plausible, especially since it has a cross engraved on its surface. In the final analysis, there is one very powerful, indeed overwhelming, reason to credit the Stone's authenticity, if not as Jacob's pillow at least as the consecration throne of kings for more than a millennium. It is simply this: If the real Stone was hidden in Scotland during Edward's invasion and the Wars of Independence, why did the Scots not triumphantly resurrect it after their liberation? Was that not the moment for the monks of Scone to bring the Stone out of hiding and enthrone their victorious warrior king, Robert the Bruce, upon it? Yet no such thing happened. The conclusion is irresistible: The entire community of Scotland knew that Edward had truly taken the Stone.

So, while it is intriguing to entertain the possibility that the Stone of Destiny, fashioned from a meteorite, lay in some English antiquarian's London garden, possibly to be destroyed in the wartime Blitz, the balance of historical evidence suggests that what you see is what you get. And where you see it now is not in Westminster Abbey, but in Edinburgh Castle. For the Stone of Destiny, after seven centuries, returned to Scotland in 1996. At the request of the then–secretary of state for Scotland, Michael Forsyth, Prime Minister John Major secured the permission of Queen Elizabeth II for the Stone to be returned to Scotland in the seventh centenary of its removal, with the proviso that it will be sent back to Westminster temporarily for coronation ceremonies. On Friday, November 15, 1996, under military escort, the Stone ceremoniously re-crossed the Scottish border at Coldstream. Then, on November 30, the feast of St. Andrew, patron saint of Scotland, a solemn service was held at St. Giles' Cathedral in Edinburgh. At its conclusion the Stone of Destiny was conveyed—on full display in its vehicle, and again with a military escort—through streets crowded with thousands of onlookers, to Edinburgh Castle. There, in the Great Hall, Prince Andrew, Duke of York, on behalf of the Queen, formally delivered the Stone into the custody of the Commissioners of the Regalia of Scotland. It was then placed on permanent display in Edinburgh Castle's strongroom, alongside the Scottish crown jewels—the Honours of Scotland, consisting of the crown, scepter, and sword of state of the Scottish monarchs. The Stone of Destiny can be viewed there by the public, restored after seven centuries to its rightful homeland, in waiting to fulfill its ancient role at the coronations of future monarchs of Great Britain.

The Holy Crown of St. Stephen of Hungary

Scotland is by no means alone in possessing mystical regalia associated with the inauguration of its kings. The closest parallel is to be found in Hungary, where even more national importance is attached to the Holy Crown of St. Stephen. The history of this crown (which includes temporary residence in America) is rich and colorful. According to tradition, the Holy Crown was that of St. Stephen, the first king of Hungary (1001–1038) and the country's first Christian ruler. Yet, although most of the coronation regalia can indeed be authenticated as dating back to his reign, the crown named after him appears to be of later vintage. Careful examination of the Holy Crown, however, has revealed that it is an amalgam of more than one crown. It divides into three main parts. The first is called the *corona graeca* (Greek crown), the basic diadem that sits around the wearer's head. This features nineteen arched panels containing religious images of Byzantine origin. At the front is a depiction of *Christ Pantokrator* (Ruler of All), flanked by pictures of the archangels St. Michael and St. Gabriel. It is also ornamented with pearls and semiprecious stones and the inscriptions are in Greek. Four pendants, known as *pendilia,* hang on chains from the diadem on either side, with another at the back—again in Byzantine style. There is no mystery about this: It is very obviously a Greek crown and in fact it was sent by the Byzantine emperor to the wife of King Géza I (1074–1077), the shortness of whose reign makes it very easy to date with accuracy.

The second part of the Holy Crown is known as the *corona latina* (the Latin crown) and consists of four gold arches, also with pictures of saints, elevating the height of the crown and making it more elaborate. Rulers attached great significance to such closed arches surmounting crowns, since they were the prerogative of kingship. This Latin crown is decorated with pictures of the first eight Apostles chosen by Christ and with seventy-two pearls, commemorating the number of his disciples. Again, the history of this portion of the Holy Crown is straightforward: It was added to the basic diadem in the reign of Béla III (1172–1196). The third part of the crown is the cross that surmounts the whole structure, which was probably added as late as the sixteenth century and has stood at a distinctive crooked angle since suffering damage in the seventeenth century.

So, with the main part of the crown dating from around 1075 and its superstructure from a century later, where is the connection with St. Stephen, who died earlier, in 1038? Despite appearances, such a connection is more than likely. There is a very strong tradition that Stephen received a crown from Pope Sylvester II, presented to him by Asztrik, first abbot of the Benedictine monastery at Pannonhalma. The king's reciprocal gifts to the pope are recorded, though not the actual dispatch of the diadem to Hungary, but it has always been believed that gold from the original crown of St. Stephen was incorporated into the later version. The gold bands forming the arches could have come from an earlier, simpler diadem; indeed, the lettering on the inscriptions is of a style that was abandoned after about 1050, suggesting an earlier origin for the *corona latina.* The decisive evidence is the fact that the rest of the regalia definitely did belong to St. Stephen: The elaborate coronation mantle actually has an inscription embroidered into it stating that it was made on the instructions of St. Stephen and his wife Queen Gizella in 1031. Similarly, the short scepter is of a style briefly favored by monarchs of Stephen's generation, but not before or after. The orb set in the top of it is a globe of rock crystal, ornamented with engravings of lions, the work of Saracen craftsmen of the Fatimid Empire in the tenth century. The larger orb that the king carries in his other hand is not part of the original Stephanian regalia, but dates only from the coronation of Charles I in 1310.

Successive kings of Hungary, therefore, at their coronations, knew they were cloaked in a mantle that had been worn by St. Stephen, crowned with his ancient diadem and holding a scepter that had once been grasped in his right hand. That same right hand also survives, although it is not part of the coronation regalia. Some time after the king's death, his right hand was separated from the rest of his body and preserved as a sacred relic. It still reposes today in St. Stephen's Cathedral in Budapest, extremely well preserved. Known as the "Holy Right," it is carried in procession every year. Although St. Stephen's feast is on September 2, his national day, which is also a public holiday, is observed throughout Hungary on August 20.

Probably no other single national symbol anywhere is so passionately regarded as the Holy Crown of St. Stephen, not even the original U.S. Declaration of Independence; the Holy Crown has acquired a huge political and cultural, as well as religious, significance. It first became known as the Holy Crown in 1256. By the fourteenth century its totem significance had become so great that it was regarded as more important than any of its wearers. Uniquely among European monarchies, the crown (meaning the object) acquired a legal personality. A doctrine evolved concerning it and no king was considered legitimate until he had been crowned with it. This was most dramatically illustrated in the case of Charles I who was crowned three times: On the first two occasions a different crown was used and not until he was finally invested with the Holy Crown in 1310 was his position considered unchallengeable. By 1401 the royal seal was engraved with the words: *The seal of the Holy Crown of Hungary*, rather than being described as the seal of the king, as would have been customary elsewhere.

During the three centuries' rule of St. Stephen's own Árpád dynasty (1000–1301) the crown was kept at Székesfehérvár, the city where Hungarian kings were historically crowned (like Scone in Scotland). Later it was moved to other locations: Visegrád, Pozsony (Bratislava), and Buda. It came closest to being lost in 1849, after the failure of the rebellion raised by Lajos Kossuth, who fled from Budapest with all the crown jewels, including the Holy Crown. Kossuth buried them in a wooden box in a forest in Transylvania, where they remained for four years before being recovered in 1853. Although the new, young Emperor Franz Josef had been summoned to the thrones of Austria, Hungary, and seven other kingdoms during the revolutionary year of 1848, his rebellious Hungarian subjects had to wait until June 8, 1867 before he was finally crowned apostolic king, along with his beautiful wife the Empress Elisabeth, in the Matthias Church in Budapest, with a Coronation Mass specially composed for the occasion by Franz Liszt. That was not the last occasion on which the Holy Crown of St. Stephen was used to crown a king of Hungary. At the height of the First World War, on December 30, 1916, the last Habsburg emperor of Austria was crowned as Charles IV of Hungary in the cathedral of Budapest. Two years later it was all over. The Habsburg Empire collapsed at the end of the Great War and with it the apostolic kingdom of Hungary, which briefly fell under communist rule, but was quickly liberated.

After the Reds had been driven out, the former commander-in-chief of the Habsburg navy, Admiral Miklós Horthy, became a virtual dictator. Since republicanism was still repugnant to Hungarians, the Holy Crown was regarded as the repository of state power, and in 1920 Horthy was declared "His Serene Highness the Regent of the Kingdom of Hungary." A joke of the period claimed that Hungary was a kingdom without a king, ruled by an admiral without a fleet, in a country without a coastline. When the man who had been legally crowned with the Holy Crown, Charles IV, twice returned to Hungary to reclaim his throne, Horthy refused to surrender his "regency" and drove out his rightful king in 1921. Charles died in exile a year later; in 2004, however, he was rewarded with a higher crown when Pope John Paul II beatified him—the final stage before formal canonization, suggesting that another saint may soon be added to the list of Hungary's kings. Horthy lasted until 1944 when the Nazis finally got rid of him and took over the country, installing their own puppet, Ferenc Szálasi, leader of the fascist Arrow Cross Party. He took the oath of office as leader of the nation before the Holy Crown of St. Stephen. Months later, as the Red Army advanced on Budapest, Szálasi fled, taking the crown jewels with him. Again, they might have vanished from the face of the earth; but they were recovered in dramatic fashion by the U.S. Army.

During the first week of May 1945, a group of Hungarian SS soldiers surrendered to troops of the U.S. Eighty-Sixth Infantry Division near the village of Mattsee in Bavaria. Among them was Ferenc Szálasi. The prisoners were found to be in possession of ironbound chests, which had been used to store the crown jewels, but were now empty. Under interrogation, they admitted to having transferred the crown jewels to an oil barrel and burying it in nearby marshland. American soldiers were dispatched to search the area and retrieved the barrel. When they opened it, they were startled to discover the Holy Crown of St. Stephen, the scepter, and the orb. The crucial patrimony of the Hungarian nation was contained in that mud-caked oil barrel, happily intact. Knowing the political importance of the Holy Crown in conferring legitimacy on a government, and urged by Hungarian anticommunists to safeguard this treasure from the Soviets, the U.S. government ordered the crown jewels to be transported to America, where they were lodged for safekeeping in the U.S. Bullion Depository at Fort Knox in Kentucky.

From 1945 until 1978, the United States refused all demands from the communist regime for the repatriation of the Holy Crown of St. Stephen. The imprisonment, torture, and show trial of József Cardinal Mindszenty, Archbishop of Esztergom and Prince-Primate of

Hungary, as well as the brutal repression of the Hungarian uprising of 1956 made any such concession unthinkable. By 1977, however, the Hungarian regime had liberalized itself to a degree unusual within the Soviet bloc. So U.S. President Jimmy Carter took the controversial decision to return the crown to the Hungarian government, as an inducement to further reform. The crown was taken to Budapest by a high-powered delegation led by Secretary of State Cyrus Vance, Senator Adlai Stevenson, and Nobel laureate Dr. Albert Szent-Györgi, and formally handed over at a ceremony in the rotunda of the Hungarian parliament on January 6, 1978. It was then put on display in the Hungarian National Museum in the capital.

With the fall of communism, the Holy Crown was reincorporated into the Hungarian national coat of arms. Its political significance was reasserted on January 1, 2000—the millennium anniversary of the Hungarian state—when the crown, orb, scepter, and sword of state were ceremonially transported through streets lined with huge crowds to the Parliament building, where they were installed as symbols of authority under the terms of a newly passed law, the *Lex Millenaris.* This move provoked some political controversy as it was seen as the de facto restoration of the monarchy, even if there was no king. So, after a thousand years of adventures and hazards, the Holy Crown of St. Stephen now rests in Budapest, at the center of state power, the most potent symbol of Hungarian nationhood.

The British and Polish Crown Jewels in Canada

Since the Hungarian crown ended up in the impenetrable Fort Knox, this episode raises the question of other crown jewels and national treasures—and how and where they might have been concealed during the Second World War. Neither the British nor Canadian governments will confirm or deny this, but it is believed that the British crown jewels were removed from the Tower of London and shipped at some risk to Canada, where they spent the rest of the conflict in the lower basement vault of the massive Sun Life Building in

Montreal, Quebec. Completed in 1931 and centrally located on the city's Dorchester (formerly Dominion) Square, the building was then the largest office complex in the British Empire, and it appears that large stocks of gold bullion from the Bank of England also joined the crown jewels there. Canada was considered a safe haven in other ways, being comfortably across the Atlantic but politically and culturally tied to Britain and Europe. Outside Victoria on British Columbia's Vancouver Island is Hatley Castle, the grand Edwardian former residence of coal baron James Dunmuir, with its splendid gardens, stunning Pacific Ocean views, and mature forests of fir and cedar. The royal family was fond of Vancouver Island, so the property was acquired in 1940 and secret contingency plans were made to use it as royal residence in exile in the event that Hitler's planned invasion of Britain ("Operation Sea Lion") was successful. (In the late 1940s and '50s, similar planning was done by Vatican officials, who scouted out Quebec City as a possible papal residence in exile, in the event that Italy went communist.)

Canada was, in fact, so much a country of contingency planning that it continued to have highly classified plans to defend itself from U.S. invasion well into the mid-twentieth century, with a top-secret "Defence Scheme No. 1" providing for Canadian diversionary counterattacks against Minneapolis and Seattle until such time as British and Commonwealth forces could come to her aid. Obviously, this plan never had to leave its sealed file.

But the government of Poland also looked to the Dominion of Canada for help and assistance under duress. After a hair-raising odyssey across Romania, France, and England, Poland's most important national treasures arrived for safekeeping during the Second World War in Canada, where they remained until 1961. This large cache included artworks, Flemish tapestries, precious manuscripts, and—most crucially for a country that had lived through so much loss and upheaval—Poland's thirteenth-century coronation sword, *Szczerbiec*, which was considered both highly symbolic and irreplaceable.

The Holy Ampoule of the Kings of France

France, too, had a sacred treasure that was employed at the coronations of its kings. This was the Sainte Ampoule (Holy Ampoule), a reliquary containing the oil of St. Remi (St. Remigius), which was used
to annoint the kings of France at their coronations in the Cathedral
of Rheims. It was the annointing that was important, not the placing
of the crown on the monarch's head. According to legend, an angel in
the guise of a dove brought the ampoule to Remi to annoint Clovis,
first king of the Franks, after his baptism into Christianity in 496. The
ampoule was a crystal vial, within a gold and jeweled case in the shape
of a dove, containing the oil of St. Remi. After the annointing of Clovis,
the oil remained unused, as the ampoule had been placed with St.
Remi in his tomb, until it was retrieved for the coronation of Charles
II the Bald, in 869. Thereafter it was used to annoint all but three of
France's kings. At the coronation ceremony, the Bishop of Laon, who
was a peer of France, had the right to carry the holy ampoule. A canopy
was held over him by four specially designated knights who consti-
tuted a very small and exclusive order of knighthood known as the
Ordre des Chevaliers Porte-Dais de la Ste. Ampoule (Order of Knights Canopy
Bearers of the Holy Ampoule), dressed in white satin with black coats
embroidered with a white Maltese cross on which was superimposed
the image of a dove with a flask; the same cross hung from a black
ribbon around their necks. The four knights were the holders of the
baronial fiefs of Bellestre, Louvercy or Neuvizy, Souastre, and Terrier,
as vassals of the Abbey of St. Remi. Their knighthood only lasted for
the period when the ampoule was outside the tomb of St. Remi on
coronation day.

The ampoule was kept permanently in the Abbey of St. Remi and
was only removed from there for coronations, with one exception:
Louis XI insisted on having it close to him on his deathbed. The ceremony of annointing was performed on seven places on the king's body,
with apertures specially made in his coronation clothes for that purpose; a tiny sample of the sacred oil was extracted from the ampoule

with a golden needle, then mixed with blessed chrism to provide an adequate amount for the ritual. At the time of the French Revolution, the Republicans, on the principle that "to break the ampoule was to break the kings," sent a representative of the convention named Rhül to Rheims to destroy the ampoule in public. This he did on October 7, 1793, by smashing it with a hammer in the public square, in front of a large crowd. The day before, however, Jules Armand Seraine, the parish priest of St. Remi, who had taken the oath of allegiance to the Republic, and a municipal officer named Philippe Hourelle, had extracted as much of the desiccated red-colored oil as they could and divided it between themselves for safekeeping. After the restoration of the French monarchy, these precious deposits, along with some fragments of the ampoule that a couple of bystanders had surreptitiously picked up, provided sufficient oil of St. Remi, in a powdered state, to be mixed with chrism for the coronation of Charles X in 1825.

But the adventures of the Sainte Ampoule were not over yet. After the fall of the monarchy in 1830 the ampoule was largely forgotten. For the coronation of Charles X it had been enclosed in a larger reliquary than the original one and in 1978 the diocesan archivist of Rheims, Father Jean Goy, was asked to photograph it. When he reverently opened the case to look at the ampoule, he was stunned to find it empty. The mystery was solved by Father Goy himself a few weeks later when he discovered some papers chronicling that in 1906, the year of the terrible persecution of the Church and the confiscation of all its property by the anticlerical government of Emil Combes, the archbishop of Rheims had emptied the sacred oil into another container sealed with his arms and carried it away in his pocket when he was evicted from his palace between two gendarmes. A later document certified that, in 1937, Emmanuel Célestin Cardinal Suhard, the then-archbishop, had opened the bottle to take some of the holy oil for the consecration of the high altar in the cathedral. Aided by these clues, Father Goy found the sealed bottle containing the holy oil in a chest with some old files; it included a glass fragment of the original ampoule. Today, the reliquary of the Ste. Ampoule is lodged in the inappropriately secular treasury of the Palace of Tau, former residence of the archbishops of Rheims, in the custody of the Republican state that tried to destroy it. In September 1996, on the fifteen hundredth anniversary of the baptism of Clovis, the Duke of Anjou, head of the royal house of France, and the man who, had history played out differently, would have been annointed as Louis XX, visited Rheims and was shown the holy ampoule by Father Goy.

Joyeuse, the Sword of Charlemagne

One original and very important item of the French royal regalia survived the Revolution undamaged. This was Joyeuse, the Sword of Charlemagne, which was carried before the kings of France during their coronation. For centuries it was kept with the rest of the regalia, apart from the Sainte Ampoule, in the Abbey of St. Denis in Paris. It survived the destruction of the other items by the revolutionaries and was placed in the museum of the Louvre in Paris on December 5, 1793, where it may still be viewed today. Joyeuse (Joyful) is legendarily said to be the sword with which Charlemagne beheaded the Saracen chief, Corsuble. In the eleventh century the *Song of Roland* included a description of Charlemagne: "By his side hung Joyeuse, and never was there a sword to match it; its color changed thirty times a day."

The sword is 38.5 inches (98cm) long overall, the blade measuring 32.4 inches (82cm) and 2 inches (5cm) wide; the quillons that form a cross hilt are 9.2 inches (23cm) in breadth and the sword weighs 3.5 pounds (1.6kg). The gold pommel is elaborately engraved and the grip was originally ornamented with fleurs-de-lis, but these royal symbols were taken off for Napoleon's coronation in 1804. The gold cross is shaped in the form of two dragons, with lapis lazuli eyes. Experts differ widely on the date of its manufacture. The museum authorities acknowledge no earlier date than the tenth century, although Charlemagne lived in the eighth and ninth centuries. But the claim for the sword's relative modernity is largely based on its proportions which, if different parts were made at different dates (like the Holy

Crown of St. Stephen), could be irrelevant. Two experts, Sir Martin Conway and Ewart Oakeshott, considered that part of the sword could indeed date from around the ninth century and the style of ornamentation lends credence to an early origin. One French expert even favored the seventh century, in which case Charlemagne must have inherited a sword that was already venerable. It is known to have been used at the coronation of Philip the Bold in 1270 and is a significant part of French history. The town of Joyeuse in the Ardèche, which once gave its name to a French dukedom, was named after the sword. There is a rival sword of Charlemagne in the Imperial Treasury in Vienna, but it is in the form of a saber. Joyeuse is worth visiting in the Louvre, to see one of the most famous blades in history and legend: Excalibur is lost to us, but we still have Joyeuse.

The Holy Lance of St. Longinus: The "Spear of Destiny"

The Imperial Treasury in the Hofburg in Vienna houses a more sacred relic: the Holy Lance of St. Longinus, also known as the Spear of Destiny. According to legend, this is the head of the spear with which the Roman soldier Gaius Cassius Longinus pierced the side of Christ on the cross. Longinus was said to have been miraculously cured of poor eyesight by the blood that spurted from the wound, became a Christian, and was later martyred for the faith. The lance held in Vienna had a confused early history. It is sometimes called the Lance of St. Maurice, based on the belief that the martyred commander of the Theban legion was a descendant of St. Longinus and owned the lance. Eventually, it became the key ceremonial accessory at the investiture of Holy Roman emperors, at least from 1273. It is also supposed to incorporate a nail from the Crucifixion, bound onto it with gold, silver, and copper thread. The lance is decorated with artwork of the Carolingian period. In 1424 the Emperor Sigismund deposited the lance in Nuremberg, allegedly for a financial consideration received from the town council, ordering it to be kept in that city forever. In 1806—the year the Holy Roman Empire was dissolved—

Austrian officials took the lance from Nuremberg to Vienna, ahead of advancing French troops, and it has remained in the Austrian capital, with one interlude, since then.

In 1909, a twenty-year-old orphaned youth who lived in a shelter for the homeless and made a precarious living out of painting from postcards haunted the Imperial Treasury Museum in Vienna, gazing in fascination at the Spear of Destiny. He was not moved by its association with Christ, but by the mythology that claimed that all the rulers who possessed it had been militarily invincible until the moment they lost it. His name was Adolf Hitler. His fascination with the lance was reinforced by his interest in Wagner's opera *Parsifal,* in which it appears. This was the origin of Hitler's preoccupation with the occult, whose consequences we have already examined in Chapter 4. In 1938, as soon as Hitler had occupied Austria in the *Anschluss,* he ordered the SS to take the Spear of Destiny from the Hofburg Museum and return it to Nuremberg. There it was stored in the Church of St. Katherine until 1944 when it was transferred to a specially constructed bombproof vault beneath the church. There it was discovered by U.S. forces on the afternoon of April 30, 1945, less than two hours before Hitler, no longer its possessor, committed suicide.

On the orders of General Dwight D. Eisenhower, the lance was returned to Vienna in 1946. General Mark Clark officially handed it into the custody of the mayor of Vienna who, until the Hofburg Museum could be made ready to display it again, found himself obliged to deposit it for safekeeping in the vault of the Austrian Post Office Savings Bank. Today it is once more on display in the Hofburg Museum.

There have been rival claimants to be the Holy Lance. One is in Cracow, in Poland, but is believed to be a copy of the spearhead in Vienna. There is also one in Rome and there was a tip of a lance head venerated in France, believed to have been broken off the lance in Rome; the French relic disappeared after the Revolution. Yet another claimed Holy Lance is preserved at Etschmiadzin in Armenia, but most experts agree that it is probably not a spearhead at all, but the point of a staff for carrying a standard. So the Habsburg lance is the version with the most tradition attached to it. If, by some quirk of history, it is the identical spear that pierced the side of Christ (and what skeptics often forget is how jealously any object associated with his Passion would have been preserved by the faithful), then it is one of the most dramatic inanimate witnesses to history surviving in the world.

Oliver Cromwell's Head

Having looked at the ceremonial objects adorning so many crowned heads, we close here with the story of a grisly republican relic—the head of Oliver Cromwell. The only military dictator to rule Britain, Cromwell famously cut off the head of King Charles I. But after Cromwell himself died, *his* head endured some misadventures. Cromwell, lord protector and "Chief of Men" to his admirers, but remembered as a butcher by many more, was a *regicide*—one of the signatories of the death warrant of his sovereign. When his own (natural) death approached, Cromwell approved arrangements for a state funeral fit for a king, after which he was entombed in Westminster Abbey. When the monarchy was restored two years later, his body was exhumed and posthumously beheaded. The severed head passed through various hands and several owners. Some Englishmen remained ambivalent about Cromwell's legacy—some even viewed him in a slightly positive light—and in 1914 First Lord of the Admiralty Winston Churchill actually suggested that a new battleship be named after him. King George V was horrified, the Royal Navy was not amused, and Churchill rapidly moved on to other, more productive ideas for the Senior Service. A statue of Cromwell had already been erected in 1899 outside Parliament with the help of an anonymous donor (actually the former Liberal prime minister Lord Rosebery), though the royal family, needless to say, did not contribute any funds. By the late 1950s, a Cromwell Association had been active for some two decades, and it seemed that the time had come to lay Cromwell's head to rest once more, although a secret burial place was required in order to ensure it would be left undisturbed—given the deep (and understandable) loathing for Cromwell even today in many parts of the British Isles.

Arrangements were made to bury (or "immure") the head at Cromwell's old Cambridge College, Sidney Sussex, where he had been an undergraduate and fellow commoner. An undisclosed place was selected by college authorities within the antechapel, just outside the college's rather high-church chapel (which would not have pleased the hard-line Puritan Cromwell). On March 25, 1960, the head was interred in a secret ceremony in this discreet location—presumably to remain there until the end of the world.

Chapter 11

(VERY) PRIVATE BANKING

*J*he Finance 101 class you took might have seemed as dry
as dust, but in fact Abba and Monty Python probably got
it right: "In the rich man's world," money can be funny,
from the "romance of the ruble" to the "sunburnt splendour of the
Australian dollar." But, more often, it's deadly serious business, with
its own sanctuaries and vaults of absolute privacy and security—in
some cases far more impenetrable than Fort Knox.

Rothschilds, London

"Money is the god of our times, and Rothschild is his prophet"—or
at least that's what writer and poet Heinrich Heine once said. He was
certainly right that a large slice of the world's population long ago
embraced a materialistic, credit-fueled lifestyle and consumerist mind-
set—making the recent global economic turmoil and banking meltdown about as pleasurable as having one's oxygen hose sliced in two
while scuba diving in deep water. But Heine's reference to the House
of Rothschild is also telling: Money and banking have their own mystique and secrets, and for centuries no name carried more cachet than
that of Rothschild. Today, the Rothschild banks no longer constitute
the world's leading financial institution, but they remain a respected
boutique family firm operating globally from the sign of the "Five
Arrows" at their historic New Court, St. Swithin's Lane location in
London—where the English branch of the family has been based for
some two hundred years. They profited from Napoleon and outlasted
the Nazis, and today their third building on the same site is under

construction. N. M. Rothschild & Sons chairman Baron David de Rothschild commissioned fashionable "star-chitect" Rem Koolhaas to design a gleaming new ten-story building with a "sky pavilion," offering contrasting, unobstructed views of the adjacent old Church of St. Stephen Walbrook. The ancestral portraits, memorabilia, and framed old accounts will no doubt be on display discreetly. If you have the temerity to drop in unannounced when the new headquarters building opens in 2010 or 2011, you might ask a Rothschild whether they still follow their canny personal investing strategy of one-third financial assets, one-third land and property, and one-third art and collectibles. It's not easy to invest alongside the Rothschilds, but you can buy your own small, indirect stake in their empire by purchasing a few shares of Jardine Strategic, one of several publicly traded companies associated with another mystique-laden entity: grand old Sino-Scottish "hong" (trading company) Jardine Matheson with its raffish beginnings in the opium trade. Incorporated in Bermuda and operationally based in Hong Kong at Jardine House with its ship's porthole-style windows at 1 Connaught Place, Jardines holds a 21 percent ownership stake in the unlisted Rothschilds Continuation Holdings, a vehicle originally conceived to provide for continuity in the event that family partners commissioned as officers in the British forces were killed on active service.

Banks That Are No More

If the Rothschilds have survived and continued to thrive as a boutique firm, the same cannot be said of so many other once-great institutions. High finance remains a story of ambition, innovation, change, and upheaval, and any exploration of the remaining private temples of money requires a detour through a rather sad—if fascinating—graveyard of failed, merged, evaporated, or erased firms. Until the world financial chaos of 2008 hit—taking down so many storied names—the most interesting example was that of Barings, the once supremely influential British merchant bank that Cardinal Richelieu called one of the six great powers of Europe (the others being England, France, Russia, Austria, and Prussia). But if you go in search of its elegant partners' room, remodeled in the 1920s by architectural genius Sir Edwin Lutyens, you won't find it—it's gone, along with its unique rabbit warren of a headquarters at 8 Bishopsgate in London. The firm's self-confidence was such that its letterhead carried only its address—there was simply no need to add the name "Baring Brothers & Co." In 1995, the gentlemen merchant bankers of Barings went bust when Nick Leeson, a Singapore-based employee, overwhelmed the firm with his unauthorized, hidden tsunami of bad trades. Highly competitive and financially rewarding fields have always attracted their share of roguish "wide boys," city slickers, whiz kids, self-proclaimed "masters of the universe," and smooth killers. Some, like Leeson, end up in Singapore's Changi Prison or similar places. The implosion of venerable American firm Kidder, Peabody & Co. in 1994 was alleged to have been a consequence of the fraud of flamboyant bond trader Joseph Jett—a roommate of one of this book's coauthors at Harvard Business School c. 1985–1986—who was ordered to forfeit his massive bonuses, fined, and barred from the securities industry.

Interesting vestiges of past greatness can be found here and there, sometimes if only as brand names. Swiss banking giant UBS acquired the genteel small investment bank Dillon, Read & Co., and later reused its name for a hedge fund business that was eventually decommissioned. One wonders what happened to all of Dillon Read's wonderful antique rolltop desks and the courtly liveried staff who used to work at its graceful former headquarters at 46 William Street in New York. Elements of the once much more significant House of Morgan do live on at Morgan Stanley and J. P. Morgan Chase, but one wonders if J. P. Morgan himself would still see any undiluted Morgan ethos left. His signature phrase—"first class people doing business in a first class way"—isn't much heard anymore, but rich condo buyers in Manhattan can now live the J. P. Morgan lifestyle, so to speak. His magnificent building at 23 Wall Street was sold and is now being redeveloped by French designer Philippe Starck, who is known for his impossibly chic interiors at such hotels as the Delano in Miami's

South Beach and the Mondrian on West Hollywood's Sunset Strip. It probably would not be to J. P. Morgan's taste; he preferred to have oak paneling and a massive chandelier in his 23 Wall Street banking hall. The façade of 23 Wall Street still has the scars of a 1920 terrorist bombing by anarchists, who put dynamite and heavy iron pieces into a horse-drawn wagon before detonating it next to the building. Several dozen people were killed, and hundreds injured, but the then-sturdy House of Morgan merely picked up a few pockmarks.

The Great Survivors: Goldman Sachs and the House of Lazard

A short walk from the former House of Morgan is 85 Broad Street, a relatively nondescript office tower that is the headquarters of what is probably the greatest financial firm of all time: Goldman Sachs. Goldman seems to provide positive proof that nice guys really do come out ahead over the long run; its clever, ferociously hardworking, generally public service–minded, and ethical team players seem to have preferred a low-key headquarters. Whether that will still be the case when their new HQ is completed at 200 West Street remains to be seen; it's been designed by architects Pei Cobb Freed, whose founding partner is architect philosopher-king I. M. Pei—designer of the glass pyramid in the center of the Louvre courtyard and other modernist icons. Like the alumni of strategy consulting firms McKinsey, Bain, and BCG, Goldman alumni seem to be everywhere one turns in public life: former White House Chief of Staff Josh Bolton, New Jersey Governor Jon Corzine, World Bank President Bob Zoellick, one-time U.S. Treasury Secretaries Henry Paulson and Robert Rubin, and Australian politician Malcolm Turnbull, to name only some obvious examples.

A more colorful survivor of the financial world's changes and upheavals is the House of Lazard, long known for its purposefully shabby offices at One Rockefeller Plaza ("One Rock")—though now moved to nearby 30 Rockefeller Plaza—and more elegant digs at what used to be its separate Lazard Frères and Lazard Brothers entities in Paris and London. In New York, partners were expected to lavish money and attention on their residences rather than their offices. Lazard is no longer run and controlled by the person some used to call the "Sun King"—Franco-American billionaire and hereditary Lazard banker Michel David-Weill. A highly complex and cultivated man, he sometimes preferred the simple fare of a liberally buttered and salted baguette to the luncheons prepared by his personal French chef. Focusing on pure advisory work in the boardrooms and corridors of power and carefully cultivating its mystique, David-Weill spoke of Lazard as an *"haute banque d'affaires* vis-à-vis the world"—a phrase ideally uttered after taking a fully inhaled drag on one of his signature Cuban cigars. A baptized Catholic with strong Jewish family roots (if no particularly strong known spiritual interests), David-Weill likely drew from his two religious traditions the wisdom that riches and influence can't banish the disappointments, betrayals, and pain of life. For a time his successor to lead this firm of "great men" appeared to be his difficult but talented son-in-law, Edouard Stern, himself the heir to a banking dynasty that served the French aristocracy. Stern, called the "Mozart of finance," later divorced David-Weill's daughter, pursued ever more risky and unwholesome extracurricular activities, and ended up murdered by his prostitute-girlfriend in 2005. He was found dead in his Geneva bedroom, shot four times and wearing a latex rubber suit with a dildo lodged in his rectum. Taki Theodoracopulos, the well-known Greek playboy–conservative columnist, felt the need to violate the injunction against speaking ill of the dead when he wrote: "[Edouard Stern] was not only ruthless and a terrible bully, he was as close to being a monster as anyone can be and still be free to walk around in polite society."

The Wealth Managers, Including Coutts & Co.—the Queen's Bankers

Scandal isn't exactly helpful to private bankers seeking to reassure rich clients, so those firms involved in what is now usually termed "private wealth management" try to stay off the police blotter whenever possible. A wide spectrum of firms around the world competes in the private wealth management arena, from large global banks to small specialist asset managers and "family office" providers. In America, long-established trust companies have traditionally been the market leaders, having been set up in many cases to manage the assets of their founding families: U.S. Trust (now part of Bank of America, but founded in 1853 by and for the Astors, Whitneys, Cornings, and others); Northern Trust; Glenmede Trust (for the Pews of Philadelphia); Bessemer Trust (for the Phipps family, partners of Andrew Carnegie); and Wilmington Trust (for the du Ponts). In Britain, the undisputed equivalent is Coutts & Co., founded by a Scot in 1692 at "the sign of the Three Crowns"—and typically still referred to as "the Queen's bankers." Until relatively recently, Coutts bankers wore frock coats and were required to be clean-shaven (if male)—and bank correspondence was delivered to and from Buckingham Palace by a brougham (horse-drawn coach) from the Royal Mews until London traffic made that tradition too difficult to continue.

In a spirit more old money than contemporary bling, the Coutts head office at 440 Strand in London has an indoor garden court for the enjoyment of clients—a "pleasure dome" with comfortable settees, and an exquisite indoor pond with ornamental carp, a traditional Asian symbol of prosperity and good fortune. The Chinese wallpaper in the Coutts boardroom came from the first British Embassy in Peking in 1794. Even Gilbert and Sullivan did their bit to immortalize the bank, with a song in *The Gondoliers* including lines about "the aristocrat who banks with Coutts, the aristocrat who hunts and shoots." Despite its traditions, the investment approach has always been up-to-date, drawing such clients over the centuries as Bram Stoker, Chopin, Berlioz, Tennyson, King George III—and, it is said, latter-day entrepreneur Sir Richard Branson of Virgin Atlantic fame. The bank's checks are distinctive, and those used by members of the royal family include the individual's monogram with the appropriate heraldic crown or coronet. Coutts is now part of the RBS (Royal Bank of Scotland) Group—a large financial conglomerate that hasn't been spared from the recent economic turmoil. In any case, new money is very welcome these days, with Coutts providing specialized services for expatriates, "inpatriates," sports and entertainment figures, and female entrepreneurs.

The Swiss Banks: Models of Discretion

Although offshore jurisdictions have long competed aggressively for private wealth, in some specific cases they do fit W. Somerset Maugham's description of "sunny places for shady people," with somewhat more lax standards than you would find in London, Zurich, or any other truly first-world environment. Even today, despite the global economic mess that has also wreaked havoc on Switzerland's financial institutions, no one outdoes the Swiss in managing private wealth. Recent events at Zurich-based powerhouse UBS show that the Swiss can make the same disastrous judgments one sees elsewhere— from their investments in U.S. subprime mortgages to banker Bradley Birkenfeld's alleged smuggling of diamonds in a toothpaste tube on behalf of a client. But just as the Swiss watch industry retooled for success after losing market share to cheap, reliable Asian quartz watchmakers by concentrating on high-end mechanical watches and high-fashion fun watches (e.g., Swatch), Swiss bankers have shown themselves reasonably good at creative reinvention after an extended crisis. Old stereotypes about the shadowy "gnomes of Zurich," secret numbered accounts, high fees, statements sent in unmarked brown envelopes, and discreet rooms for clients to clip coupons off their unregistered bearer bonds don't really capture the essence of Swiss banking anymore—if they ever did. Swiss banking is actually quite varied, including the unique Italian-Swiss flair of Lugano with its relatively Mediterranean vegetation and "molto snob" clients. The large and somewhat antiseptic headquarters of UBS at Bahnhofstrasse 45 in Zurich, and of Credit Suisse at nearby Paradeplatz 8, exude the quiet professionalism of major global institutions. The old Latin saying,

Pecunia non olet (Money has no smell), seems particularly apt here, as the big Zurich players were never known for being colorful. (The saying comes from Roman Emperor Vespasian, who instituted a tax for using public lavatories, noting that the revenue itself was odorless.)

The Swiss have also taken a lot of heat in recent years for their handling of dormant or unclaimed accounts, especially accounts established by Jews and other Europeans who were later murdered by the Nazi regime—not to mention the current view that the country cooperated with neighboring Nazi Germany more than was absolutely necessary. According to Swiss banking law, dormant accounts eventually become part of the bank's assets if unclaimed by a legal heir, and it's true that Swiss bankers did not go to extravagant lengths to find possible heirs if none appeared on their doorstep. However, Winston Churchill's late 1944 characterization of the Swiss and their compromises still rings true:

> Of all the neutrals Switzerland has the greatest right to distinction. She has been the sole international force linking the hideously sundered nations and ourselves. What does it matter whether she has been able to give us the commercial advantages we desire, or has given too many to the Germans, to keep herself alive? She has been a democratic state, standing for freedom in self-defence among her mountains, and in thought, in spite of race, largely on our side.

At the pinnacle of the Swiss banking world are the true remaining private banks—Banquiers Privés and Privatbankiers—which remain unlimited liability partnerships owned by family partners of Calvinist origin formed at the time of the French Revolution. Despite their relatively diminutive scale, together they manage literally trillions in assets. There are fourteen still in existence, mostly based in Geneva and Basel, though some are run from Zurich, Lausanne, St. Gallen, and Lucerne. Most represent the crème of the *haute société protestante* that intermingles the Swiss private banking elite with certain top-drawer circles in France and Germany. Until recently, they were so discreet that the brass plates on their buildings used to carry only the initials of the name of the bank—which, when combined with the country's strictly enforced bank secrecy laws, gave them a unique air of personal discretion. The two most important are Pictet & Cie, founded in 1805, and Lombard Odier Darier Hentsch, founded in 1796. Pictet, now with offices in thirteen countries, is run from a brand-new, ultrasecure headquarters building at Route des Acacias 60, built with sturdy six-ton (5,448kg) façade blocks, sixty-five meeting rooms, twenty-six elevators, and five hundred underground parking spaces—a luxury in Geneva. By contrast, Lombard remains in its elegant old-style large town house at Geneva's Rue de la Corraterie 11, even as its investment offerings and global expansion have kept pace with Pictet.

Private wealth managers, especially the remaining true private banks, promise clients asset preservation and protection—and here is where the real controversy and tensions lie. Individuals have an obligation to observe the laws of their country and to fulfill such other duties as are required of citizens, including the payment of taxes. At the same time, over the centuries, people who trusted their governments around the world have seen the value of their currencies eroded and their assets confiscated, and not just in places like Venezuela and Zimbabwe. U.S. and UK citizens have seen the purchasing power of the dollar and the pound sterling evaporate by 91 percent and 97 percent, respectively, since 1945, thanks to inflationary policies (and policy mistakes) of the Federal Reserve and the Bank of England. Those living in countries more directly exposed to war, revolution, hyperflation, and chaos have found the arguments of Swiss (and Liechtenstein) private bankers even more persuasive, and so they have regularly violated their own countries' laws to safeguard their assets. Assets parked in Geneva in 1900 would have grown exponentially by now, but those left in Paris, Berlin, Buenos Aires, or Salisbury (later renamed Harare) would probably have been largely wiped out one way or another.

The country of Liechtenstein, its princely family, and their banking and wealth management group, LGT, have recently found themselves in a heated dispute with the German government. The fortyish acting head of state, Crown Prince Alois, has pointed out that the German government bought stolen data from a criminal who was a former LGT employee in order to seek out possible cases of German tax evasion. The crown prince, a graduate of the Royal Military Academy Sandhurst in England, who then commanded Coldstream Guards soldiers with a German accent that sometimes startled the Brits at Wellington Barracks in London, has sturdily stood his ground at the Castle in Vaduz and at the nearby LGT headquarters at Herrengasse 12. No one disputes that German citizens have a duty to obey German tax laws, or that such citizens have a right to call for lower or simpler taxes through their political process; but the government's buying of stolen data from criminals in other countries in violation of their laws seems like a step too far.

The German Private Banks: Oppenheim, Warburg, and Others

Given Germany's historic combination of economic vitality and periodic upheaval, it's no surprise that private banking services have always been a stable business within the country, in Frankfurt, Cologne, Hamburg, and other traditional financial centers. The grandest and largest of the bunch is still Sal. Oppenheim—sometimes written as Salomon Oppenheim jr. & Cie—founded in Bonn in 1789, and later moved to Cologne, where it flourished. In 2007, it made the momentous decision to move its headquarters outside Germany, to a distinctive new building at 4, rue Jean Monnet in Luxembourg—although most of its operations remain in Germany. The leader of the family contingent in the bank is First Deputy Chairman Baron Friedrich Carl von Oppenheim, who is a German nobleman proud of his Jewish heritage. Of a similar character is the smaller private bank M. M. Warburg & CO, which reopened in its impressive Ferdinandstrasse 75 building in Hamburg after the horrors of the Second World War. The Warburgs have been eminent bankers for generations in several countries, not only in Germany, where Max Warburg was an adviser to (and personal friend of) the last kaiser, Wilhelm II. His brother Paul Warburg became vice chairman of the Federal Reserve in the United States, something that conspiracy theorists like to note. Most interesting of all may be the late Sir Siegmund Warburg, a classical scholar who went on to found a new and highly successful London merchant bank from scratch after the war; it was later acquired by UBS. Sir Siegmund's only eccentricity was to endow a new institute for the study of graphology (handwriting analysis) at the University of Zurich. Sir Siegmund used to repeat a saying he had heard from his grandfather: "It was the Warburgs' good fortune that whenever we were about to get very rich something would happen and we would become poor and had to start all over again."

Of a different character was the German Privatbankhaus Schacht & Co., founded in Düsseldorf in 1953 by the oddly named Dr. Hjalmar Horace Greeley Schacht. Schacht was Hitler's president of the Reichsbank (1933–1939) and minister of economy (1935–1937), and brought some credibility to a Nazi leadership group that was largely made up of thuggish riffraff. (Hermann Göring was also sometimes said to elevate the tone of the Nazi inner circle, as he was at least an officer and decorated fighter pilot in the First World War, but this was entirely relative, given his drug addiction, corpulence, and tendency to grab vast quantities of other people's property.) Never a Nazi party member officially, Hjalmar Schacht is credited with changing the name of a country in light of Nazi racial theory: Persia became known as Iran, which means "land of the Aryans." He was also an enthusiastic Freemason from 1906, but the Nazis turned a blind eye to that, since his expertise was useful—despite the Party's frequent and bizarre railing against "Jesuits and Freemasons" (two bodies that would have had no overlap in membership or aims at the time). As Schacht's star fell and as he got drawn into various plots, he was imprisoned in the Dachau concentration camp at the end of the war, and was later tried and acquitted at Nuremberg—probably the only concentration camp survivor to be tried at the war crimes tribunal. Before he died in 1970, he had successfully relaunched himself as a private banker and economic adviser to various nonaligned governments, including Indonesia's.

A Well-Connected American House: Brown Brothers Harriman & Co.

The Warburgs and Dr. Schacht were well known to another privately owned bank of particular interest to conspiracy theorists— Brown Brothers Harriman & Co., which even now remains a true partnership bank. Although it outgrew its historic 59 Wall Street building and moved to new quarters in 2003, it remains in its rarefied, WASP-y, clublike buildings in Philadelphia at 1531 Walnut Street, and in Boston. Famous partners in the twentieth century have included Senator Prescott Bush, father and grandfather of two U.S. presidents, and W. Averell Harriman, who served as U.S. ambassador to Stalin's Soviet Union during a critical period (1943–1946), when the United States tacitly agreed to give the Soviets a sphere of influence (and later much more) in Central and Eastern Europe. (Harriman later went on to become Secretary of Commerce, Governor of New York, and third husband of Winston Churchill's ex-daughter-in-law Pamela Churchill Harriman—who herself years later helped launch Bill Clinton on the Washington scene.) At 59 Wall Street, Prescott Bush and Averell Harriman were among the substantial number of Brown Brothers partners drawn from the ranks of Yale's Skull and Bones who later occupied major government posts—a fact that continues to interest more than a few bloggers determined to find the fingerprints of occult puppet masters behind world events. (Those looking for a spy story on Wall Street would actually do better to look into the career of banker and British intelligence operative Sir William Wiseman, longtime partner of Kuhn, Loeb & Co., whose then powerful firm was linked by marriage to the Warburgs, and later merged with Lehman Brothers.) Still, there is no denying the financial clout and importance of Brown

Brothers during its long heydey, even if today it is considered a boutique firm. Young trainees from other financial centers used to consider it a great privilege to do a stint at 59 Wall. One of those trainees in the early twentieth century was Montagu Norman, later to become both Governor of the Bank of England (1920–44) and a good friend of Dr. Schacht (Norman was also to become godfather to one of the German central banker's grandchildren). The enigmatic first and last Lord Norman, with his "half patrician, half priestly" manner, became the most eminent banker in the world. A small world, you might say.

C. Hoare & Co.

Brown Brothers has a kind of twin across the Atlantic, but this London counterpart has no reputation for spookery or political intrigue. We are referring to C. Hoare & Co., private bankers "at the sign of the Golden Bottle" at 37 Fleet Street in London since 1672. Its intimate-scale banking hall has a remarkable antique cast-iron and bronze stove at its center, while the current generation of Hoare family owners ensure consistent, hands-on attention to clients' money matters—freeing those clients to focus on their businesses, country pursuits, philanthropy, or whatever else they choose to do with their time and financial independence. During the banking meltdown of 2008, the phones at 37 Fleet Street were apprarently ringing off the hook with rich people eager to transfer their accounts to Hoares, given that private bank's deliberate and highly strategic insulation from the world's expanding cesspool of toxic securities.

The Enduring Allure of Gold

Given that dramatic change and crisis are more common in human (and financial) history than stability—and thinking of the many periods when paper assets became worthless—maybe one might want to own a bit of gold, just to be on the safe side? A "barbarous relic" to some, gold has come back into fashion as the "hard" asset class of last resort. The glamorous two-year-old "global briefing" magazine *Monocle* reported in early 2008 on a strong uptick in the number and frequency of secretive "daily bullion flights between the world's leading financial hubs—welcome aboard Bullion Air." Owning gold is something of a bet against innovation and progress, since normally one should prefer to own stock in profitable, growing companies rather than bars of metal that pay no dividends or interest, and actually cost you a fair amount of money to store and protect. Still, the lure of gold is eternal, and it's not a bad hedge against the Four Horsemen of the Apocalypse. In the early 1960s, Queen Elizabeth II was a luncheon guest at Hambros, the distinguished merchant bank of Danish origin then located grandly at 41 Bishopsgate (it later was absorbed into a large French bank). To create a touch of drama, the Hambros staff secretly built within its vault a three-foot (1m) high pile of precious metals—an amazing collection of bars and coins from many sources—then worth precisely £1 million. Everyone had great fun seeing this physical display of a fortune, including the Queen, who was persuaded to accept a small, three-troy-ounce gold "smuggler's bar" as a souvenir. It is worth reading the words General Charles de Gaulle spoke to British historian Paul Johnson:

> Gold is absolute objectivity. It is blind, like justice. It is pure, like a virgin. It has no politics and no ideology, no likes or dislikes, no friends or enemies. All it recognizes is its possessor, whom it serves faithfully so long as he has it.

Chapter 12

UNIVERSITY SECRET SOCIETIES
AND DUELING CORPS

*I*f you somehow managed to slip a charitable contribution under the forbidding doors of the Skull and Bones tomb at Yale University, would the denizens of that society have the audacity to cash it (and even send you a tax receipt)? It's not a totally outlandish question, as the one thing that Skull and Bones shares with the March of Dimes, the Salvation Army, and the American Cancer Society is fully tax-exempt charitable status. Perhaps only in America, a nation of "joiners" with a long fascination with elite college societies, could the world's most desperately secretive and emphatically closed society be considered a legitimate educational charity.

Of course, other universities have secret societies, but what greatly enhances the mystique of the Yale senior societies (as they are formally known) is their permanent infrastructure—their distinctive and elaborate halls, *tombs* in college parlance, some with spooky, whimsical flourishes that could have been devised by H. P. Lovecraft.

The Apostles of Cambridge and the Bullingdon Club of Oxford

In England, by contrast, Cambridge University is home to the Conversazione Society—an internationally known secret society normally referred to as the Apostles, founded in 1820, with a membership roll that has included John Maynard Keynes, Bertrand Russell, Ludwig Wittgenstein, E. M. Forster, and at least two Soviet spies—Guy Burgess and Anthony Blunt. But the Apostles, for all their history, intense intellectual debate, and left-wing intrigue, have no permanent digs—

only their "Ark" with its collection of papers, handwritten notes, and list of members living and dead. "Embryos" (potential members) meet "Apostles" and "Angels" (current and alumni members) discreetly, in various Cambridge rooms, where their oath of secrecy can be administered along with a supposed curse. High-flying politician and writer Harold Nicholson spoke of a "militant, Masonic atmosphere, as of some secret society which was to reform the world."

In a very different vein are the elite, long-established Oxford and Cambridge dining societies, known for their high-spirited antics, white-tie suppers, and frequently recharged champagne glasses. If Brideshead lives on, it is in clubs like Oxford's Bullingdon, whose colorful membership has included London's mayor, Boris Johnson, Poland's foreign minister Radosław "Radek" Sikorski, and possibly the next UK prime minister, David Cameron. Yet if you visit Oxford, you will find no elegant building marked "Bullingdon Club"—there simply isn't one.

If Britain's university towns aren't exactly crowded with secret society buildings, at times the United States seems to give the opposite impression—especially with its dense concentration of Greek-letter fraternities and sororities, in some places as numerous as Starbucks and Dunkin' Donuts outlets. Even the infinitely more elite societies of Harvard, Yale, and Princeton acknowledge their debt to the original Greek-letter fraternity, Phi Beta Kappa, founded in 1776. Although it gave up its secrets and became the country's preeminent honor society for academic excellence long ago, it created the imprint for hundreds of other organizations: the adoption of two or three Greek letters to represent a secret motto encapsulating a fraternity's particular mission or specific high-minded ideals. The meaning of the letters is revealed during initiation rites, typically awkwardly phrased nineteenth-century creations based loosely on cribbed Masonic rituals—many of which circulate on the Internet these days. After having lost their popularity during the campus counterculture and unrest of the 1960s, fraternities bounced back in the 1980s and 1990s, only to lose steam again in the face of political correctness, lawsuits, crackdowns on underage drinking, and the decreasing leisure time of undergraduate life.

Individual chapters represent a vast range of styles, in terms of spirit and architecture—from ramshackle firetraps to opulent patrician mansions, with members aspiring to run Boy Scout troops or opium dens. Even modest fraternity houses tend to have a chapter room that has been literally consecrated for use as a ritual space. However, mass-produced (and occasionally goofy-looking) robes, altar cloths, lamps, ceremonial swords, and T-shirts can be ordered online from licensed "paraphernalia" suppliers, and few members take the "spiritual" dimension too seriously.

Princeton's Eating Clubs

Tiffany—not T-shirts—has traditionally been the preferred style of the Ivy League's clubs and secret societies, and, in fact, the famous New York jeweler has been the maker of the silver pins for Skull and Bones for generations. But not everything is quite as it appears, with Princeton as a perfect example. Princeton University's strikingly beautiful and well-groomed campus exudes a certain timelessness—but its Gothic architecture has a bit of Ralph Lauren's costume department about it. Most of it was assembled (with skill and vision) in a relatively short time. Until the late nineteenth century, the place was still the small, if good, Presbyterian "College of New Jersey." Today it is one of the world's greatest centers of learning (benefiting from the nearby Institute for Advanced Study), and has the good sense not to try to do everything well (it still has no law, medical, or business schools). Its alumni are famously and generously loyal, and the pleasantness of both the campus and the adjoining town shows that classical architecture and human-scale urban design work, regardless of actual age and weathering. The glamour of Princeton is also undeniably connected with its handsome "eating clubs" on Prospect Avenue. Despite their relatively new construction, they nonetheless developed an instant patina during the Jazz Age. F. Scott Fitzgerald called the Ivy Club "detached and breathlessly aristocratic," and the Cottage Club boasted a new library designed to replicate one at Merton College, Oxford. Cap and Gown (once irreverently called "Clap and Groin") today has an alumni membership that ranges from Donald Rumsfeld to Brooke Shields, and Quadrangle's alumni group includes Amazon founder Jeff Bezos. Even Ralph Nader was a clubman during his undergraduate years. Today, ten eating clubs remain in operation, all coed. Five select their new members by the fraternity rushlike process called "bicker," while the remaining five are essentially open to all comers. No one is turned away. Some three-quarters of undergraduates eventually join, with all the instant elegance F. Scott's memory can bestow.

Harvard's Final Clubs

If today's hardworking Princeton students still (occasionally) dream of endless lawn parties and croquet, Harvard and Yale undergraduates gravitate to their own distinctive lore and legend. Unlike Princeton, Harvard and Yale developed more gradually and organically, before the idea of a "campus" even existed, and so their older buildings and quadrangles gently filled vacant areas among city streets in Cambridge and New Haven—and in a variety of architectural styles. Harvard men had their stereotypes—pale, effete intellectuals; self-assured Boston Brahmins; and cultured foreigners. One's roommate could turn out to be a future Latin American *presidente*—or maybe the next Aga Khan.

Harvard's club scene also developed gradually and with variety: the Hasty Pudding Club-Institute of 1770, with its raucous theatricals in drag and Indian pudding made with cornmeal and molasses; the Lampoon, with its humor magazine edited from a "mock-Flemish castle," run by officers with kooky titles like Ibis, Narthex, Sackbut, and Hautbois; and, for the academically distinguished, the Signet Society, with its genteel clubhouse and heraldic shield on Dunster Street. Still at the pinnacle of this diverse system of clubs and societies are the so-called "final clubs," final in the sense that the other Harvard societies were traditionally regarded as mere waiting rooms for "punching season"—the selection process for the final clubs. There are eight final clubs still in existence, and they and the university broke official ties in the mid-1980s when the clubs chose to remain all-male. Preeminent among them is the Porcellian Club—"the Porc"—founded around 1794 at the time of a legendary pig dinner, and still using the motto *Dum Vivimus Vivamus* (While we live, let us live). Teddy Roosevelt, Oliver Wendell Holmes, and George Plimpton were well-known members, but Teddy's cousin FDR was not selected—supposedly giving him a chip on his shoulder for life. The Porc's Massachusetts Avenue clubhouse, across from Harvard Yard, seems to lack any visual interest for passersby, which is probably intentional. More visually striking on the outside is Jack and Bobby Kennedy's final club, the Spee, at 76 Mount Auburn Street, designed in a kind of "Georgian moderne" style. A short walk away is the pleasant Fox Club, at 44 John F. Kennedy Street, which has had its own interesting spectrum of members ranging from Bill Gates to T.S. Eliot. The final clubs try to stay out of the news, but they resurfaced in 2006 when Senator Ted Kennedy publicly resigned from his club, the Owl, which he joined in 1954—as a contemporary gesture of political correctness.

Yale's Senior Societies: Skull and Bones and Its Rivals

Harvard and Princeton may have their points of interest, but for collegiate secret society researchers and connoisseurs, Yale remains the ultimate mother lode. As at Harvard, there is a diverse array of other long-established social clubs, embracing St. A's (St. Anthony Hall), the "Lizzie" (the Elizabethan Club, with its first editions and cucumber sandwiches), Mory's (a kind of private restaurant where the Whiffenpoofs sing) and a couple of fraternities, including DKE (Delta Kappa Epsilon). All these groups bear the stamp of the Yale man of legend, a cheerful, driven, All-American go-getter and high achiever. That special "Old Blue" spirit mixed lineage with meritocracy and, at least until the 1960s, most Yalies strove earnestly to work "for God, for country, and for Yale." Indeed, their heartstrings were tugged when-ever *Bulldogs* or *Boola Boola* were mentioned. High academic, literary, or sporting achievements could make one a candidate for Bones or for one of the other senior societies, regardless of wealth or family background. In fact, the mystique of the Yale societies was so great that it spawned a whole group of imitators elsewhere: At Dartmouth, one can stroll by Sphinx, Casque and Gauntlet and others; at the University of North Carolina–Chapel Hill, there are the buildings of the Orders of Gimghoul and of the Gorgon's Head; even Berkeley, for all its grungy street theater and left-wing shibboleths, maintains its own senior society modeled on Bones—the Order of the Golden Bear, with its seat in a rustic, historic, early-California log structure at the center of the campus.

Yale currently has ten "aboveground" societies with halls or tombs, and a fluctuating number of more ephemeral "belowground" societies without any permanent real estate. The former group, in order of tra-ditional precedence, is Skull and Bones, Scroll and Key, Wolf's Head, Berzelius, Book and Snake, St. Elmo, Elihu, Manuscript, and Mace and Chain. Elihu, which is pleasantly housed in a former Tory tavern from colonial times, is the only one that describes itself as a "nonsecret senior society." All are now coed, but the heated internal dispute over admit-ting female members did particular damage to Bones and its esprit de corps. Alexandra Robbins, an enterprising and vivacious journalist who was herself a Yale graduate and a member of the prestigious rival society Scroll and Key, was able to pierce the previously impenetrable veil of Bones, thanks in large part to the society's loss of nerve and the disgruntlement of many of its members. Her off-the-record interviews resulted in the original 2002 exposé *Secrets of the Tomb.* We will not repeat information widely available there, but there are still some interesting questions that remain unanswered.

Over the years, *The Economist* magazine has carried a surprising amount of coverage on Skull and Bones, some of it admittedly tongue-in-cheek. The magazine's "Good Network Guide," which ran in 1993, devised a 0–5 ratings system for elite networks, and gave

Bones a 2 for Power, 4 for Secrecy, 2 for Organization, 0 for Strength of Beliefs, 5 for Peculiarity of Rituals, and 5 for Exclusivity. It also suggested that Bones "may have passed its 'best before' date"—presumably because of its bruising internal civil war over female membership, pitting factions of alumni and current members against one another. Given the intensely masculine character and tone of everything about Bones since 1832—a kind of richly textured High WASP machismo—one could see that the "Bones life" (as it's sometimes called internally) would probably never be the same. As a society that only selects fifteen new members a year on one college campus—and has only several hundred living members—the international prominence, overwhelming success, and intense drive of its initiates is justly famous. News stories in recent years have tended to mention both Presidents Bush and Senator John Kerry, but one could just as easily have plucked out such Bones names as FedEx founder Fred Smith, self-made private equity multibillionaire Stephen Schwarzman of the Blackstone Group, or even talented political satirist Christopher Buckley (himself the son and nephew of three Bonesmen). The list could easily go on.

However, as an organization that has carefully cultivated its aura primarily through a grand, aloof form of noncommunication with the outside world, Bones seems to have been at a loss for words on those occasions when it does feel the need to say something about itself. Some students "tapped" for membership do need a bit of convincing, so here is one line Bones has used to describe itself on occasion, in a spirit of saying as little as possible while seeking to reinforce its mysterious allure: "The life which we invite you to share in our society is based on such intangible factors that we cannot meaningfully convey to you either its nature or its quality." However, the U.S. Internal Revenue Service requires charitable organizations to be a bit more—well—specific, so RTA Incorporated (the legal name of Skull and Bones, formerly the Russell Trust Association) explains its existence and 501(c)(3) public charity status in the following way from its New Haven post office box address:

"Educational Programs—structured programs of intellectual inquiry, sensitivity training and personal development for students of Yale University focusing on topics of intellectual, political or cultural importance. Recent topics have included homeland security, corporate governance and US international relations."

Sensitivity training? It's hard to imagine Bonesmen of years gone by using that kind of language. Given what is now known and confirmed about the goings-on within that austere-looking, essentially windowless "Greco-Egyptian" tomb (with dashes of Gothic) at 64 High Street in New Haven, it's clear there are elements that are typical of other "initiatic" societies and some elements that are truly unique to Bones. In the former category, for example, those coming to their Bones initiation must not wear or carry metal. As in Freemasonry and elsewhere, this can signify that the neophyte arrives "penniless"—in a symbolic state of poverty—while ensuring that any bumps while blindfolded or any roughhousing are relatively harmless. Another example is the ceiling decoration of the sanctuary, interchangeably called the Inner Temple and Room 322 in the case of the Bones tomb. As in some other esoteric societies, the ceiling is painted with stars in a kind of celestial canopy—which can represent the new world into which the initiate is being reborn. Bones members also receive a secret name to be used at all times within the tomb (but never outside), with the names assigned or chosen according to certain formulas and customs that have gotten wide reportage and more than a few laughs in recent years. (George W. Bush, it's been reliably reported, couldn't think of any name to take, so he used "Temporary"—which in time became his name for life within "the Order," as members also refer to their society.) Taking a new secret name is common in esoteric orders, as is the uncharitable tendency to refer to nonmembers and to the outside world as profane or "Barbarian" (the latter being the preferred Bones usage).

Then there are the things genuinely unique to Skull and Bones. In contrast to most other secret societies, Bones has a rite of initiation that is loud, chaotic, and deliberately disorienting, as it seeks to create an otherworldly atmosphere—but not through the usual air of dignified solemnity. Building on this sense of being in a world apart is the use of "Skull and Bones Time," with clocks within the tomb (including a now-famous grandfather clock used in secret group photos) set five minutes ahead of the rest of the world. Finally, as part of the intense bonding process bringing together fifteen new members of a particular year's "club" or "delegation," members are required to reveal their personal sexual history in detail in a series of guided discussions. This last element (depending on one's view) is either luridly fascinating or deeply disturbing, or both. Certainly it was not instituted with a future coed membership in mind.

Rivals to Skull and Bones

It is interesting to compare and contrast the Bones experience with the inner workings of the other Yale senior societies, beginning with its most distinguished rival, Scroll and Key—which has a membership roll rivaling Bones in its impressiveness. Those passing through the ornate, exotic-looking Moorish tomb of "Keys" at 444 College Street have included *Newsweek International* editor Fareed Zakaria, Yale president and Commissioner of Baseball Bart Giamatti, cartoonist Garry Trudeau, philanthropist Paul Mellon—not to mention such other worthies as Cole Porter, Cornelius Vanderbilt, Sargent Shriver, Dean Acheson, and even best-selling pediatrician-author Dr. Benjamin Spock. Since 1844, Keys men (and now women) have always had a certain urbane flair, and they are the only secret society that puts on a regular public performance of a sort: At midnight after their twice-weekly meetings, they gather outside their tomb door to sing "The Troubador," an ancient song of courtly love. No less than Bones, they guard their own arcana, and Keys exists legally under the name of the Kingsley Trust Association. Internal documents and memoirs refer to "the Society known to the world as Scroll and Key"; to members, its actual name is C.S.P.—*Collegium Sanctum Pontificum* (College of the Holy Pontiffs). With the Roman god Jupiter as their mythological patron (in contrast to Bones' Eulogia), members swear during solemn, part-Latin rituals to perform "their pontifical duties with zeal and fidelity." A bit sophomoric? That's for you to decide.

As with all the Yale senior societies, the main "program" of Keys is a year of revealing one's personal life stories and taking part in structured discussions and debates about major political and cultural issues of the day. Whatever else one may say about them, over the years these societies have selected a mix of rather talented and ambitious students and forced them to grapple with the big questions facing their generation while savoring a rarefied, highly private bonding experience. The usual background noise and temptations of elite university clubs were (and are) typically excluded, whether cocktail shakers and tinkly piano music or the more recent generations' gravitation toward mind-numbing cannabis pipes and pounding live rock and techno. The popularity of the Yale senior societies has remained reasonably constant, drawing actress Jodie Foster, CNN program anchor Anderson Cooper, and political commentator David Gergen to Manuscript during their undergraduate years; Senator Joe Lieberman and legendary investor and philanthropist Sir John Templeton to Elihu when they were Yale students; and journalist Bob Woodward of Watergate fame, CIA director Porter Goss, and African-American public intellectual Henry Louis Gates, Jr. to Book and Snake, with its classical white Greek temple and iron fencing of Caduceus-like intertwined snakes at 214 Grove Street.

Sometimes unfairly overlooked (or overshadowed) is Wolf's Head, long regarded as the third-ranking society after Bones and Keys—and the only one to have had two tombs of considerable architectural distinction designed by notable architects. Its first, conceived by McKim, Mead, and White and built in 1884 at 77 Prospect Street, has a slight flavor of old Heidelberg or some other German university. This hall was sold to the university (which still uses it for academic purposes) when Wolf's Head member, oil baron and philanthropist Edward Harkness underwrote the costs of a new tomb (in addition to funding, rather generously, the creation of an Oxbridge-style house/residential college system at Harvard and Yale). The new hall was built in 1924 at 210 York Street according to the designs of an American architect of genius—Bertram Grosvenor Goodhue. Described by the author of the official current Yale campus guide as "a romantically ruina-ceous English Cotswold manor on steroids," it is the largest of the senior society properties—and also surrounded by a high stone wall. For its dedication, member and Pulitzer Prize–winning author and poet Stephen Vincent Benét composed a strictly private poem, which now hangs inside. Although not exactly his best or most memorable lines ("When the wind blows over New Haven, bitter with snow . . . May there be a fire on this hearth, with logs aglow, and fellowship in this Hall . . ."), it was a fitting gesture. That particular fellowship has included Baltimore Mayor Kurt Schmoke; British Labour MP, former government minister and bon vivant Geoffrey Robinson; sometime Yale president Benno Schmidt; and conservative philanthropist (and Catholic convert) Lew Lehrman, among others.

Now that even Skull and Bones members appear to have spilled the beans, is there anything left to discover about these storied soci-eties? Yes, and the remaining mystery mostly has to do with Bones' origins. Members, researchers, and conspiracy-minded outsiders all seem to agree (rightly or wrongly) that the origin of Bones was as a chapter or branch of some kind of German society, presumably a student "corps" of some kind. Does this ring true? What was it, and does it still exist? Even Bonesmen and internal society histories seem to be a bit vague on this point. The founder of Bones, General William Russell, did study in Germany (a fashionable thing to do in the nine-teenth century and beyond), and indeed the tomb itself is almost lit-erally littered with Germanic memorabilia. However, as we'll see in the remaining part of this chapter, there is very little in the rituals and iconography of Bones to suggest any connection whatsoever with German student "corps" as they were then or are now.

Intriguing, however, is a print in the tomb that appears to make a specifically Illuminist reference, with a drawing of skeleton remains and the words from what is believed to be the Regent degree, one of the higher grades of initiation of the Illuminati: *Wer war der Thor, wer Weiser, wer Bettler oder Kaiser? Ob Arm, Ob Reich, in Tode gleich* (Who was the fool, who the wiser man, beggar or emperor? Whether rich or poor, all are equal in death). Such symbolic messages were common in German Masonic and quasi-Masonic circles of the period, as was the use of human skeletons and death's-head badges. Admittedly, even in Catholic symbolism, as used in Central Europe, such macabre *memento mori* symbols were common and accepted as reminders of mortality. German Masonic and other esoteric lodges went rather heavy on such stuff, even occasionally using full-sized human skeletons as holders of candelabra.

In the early 1900s, two of the largest and most prestigious German Masonic lodges were the Three Skeletons in Breslau (now Wrocław, Poland) and the United Death's Head and Phoenix in Königsberg (now Kaliningrad, Russia). In the case of Bones, until the final goodies come out, the most plausible story is that it borrowed (or descends in some way) from an esoteric, perhaps quasi-Masonic, society that was operating c. 1830—not a student corps. Watch this space, as they say.

The German University "Corps"

If America's elite college societies are discreet, the German student corps operate under conditions of still greater secrecy, since their ethos is considered so politically incorrect. A cult that, historically, revolved around the concept of the *Mensur* (duel), fought with the *Schläger,* or German broadsword, and advertised for the remainder of the combatant's life by the "boasting scar" deliberately acquired on his face does not sit easily in the nervous democracy that is modern Germany—a country obsessed with avoiding any association with militarism. Yet today there are still more than two hundred German and Austrian corps, as well as a resurgence of such societies in post-communist Poland, testifying to the continuing appeal of this tradition to young men. Corps members wear ribbons across the breast, displaying the colors of their unit, matched by a peaked cap; on formal occasions they don a full uniform, including a tunic ornamented with frogging, like a nineteenth-century hussar's costume.

The origins of the German student "corporations" go as far back as the fifteenth century, but the oldest body surviving today dates from 1716. They arose because students often had to travel a long distance between university and home, so they formed groups, for company and protection. Because they carried enough money to see them through a university term, they were a target for robbers and this may be why they were originally motivated to master the use of the sword: Only students and noblemen were authorized to carry swords. Today the corps are divided into five main groups, though there are others. First is the Kösener Senioren-Convents-Verband (Kösen Senior Corps), the oldest body, which consists of 105 German and Austrian corps, with a political outlook traditionally described as "liberal," though in the context of the corps, such political terms have a nineteenth-century meaning. Then there is the Weinheimer Senioren-Convent (Weinheim Senior Confederation); this encompasses sixty corps, with a similar nineteenth-century liberal tradition. Curiously, the Weinheimer "convent" also has formal links with the Tau Kappa Epsilon college fraternity which has more than 270 chapters in the United States and Canada. The Coburger Convent is composed of one hundred corps, and its political tradition is conservative. Next comes the Deutsche Burschenschaft (German Fraternity), which purists regard as a different institution from the corps. Though its organization today is very similar to that of the corps, historically it had a nationalist outlook, though today it emphasizes tolerance and diverse recruitment. The Catholic student corporations, which for reasons of canon law and papal condemnations do not duel, are grouped within the *Cartellverband der katholischen deutschen Studentenverbindungen* (Union of Catholic German Student Associations). It should be emphasized, once again, that the political labels attached to these groups refer to positions they held around the time of the 1848 revolutionary upheavals and cannot be translated into similar allegiances today. The corps are nonpolitical, but might be described as moderately conservative insofar as they uphold ancient traditions that are frowned upon by politically correct leftists today.

To describe around two hundred corps in detail would be beyond the scope of this book; but here we take a look at a few representative examples of the various traditions and, as our chief interest is in places, we shall concentrate on those that have the most interesting headquarters—the discreet and exclusive sanctuaries within which the members gather to perpetuate their old traditions. The—to English speakers—incongruous term *convent* simply refers to a corps, a group of men assembled together. Despite their distinctive individual traditions, there are certain features that are common to most corps. For example, they have two kinds of membership: the current student members and the alumni who remain part of the corps for life (the *Altherrenschaft* [Senior Gentlemen's Association]). In each corps there are three key officers: the *Senior*, effectively the president, who adds a single "x" to his signature; the *Consenior*, who teaches fencing and supervises the *Mensur*, and who adds a double "xx" to his signature; and the *Drittchargierter*, or secretary, distinguished by a triple "xxx" after his signature. Very important to each corps are its colors (*couleurs*), displayed on a sash worn across the chest, most frequently, but not invariably, tricolor. Originally, each color had a symbolism: white for the nobility (though most corps are completely democratic in their recruitment, a few cherish an aristocratic tradition), black to signify devotion to the sword, blue for camaraderie, and so on. By reading the three colors of a corps, it is theoretically possible to deduce its priorities, though most corps today have similar values, the chief being character formation and forging friendships for life.

It was this spirit of brotherhood that provoked Hitler's distrust of the corps: He was jealous of any loyalty that cut across that owed to the Nazi Party. Although in the popular imagination of non-German observers, the corps, with their dueling scars and their hierarchical traditions are perceived in caricature as pro-Nazi, the historical reality was altogether different. Some were disbanded even in the early days of the Third Reich for refusing to expel their Jewish members. On the other hand, as early as 1921, the Kösener Senioren-Convents-Verband passed regulations to exclude Jews, in the reaction against Germany's defeat in the First World War. This aroused the outrage of Walter Bloem, the distinguished German novelist and member of two corps, who wrote a novel called *Brotherhood* that featured a fictitious dueling fraternity. Despite this blot on the reputation of the fraternities, it is only fair to record that the Kösener Convent group and many other corps made a stand for their Jewish brethren later, under the Third Reich, when it was dangerous to do so, leading to the total suppression of all the corps. The Corps Austria Frankfurt am Main, for example, which belonged to the Kösener Convent (abbreviated as KSCV), refused to implement Hitler's 1935 decree on Aryan restrictions for membership, so was suppressed the following year. Its "old boy" *(Altherren)* branch was forcibly disbanded by the Gestapo in 1939. There were many similar instances of anti-Nazi resistance by the corps, which had long nurtured a tradition of liberal nationalism. Those executed following the July 1944 plot against Hitler included men like Ulrich von Hassell, German ambassador to Rome, who was a corps member. Only after the fall of the Third Reich were the corps gradually able to resume their activities. Today they are assailed from the other side of the political spectrum by politically correct leftists who loathe their cultivation of tradition.

So its private home, the Corpshaus, has become a closely guarded sanctuary for each fraternity. That said, the umbrella organization for the most senior corps, the Kösener Senioren-Convents-Verband, with 105 member fraternities, meets annually at a ruined castle. The group's spiritual headquarters is Rudelsburg Castle, dating from 1050, on the east bank of the River Saale near Bad Kösen, in Saxony-Anhalt. The impressive ruins of the castle are surrounded by memorials erected by the KSCV. Here, in a great festival, the members of the constituent corps met every year from 1855 to 1934. In 1935 the KSCV was suppressed by the Nazis and after the Second World War Rudelsburg was in communist East Germany. The patriotic monuments the students had put up were mostly destroyed by the communists, but have now all been restored. Covert corps activity in East Germany grew more overt as the regime became more shaky and was quite open from 1987 on. Since 1995 the KSCV has resumed its annual congress at Rudelsburg, in much more congenial conditions since the ruins now house a restaurant. The restored monuments include the Pillar to the Fallen, a war memorial put up in 1872, destroyed by the Reds in 1953, and now rebuilt; the Emperor William I Obelisk, erected in 1890, destroyed, and restored; the Young Bismarck Monument, showing the German chancellor in his corps uniform with dueling sword (he belonged to the KSCV Corps Hannovera Göttingen and was famed for fighting thirty-two duels in one summer term); a replica of the 1896 statue, destroyed and reerected; the Lion Monument, commemorating 2,360 members of the KSCV who fell in the First World War, now refurbished; and the very simple Alliance Stone, placed here in 1997 on the tenth anniversary of the resumption of student corps life in eastern Germany.

Such public activity as the KSCV congress at Rudelsburg is the exception rather than the rule for student corps in the unfavorable climate of the twenty-first century. More typical is the in-house atmosphere today at the home of the corps to which Bismarck belonged in his fighting days of thirty-two bouts a term—the Corps Hannovera Göttingen, in the town of the same name. The Corpshaus is an appropriately turreted Gothic building in beige stucco, at Bürgerstrasse 56–58. Its main feature is a great hall with a long table for fraternal banquets, which could serve as the stage set for *Tannhäuser*. Women are not allowed to go higher than the first floor, although the corps is renowned for throwing the best parties in town, at which young ladies are treated with old-world gallantry. The Corps Hannovera, along with similar fraternities such as the Corps Teutonia Marburg and the Corps Lusatia Leipzig, prides itself on espousing the "blue principle" (blue is the central color in its sash), which means the promotion of gentlemanly, sociable conduct. With young members living in the house and practicing their swordsmanship every day with great dedication, there is something of a monastic atmosphere about the

Corpshaus, perhaps like a medieval commandery of the Teutonic Knights. The members, in their red caps and red-blue-gold sashes, also lend the building an operatic character. The Corpshaus is not entirely discreet, since a house flag flies from the mast on top of the battlemented tower and cars parked outside are regularly vandalized by leftists with a grudge against the masculine and romantic traditions the corps represents. The members' indifference to such hostility is adequately expressed in the Corps Hannovera's Latin motto: *Numquam retrorsum, fortes adiuvat fortuna!* (Never backward, fortune favors the bold!).

If the Hannovera Göttingen has Bismarck as its tutelary genius, other corps can also boast distinguished former members. Emperor Wilhelm II belonged to the Corps Borussia Bonn, the most unrepentantly grand of all the corps; Heinrich Heine, the famous poet, graced the ranks of the Corps Guestphalia Göttingen; the composers Richard Wagner and Robert Schumann belonged respectively to the Corps Saxonia Leipzig and the Corps Saxo-Borussia Heidelberg; and, perhaps most surprisingly of all, Karl Marx, an inveterate duelist, was a member of the Corps Palatia Bonn.

When speaking of his beloved Corps Borussia and its traditions, Kaiser Wilhelm II said: "It is my firm conviction that each young man who enters a corps will find his true direction in life from the spirit which prevails in them. For it is the best education a young man can have for later life." However, as a young prince, he was not allowed to duel, and so his full membership in the corps was—strictly speaking—something that required bending the rules. The Borussia, located at Kaiserstrasse 147 in Bonn, is one of three remaining "white circle" or noble corps in Germany. Its Corpshaus has all the usual furnishings you would expect to find—drinking horns, old prints, coats of arms in stained glass, suits of armor, heraldic flags, and the like.

The Mensur

What actually takes place behind the closed doors of these sanctuaries of swordsmanship and male bonding in the cause of tradition?

The chief activity—the raison d'être—of these mainstream student corps is the *Mensur*. It is not strictly accurate to describe the *Mensur* as a "duel": The motivation is different. The opponents have no quarrel with each other, and while each must honestly strive to win, the real prize—disfigurement for life—goes to the loser. Each corps member is obliged to fight the *Mensur* a minimum number of times, typically three or four. After that, he need never pick up a sword again: He has proved himself and is a corps member for life. The *Schläger,* a combination of broadsword and rapier, has a razor-sharp blade a fraction under three feet, four inches (102cm) long. The lethal character of these weapons demands extreme precautions. The combatants wear steel goggles to protect their eyes, with a nose guard, a tunic and gloves of chain mail, additional leather padding on the sword arm, and a kind of muffler or neck brace to prevent a fatal injury. Unlike the fencing *piste* with its rapid movements forwards and backwards, in the *Mensur* the opponents stand stock-still. Beside each antagonist, similarly attired, stands his second, sword in hand. The atmosphere is an extraordinary mix of the highly formal and the totally relaxed. The referee impassively calls out the traditional instructions for each round of the fight: *"Hoch, bitte!" "Fertig!" "Los!"* But the student spectators casually swig from bottles of beer (as do the combatants between bouts), as casually as the members of an American fraternity house. Only the sword arm moves; both men are experienced fencers; but sooner or later one party makes a mistake and pays for it with an agonizing wound that pours blood. Of paramount importance is for the duelist not to flinch, or show fear or even pain: That would lead to disqualification and disgrace.

The wounded party must display complete sangfroid, even as he is led off to have his wound stitched by a medical student who is waiting in attendance. It doesn't matter if he is a novice: His lack of experience will help to make the scar more obvious. For the scar itself is a major part of the cult. In times past, men used to sew horsehair into a wound to ensure that it healed more slowly and left a well-defined scar. This is the *Renommierschmiss* (bragging scar) that will mark the corps member for life and advertise his membership of an elite, in terms of both class and courage. In the nineteenth century it was the passport to a good marriage and even today the comely girls flocking to corps parties bear out the claim of grinning members: "Chicks dig scars."

Not all corps, however, are devoted to the *Mensur.* The Catholic corps, organized in their own convent called the *Cartellverband der katholischen deutschen Studentenverbindungen,* were specifically established to oppose dueling, in accordance with Church teaching. If that sounds a bit killjoy, it is important to remember that, in the nineteenth century, the corps fought less disciplined duels with more frequent fatalities. Indeed, dueling had reached such epidemic proportions that at the University of Jena, in one week in 1815 there were 147 duels fought among a student population of 350; even in the 1840s, at the University of Leipzig, 400 duels took place, two of them fatal. So the Catholic Church sought to encourage the emergence of institutions that would offer students all the camaraderie of the dueling societies, without the concomitant contempt for life. Founded in 1856, the Catholic *Cartellverband* includes around 180 societies spread across Germany, Austria, Switzerland, Belgium, France, Italy, Poland, Hungary, Slovakia, and even Japan. They, too, have their caps, colors, and traditions. Their nonviolent character means that many churchmen are members, including Pope Benedict XVI (Pius XII was also a member) and the roll includes one canonized member, St. Józef Bilczewski, archbishop of Lwów/Lemberg (now L'viv in Ukraine) and three Blesseds. Although Catholic grandees destined for holy orders occasionally joined one of the dueling corps in bygone days—for example, the distinguished Bishop von Ketteler of Mainz—a dueling scar and a bishop's miter are today considered quite incompatible. The Catholic fraternities also have some fine houses, perhaps above all Guestfalia Tübingen.

An unexpected consequence of the collapse of communism in Central and Eastern Europe has been the resurgence of the Polish corps, complete with caps, uniforms, and colors. The earliest ones were founded by nineteenth-century Polish students at the Baltic universities in Riga and Dorpat (now Tartu, Estonia). The most prominent today include the Arkonia, Warsaw, established in 1879, and restored in 1995; the Sarmatia, Warsaw, founded in 1908 and restored in 1993; the Lechia, Poznan, established in 1920 and reactivated in 1993; and at least half a dozen others.

The survival of Academic Fencing, as the art of the *Mensur* is called, within the mainstream corps is a triumph of romanticism over political correctness. It is an entire culture in itself; as it happens, the man who is now regarded as the leading authority on this culture is currently based in the United States: J. Christoph Amberger. A Berliner by birth and a member of both the Corps Hannovera Göttingen and the Corps Normannia Berlin, Amberger has seven *Mensuren* to his credit. His book *The Secret History of the Sword: Adventures in Ancient Martial Arts,* published in Baltimore in 1997, is regarded as the definitive work on the subject. It is not the first work published in America to deal with the dueling corps: In 1880 Mark Twain devoted four chapters of his book *A Tramp Abroad* to a description of the student corps and their duels, as witnessed by him in Germany. He observed:

> All the customs, all the laws, all the details, pertaining to the student duel are quaint and naive. The grave, precise, and courtly ceremony with which the thing is conducted invests it with a sort of antique charm.

That charm survives today—behind closed doors, in the secret sanctuaries of honor.

Chapter 13

JOLLY GOOD FELLOWSHIP

"*J*eeves," I said, "we start for America on Saturday."

"Very good, sir," he said, "which suit will you wear?"*

That dialogue between Bertie Wooster and his imperturbable man Jeeves, both the creations of the comic genius P. G. Wodehouse, resonates from a very special world—a world as fantastic as Disneyland and, to the sympathetic observer, just as entertaining. It is a sheltered and exclusive place, entered like a secret garden by an unobtrusive door in the wall to which only a privileged few possess the key. Bertie and his chums are inhabitants of Clubland and that private world is arguably the most impenetrable sanctuary of all.

Clubland is the collective term—employed as long ago as 1878—for the most exclusive gentlemen's clubs in London and, subsequently, around the world. Although it is now a global phenomenon, even if on a very small scale, it is essentially an English invention. The image of padded armchairs, candlelight blinking on polished silver, port circulating in paneled rooms, and soft-footed servants tending to members' every need is an Edwardian vignette of discreet luxury that has long disappeared from most English country houses but still survives, at least to some extent, in clubland. Admission to this magic circle has always been by election, with the portals jealously guarded by existing members. The traditional style of voting was to place ivory balls in a box: white balls from those members approving of a candidate, black balls from those blocking his admission. Unpopular candidates could accumulate a startling number of black balls: On election day it was always a bad sign if the club secretary peered inside the box full of

---

* Quote from "Extricating Young Gussie" by P. G. Wodehouse.

ivory globes and grunted, "Caviar." Nowadays blackballing of members is done more rarely and discreetly; if a candidate's prospects are hopeless, the club secretary will have a quiet word with his proposer and seconder, and his name will be withdrawn.

London's Private Clubs

The lore surrounding London clubs amounts to an entire culture and mythology. It was translated brilliantly into fiction by P. G. Wodehouse, quoted above. His character, Bertie Wooster, was a member of the Drones Club (fictitious, but based on the real-life, though now defunct, Bachelors'), where the members, mostly ill-behaved and intellectually challenged young men of impeccable backgrounds, were categorized as Eggs, Beans, or Crumpets. Bertie's fast-changing girlfriends belonged to the debutantes' club, the Junior Lipstick. Jeeves himself was a leading light in the Junior Ganymede, a club for gentlemen's gentlemen, where superior valets and butlers congregated and kept a book in which all the foibles of their employers were recorded. Other clubs invented by Wodehouse were the Negative and Solution (for photographers) and the Senior Bloodstain (for private investigators). Yet the real world of clubland was scarcely less colorful than the rich products of the Wodehouse imagination. It was in gentlemen's clubs that such traditions originated as ironing newspapers before setting them out for members' use and boiling silver coins, to ensure cleanliness, before giving them in change. The object of a good club is to provide a home away from home for every member, wining and dining him splendidly, isolating him from the outside world, and, above all, offering him sanctuary from his womenfolk. For most of clubland's history, its discreet habitats had the primary purpose of providing refuges wherein the British male could seek protection from his natural predator: woman.

White's: The Oldest Club
The oldest surviving gentlemen's club is White's, in London's St. James's Street. White's was founded in 1693, the only club that can

claim a seventeenth-century pedigree, and its preeminence is undisputed. Originally, it was a coffeehouse established by an Italian named Francesco Bianco, who Anglicized his name to Francis White. In its early days, it had a reputation as a resort where young noblemen were fleeced by professional gamblers; whenever Jonathan Swift, the great satirist, passed White's, he was accustomed, quite unsatirically, to shake his fist at the building and curse it fervently. The club has been in its present premises, a beautiful house at the top of St. James's Street, since 1753; the famous bow window was installed in 1811, where the entrance had formerly been. This fact is still evident today if one looks at the row of five windows on the floor above, behind their wrought-iron balconies: The larger, arched window directly above the ground-floor bow window is in the center of the frontage. The modern entrance, up a short flight of steps, is slightly on the right-hand side of the building. Like most senior clubs, White's has an imposing staircase, its effect amplified by a large mirror, and ornamental pillars are a prominent feature within the house.

The vantage point of the bow window immediately became the exclusive preserve of the great dandy Beau Brummell and his circle (they called it the "bay window"), who disdainfully surveyed the street outside: It was said that a nod of acknowledgment from Brummell in the window could make the fortune, socially speaking, of the favored acquaintance passing by. The Beau once redeemed a debt simply by giving his arm to his creditor while walking the short distance to White's from Brooks's across the street. On the other hand, as Henry Luttrell recorded, the critical arrow "shot from yon Heavenly Bow at White's" might land with devastating consequences:

> On some unconscious passer-by
> Whose cape's an inch too low or high;
> Whose doctrines are unsound in hat,
> In boots, in trousers or cravat . . .

White's was described by a Regency social commentator as "*the club from which people have died of exclusion.*" Later, in Victorian times, Disraeli called membership in White's a supreme human distinction, equivalent to becoming a Knight of the Garter: He attained the office of prime minister, an earldom and the Garter—but never won admission to White's. The club was famous for high-stakes gambling. Brummell won £20,000—an enormous sum in the early nineteenth century—from George Drummond, of Drummond's Bank, on one day in the club. Lord Robert Spencer, brother of the duke of Marlborough, lost his entire fortune there, but recouped it by running a faro bank from which he retired, never to play again, with a profit of £100,000—around £5 million ($7.4 million) in today's money. Another famous Regency buck, the second Lord Alvanley, bet £3,000 there on one of two raindrops running down the windowpane of the famous bow window. The betting books at White's, going back to 1743, furnish an intriguing social history. One member bet £1,000 that a man could survive for twelve hours under water. A penurious volunteer was found and was sunk in a boat to test the theory: The experiment failed, the member lost £1,000, and the human guinea pig lost his life—not clubland's finest hour. Today, modern technology has been enlisted to serve the sporting interests of members, with horse racing available on television. Harold Macmillan, the former prime minister, said that White's had the ideal membership composition for a London club—two-thirds gentlemen and one-third crooks.

Even in modern times, there was no shortage of rakes and eccentrics. In the twentieth century a member entered the club one day with a fighting cock (totally against the law) perched on his shoulder. Two famous fighting cocks among the members were the novelist Evelyn Waugh and Winston Churchill's son Randolph, who carried on a guerrilla war against each other on the premises for twelve years. One day in 1964 Waugh learned that Randolph Churchill was in the hospital for an operation to remove a lung; but, he was assured, the trouble was "not malignant." Waugh remarked to Lord Stanley of Alderley, in White's, that it was a typical triumph of modern science "to find the only part of Randolph that was not malignant and remove it." Stanley reported this sally to Churchill and, on his release from the hospital, the two antagonists were reconciled.

Less reconcilable were the differences that lay behind a famous episode during the postwar Labour government. Aneurin Bevan, the outspoken Welsh socialist Member of Parliament, intemperately described the Tories—many millions of his fellow Britons—as "lower than vermin." Shortly after this outrageous utterance, Air Marshal Sir John Slessor tactlessly took Bevan to lunch at White's. A member, the Honourable John Fox-Strangways, expressed his feelings by kicking Bevan down the steps of the club; he then went back inside and resigned, to avoid embarrassing White's. The most highly placed member to resign was King Edward VIII: When he abdicated the British throne to marry Wallis Simpson, he thought it appropriate simultaneously to terminate his membership in White's. He may have regretted that more than the loss of his crown.

Boodle's, Brooks's, and Others of Distinction

Many of the old clubs of London that were founded as a result of the fashion set by White's no longer exist: Wattier's, the Cocoa Tree, and Arthur's are just a few of the casualties of time. Yet a heartening number still survives. Next in antiquity after White's, and its near neighbor on St. James's Street, is Boodle's. This club was established in 1762 and originally had a Whiggish atmosphere, in contrast to the Toryism prevailing at White's, though in both cases political affiliations are a thing of the distant past. The club was named after its original headwaiter, Edwin Boodle, and is famous today for its elegant first-floor saloon, one of the finest rooms in London. The plaster work here and throughout the building is superb, giving the house a classic character, its elegance reinforced by Adam fireplaces. The coffee room (as the dining room is still called in traditional clubs, recalling their earlier existence as coffeehouses) is a noble, high-ceilinged chamber graced by a large painting of a stag hunt. Horses rival humans in the club's portraiture, including a painting by George Stubbs and pictures of Grand National winners.

Historically, Boodle's had so many baronets among its members that it used to be said that if the porter called out "Carriage for Sir

John!" at least a dozen men would turn around. Beau Brummell was a member here too and Boodle's had a bay window of its own where an elderly duke once liked to sit "watching the damned people get wet." Long after the development of modern sanitation, a lobby containing chamber pots remained at the service of older members who could not accustom themselves to newfangled conveniences. Even if the club became nonpolitical, plenty of Members of Parliament belonged to it, as an old verse recorded:

In Parliament I fill my seat
With many other noodles,
And lay my head in Jermyn Street,
And sip my hock at Boodles.

Yet the club was not just a clique of fashionable beaux and gamblers: It had an intellectual membership, too. This, in its early years, included Adam Smith, author of *The Wealth of Nations;* David Hume, the philosopher; and Edward Gibbon, the historian, who presented a copy of his classic work, *The Decline and Fall of the Roman Empire,* to King George III, who graciously observed: "Another great, fat book—scribble, scribble, scribble, eh, Mr. Gibbon?" It was Boodle's that was famous for boiling coins before giving them in change to members, a practice now, sadly, discontinued. Its famous culinary dish is Boodle's Orange Fool, a triflelike dessert with a sponge-cake base. In more modern times well-known members have included the urbane film star David Niven and Ian Fleming, the creator of James Bond.

The third in the trio of historic clubs that can claim descent from the sanctuaries of the eighteenth-century rakes and Regency bucks is Brooks's, facing Boodle's on the opposite side of St. James's Street and founded in 1764, moving to its current premises in 1778. Among its founding members were two British soldiers destined to play an ill-starred role in American history: General Burgoyne and Lord Cornwallis. The club is a large building with its brick frontage divided by half a dozen stone columns beneath a classical pediment and a

balustrade around the roof, standing out from its neighbors on
the west side of St. James's Street, designed by the architect Henry
Holland. The memory of Charles James Fox, the Whig statesman
and reckless gamester whose portrait hangs above the chimney-
piece in the hall, dominates the history of the club. Brooks's does not
boast a bow window like White's and Boodle's, but it has the Great
Subscription Room, created by John Adam, as its architectural glory.
Here Fox, Brummell, and other hell-raisers and party-animals of the
time gambled extravagant amounts of money in all-night sessions.
The claim that the curved section cut out of one of the tables was
made to accommodate Fox's prodigious belly is a good clubland tale,
but in fact it was the standard design to afford room for the croupier. The library, a long yet intimate room crowded with comfortable
leather sofas and armchairs, is ornamented with portraits of members of the Society of Dilettanti in fancy dress, painted in the 1740s,
including Sir Francis Dashwood, president of the Hellfire Club, incon-
gruously habited as a Franciscan friar. The composer Sir Edward Elgar
was a member, noted for regularly using the club telephone to call his
home in Worcestershire so that he could listen to his dogs barking.

Other London Clubs of Distinction

Yet if these three establishments are the crème de la crème, there are
plenty of other clubs in London maintaining ancient traditions that
have historically embraced a considerable degree of eccentricity and
outrage. The stateliest is the Athenaeum, in a custom-built classical
building in Pall Mall, clubland's other great thoroughfare leading onto
St. James's Street. Standing on a corner site between Pall Mall and the
Duke of York's Steps, the building's most striking external feature is a
classical frieze, based on a design at the Parthenon, which stands out
in bold relief from the light stonework. The theme throughout is a
far from understated Greek pastiche. The Athenaeum has enormous
dignity: Nothing could be further from the gaming-hell atmosphere
of the more worldly institutions in the rest of clubland. Its cathedral-
like gravitas may partly be attributed to the large number of bishops

among its membership; it is a standing joke in clubland that the noto-rious propensity of visitors to lose their umbrellas at the Athenaeum must be due to sticky-fingered clerics.

The Athenaeum was founded by John Wilson Croker (who first coined the name "Conservative" for the old Tory Party); Sir Thomas Lawrence, the painter; and other friends in 1823, to provide a sanc-tuary for intellectuals in clubland. Members have included Sir Walter Scott, Charles Dickens (whose chair is preserved in the club), William Makepeace Thackeray, Charles Darwin, and Herbert Spencer, who famously reproached a young man who beat him at billiards there, with the words: "Proficiency in billiards is the proof of a misspent youth."

A line of dialogue in Noël Coward's *Present Laughter* epitomizes the club's reputation:

"You ought never to have joined the Athenaeum Club. It's made you pompous."
"It can't have. I've always been too frightened to go into it."

The Athenaeum, however, completely failed to intimidate the irrepressible F. E. Smith, Earl of Birkenhead. When he was Lord Chancellor, walking each day to the House of Lords he developed the habit of stopping off at the Athenaeum, to which he did not belong, to use the lavatory. After several weeks, he was challenged one day as he emerged by an embarrassed servant, who asked: "I take it you are a member here, sir?" "Good God!" exclaimed Birkenhead, gazing around him. "Do you mean to tell me this place is a club as *well*?"

The Athenaeum's neighbor in Pall Mall is the Travellers', also notable for appearing in the opening chapter of Thackeray's novel *Pendennis,* even though the author was blackballed for membership. The staircase has a brass handrail that was installed to assist the great diplomat Talleyrand, who was a member when he served as French ambassador in London, in mounting the stairs. Today the handrail is suitably inscribed to commemorate its origin and the Travellers' is still home to foreign diplomats. Among the many splendid rooms, the library with its elegant pillars is particularly impressive. This club has changed dramatically in character. Formerly the stern tradition was that members did not speak to one another, going so far in unsociability as to bring books and newspapers to the dinner table. Today, by contrast, the Travellers' is one of the liveliest clubs in London, having added dinner events with famous modern explorers and travel writers to its longstanding reputation of being "associated with a cultivated, cosmopolitan view of the world." Its founding rule that candidates for membership must have traveled at least five hundred miles in a direct line from London is meaningless in today's jet-setting age. Candidates' proposers are now expected to note some of the more exotic countries their prospective members have visited; but, as has been observed, Travellers' members are congenial folk, more obviously so than their incommunicative predecessors in the club, and if they like somebody they are sure to find some pretext for admitting him.

The tradition of monastic solitude, to which the Travellers' was formerly subject until its transformation, has always been an element of clubland life. That might seem perverse, in institutions theoretically established to promote conviviality, but there is logic to it. While it might appear axiomatic that clubmen should be clubbable, the competing claim was that members should treat their clubs like their own homes—in effect, as sanctuaries. That implies a degree of detachment, a desire to be untrammeled by social obligations to other people, to slip into the comfort, metaphorically speaking, of house slippers. Hence the self-absorption and isolation that could seem churlish to outsiders. A possibly extreme example was the case of a new young member in a London club who, encountering an older member, politely said, "Good morning." To this well-intentioned greeting, his senior barked in reply, "Good morning, good morning, good morning, good morning, good morning, good morning, *good morning!* Now, let that do you for a week!"

Not all clubs are housed in palatial buildings. Two of the best— Pratt's and the Beefsteak—meet in cramped quarters, the former in a basement near St. James's Street, the latter in a room above a shop, in a district some distance from from the mainstream Pall Mall–St. James's Street axis of clubland.

Pratt's is a truly private club, being owned by the Duke of Devonshire. It owes its name to a former croupier at Crockford's, the famous gaming club, who retired to this house just off St. James's Street under the auspices of the seventh Duke of Beaufort. The basement kitchen is the very basic home of the club. During the Second World War, Winston Churchill grilled steaks here for his fellow members after toiling late into the night for the war effort. Members still dine late off simple grills (the club stays open until the last member leaves). The walls are covered with the bric-a-brac contributed by members over the years since its founding in 1841, notably a small statue of Buddha presented by a famous Oriental traveler who claimed to have bought it at a London open-air market. All the staff are known as George, for the convenience of members whose memories may have been dulled by port; when, for the first time, a waitress was engaged, she was immediately christened Georgina. The small size of the premises necessarily makes the club intimate and convivial.

At the Beefsteak, all the staff are similarly called Charles. This is the successor to a variety of clubs called the Beefsteak, beginning in 1709, and revived in 1730, when the members wore blue coats with buff waistcoats and buttons inscribed "Beef and Liberty." The artist William Hogarth was among those early Steaks. The modern club, on Irving Street, near Charing Cross Road, dates from 1876. Members dine beneath a raftered ceiling displaying the club emblem of a gridiron, the paneling of the room surmounted by a collection of plates, with light provided by a large mullioned window. Its modest premises, with numbers of prosperous gentlemen seen entering, aroused the suspicions of the police a century ago. They duly launched a raid and found several men seated around a table in an upstairs room. "And who might you be?" the police inspector asked the first of them. He was told: the Lord Chancellor. "And you, sir?" "The governor of the Bank of England," was the reply. "I suppose *you* are the prime minister?" said the inspector skeptically to the next member. Arthur Balfour, who indeed held that office, pleaded guilty as charged. The inspector's reaction, when he finally discovered that these responses were true, is not recorded. The primary function of the Beefsteak is conversation. To this end, members all sit at a single table. Each, as he arrives, is obliged to take the vacant place next to the most recently seated member. In this way strangers, of very different backgrounds, are thrown together, to rise to the challenge of witty repartee. There are, of course, pitfalls: A young member once spent the entire meal telling his neighbor how to write fiction—he had not recognized his companion as Rudyard Kipling.

In their role as sanctuaries, one of the chief amenities of clubs is to defend their members against any threat of female intrusion. This role is more understated nowadays than formerly, since many clubs now admit women either as guests or to some degree of membership. Most women acknowledge the masculine character of clubland and sensibly respect its territorial integrity, while enjoying being taken to dinner on elegant premises where an atmosphere of old-world gallantry prevails. The protective tradition, however, is strong. At Pratt's the rule is that no woman is allowed to telephone the club. If any lady is so unwise as to do so, the standard response is "Madam, no married member is ever in the club." The story is told of a woman who once entered Brooks's and demanded to know if Mr. So-and-So was in the club. "I can't say, madam," replied the hall porter. "Please find out," she insisted, "and if he is, say his wife wants him." "I'm sorry, madam," was the firm rejoinder, "but members of Brooks's don't have wives."

Altogether, there are still around fifty major clubs in London, though that is a considerable reduction from clubland's Victorian heyday. Famous institutions include the Carlton Club, founded in 1832 to oppose the Reform Bill; the Garrick Club (1864), with dramatic and literary associations—the colors of its tie are said to have been inspired by the club's salmon and cucumber sandwiches; the Cavalry and Guards Club (1890); and Buck's, formed in the tradition of a private club by Captain Herbert Buckmaster, as recently as

1918. (This club's house libation, the "Buck's Fizz," has been called "a genuine contribution to the happiness of mankind.") The Turf Club (1861), with its racing connections, is still famous for having the largest number of dukes as members. There are other clubs associated with the armed services, and still others identified with specific professions or sports. Most clubs traditionally cultivated a degree of oddity, but few went so far as the Eccentric Club, which installed a clock in the bar whose dial was a crazy mirror-image of a conventional clock-face. In an increasingly conformist world, however, eccentricity is not as pronounced or as prevalent as it once was—even in clubland—though it does survive.

Not all eccentrics were attractive. The most extreme example, in nineteenth-century clubland, was the Marquess of Clanricarde, owner of a two-hundred-roomed castle and vast estates in Ireland where his tenants were rack-rented, while he enjoyed a then-princely income of £80,000 a year. But, in fact, *enjoyed* is the wrong word. Clanricarde, a notorious miser, lived squalidly. Though he belonged to the best clubs, he would dine in them off sandwiches out of a paper bag and a banana dunked in coffee. He raked in garbage bins for scraps and asked club chefs to cook strips of fat he had scavenged in this way, but was indignantly refused. Sometimes strangers, imagining him to be destitute, gave him food—a charity that would have been better extended to his Irish tenants. Clanricarde was offensive to his fellow club members, placing his thumb and fingers to his nose in an insulting gesture. At other times he would sit in the club window, licking the tip of his large nose in a grotesque fashion—surely the least clubbable of clubmen.

Clubs Outside London and in Europe

The institutions of clubland quickly spread to other parts of the British Isles and further afield. In Ireland, a very clubbable country, the doyen was the Kildare Street Club, founded in 1782 in custom-built premises on the street that gave it its name. The building was distinguished by the carvings of monkeys playing billiards in the stonework around the windows. In the late twentieth century it merged with the University Club, and moved to new premises. There is definitely something very Irish about the Kildare Street and University Club actually being situated in St. Stephen's Green. In Scotland, the New Club, established in 1787, occupies very modern premises on Edinburgh's Princes Street, with breathtaking views of the castle on its crag.

Further afield, most of the older European capitals have gentlemen's clubs after the English model. The Jockey-Club de Paris, at 2 rue Rabelais, founded in 1834 to encourage the improvement of horse breeding in France and to act as a national authority for horse racing, bears the most striking resemblance to its English counterparts. Its first president was an Englishman, Lord Henry Seymour-Conway, son of the Marquess of Hertford. Every president since 1884 has been a French duke, except for a brief period from 1914 to 1919 when it had to make do with a humble count. There is also the Travellers Club of Paris, at 25, Avenue des Champs Elysées, with a tradition of Americans among its members, housed since 1904 in the last surviving great house on the Champs Elysées, the former home of the marquise de Païva. A caricature of Second Empire opulence, its features included an onyx staircase and a bathroom decorated in Moorish style with a silver bath.

Beyond dispute, however, the most stately and luxurious club in the world is the Circolo della Caccia (Hunt Club) in Rome. It was founded by three Roman aristocrats in 1869, just a year before the papal state was overrun and forcibly incorporated into the kingdom of Italy. Its premises are the Borghese Palace, the historic home of the senior princely family of Rome: The present Prince Borghese still occupies apartments within the building. The palace is enormous, with three façades, and nicknamed the "Harpsichord" because of its irregular design. It has a colonnaded loggia and the whole place is a glory of sculpture and statuary. Inside, there are two staircases and such is the splendor of the artistic heritage it embodies that the palace is known as one of the four wonders of Rome.

The late Sir Charles Petrie, the eminent English historian, used to tell a story about himself relating to the Caccia. Traveling to Rome once, he decided to visit the Caccia, by reciprocal arrangement with his club in London. The flight was long and the weather extremely hot, so Petrie hurried into the bar, desperate for a drink. Only one member was there: an impeccably dressed Roman nobleman ensconced at the bar. As soon as Petrie spoke to the bartender, this gentleman intervened to say: "Ah, I see you are a visitor here. You must allow me to buy you your first drink." He then turned to the bartender and said: "Two of my 'specials,' please." The bartender then proceeded, conscientiously and at great length, to mix an elaborate cocktail, watched impatiently by the parched Petrie. When the drink was finally placed in front of him, overcome by thirst, Petrie swallowed it in one gulp. "Oh, sir," exclaimed his host, "please forgive me. I rudely forgot to introduce myself." Saying which, he handed him his card on which Sir Charles—who had just gulped down one of this man's "specials"— read with consternation the name: "Count Borgia." A descendant of the most famous poisoners in history may be welcome on the Caccia's membership list, but money and fame are not considered adequate credentials: J. Paul Getty was blackballed when put forward for membership in the Caccia, a personal blow that made international news at the time.

America's Private Clubs

One expects to find exclusive clubs in Rome, a city of popes and princes, of secret conclaves and Renaissance conspiracies; but was the institution of clubland capable of taking root in the motherland of democracy—in America? The answer is yes; and very successfully. The essentially sociable character of Americans and their genius for adapting social structures to meet specific local needs led them to embrace clubs, fraternities (as has already been seen), and societies on a larger scale than probably any other nation. The most direct import from Britain was the gentlemen's club, as established in cities like New York. In American English, however, the preferred term is "private club"—as a "gentlemen's club" means an entirely different kind of establishment, and one typically listed in the Yellow Pages alongside escort services and lap-dancing bars.

The best American private clubs have none of the threadbare quality of their English counterparts, and they have traditionally insisted on decorum rather than high-spirited antics (with a few exceptions—such as San Francisco's world-famous Bohemian Club, which is in a remarkable league of its own). More typical of the American interpretation of club life is the dense concentration of professionally run, highly polished, and somewhat hotel-like private clubs in Manhattan's Midtown and Upper East Side, a collection of impressive clubhouses that is only rivaled by that of London. The majority were designed by just two architectural firms, McKim, Mead and White and Delano & Aldrich. The former firm, led by the flamboyant Stanford White, whose murder by a jealous millionaire husband sparked the "trial of the century," designed the Century Association, Harvard Club, Racquet & Tennis Club, University Club, and Metropolitan Club—the last an excessively lavish Italian Renaissance palazzo commissioned by a miffed J. P. Morgan, who wanted a showpiece club for his friends who were blackballed elsewhere. More endearing is the design of the Harvard Club's vast Harvard Hall, sporting a full-sized elephant's head hunting trophy hanging from above, which would have dwarfed any smaller space. (Also endearing are the club's highly addictive popovers, served in place of rolls at lunch and dinner.)

Even more elevated in tone is the trio of clubs designed by society architects Delano & Aldrich (as in Franklin *Delano* Roosevelt and Nelson *Aldrich* Rockefeller). Having always been at the pinnacle of New York's clubland pecking order, the Union Club, Knickerbocker Club, and the Brook each displays the architectural wit, whimsy, and special touches of their designers. The Union Club, located at Park and 69th, has been described as a "Fifth Avenue Mansion gone wild." It was once known for its 100,000-cigar humidor, and still has a members' changing room with "an astounding tentlike ceiling, with hanging lanterns, as if it were a sultan's tent somewhere in Arabia"—as *The*

New York Times has reported. Some disgruntled members who claimed standards were dropping at the Union founded the Knickerbocker—"the Knick"—but asked Delano & Aldrich to create a more "slim and elegant" clubhouse, which was built at the corner of Fifth Avenue and East 62nd Street. The Knick is known for its especially good food, as is the third club in this trio—the Brook, at 111 East 54th Street. The name of the club comes from Tennyson's poem of the same name, whose lines include "for men may come and men may go, but I go on for ever." The Brook aspires to offer good conversation, food, drink, and sanctuary without end. Those privileged to enjoy the atmosphere and service on offer constitute a mix of old-line American blue-bloods and some relatively new arrivals of stature, including Henry Kissinger—who sometimes grants interviews to journalists from his luncheon table at the Brook.

If American clubs haven't—on average—generated quite as much wit, repartee, and anecdotage as their counterparts in England, there are some notable exceptions among the clubs frequented by the Hollywood and show-business fraternity. Victor Mature, for example, wanted to join the exclusive Los Angeles Country Club. When he asked to become a member, however, he was rebuffed with the response: "We don't accept actors." "I'm no actor," riposted Mature, "and I've got sixty-four pictures to prove it." The North Course at the club remains one of the most exclusive golfing venues in the world, and the club itself has long been the carefully manicured and groomed bastion of southern California's original business elite of largely Midwestern origin. Mature was by no means the last victim of the club's exclusivity: It is said that Hugh Hefner, who lives beside one of the fairways, was also refused membership.

The Hillcrest Country Club, also in Los Angeles, can claim probably the largest collection of humorous stories of any club in the world—hardly surprising, since the cream of America's most talented comedians have been members. Hillcrest, situated at 10000 West Pico Boulevard, is across the street from Fox Studios. It began its existence as an exclusively Jewish club, though it has since opened its doors to non-Jews. Besides a large initiation fee, members had to contribute to the United Jewish Appeal. Its golf course, designed by Willie Watson, opened in 1920. In the 1950s—a unique experience for any club—oil was discovered on its land, drilling began and members collected tax-protected dividends based on their original initiation fees. Memberships dating back to before the discovery of oil became so valuable they were passed down as a form of inheritance. But what lent Hillcrest even more prestige than its oil income was the plethora of Hollywood stars among its membership, including Milton Berle, Eddie Cantor, and the Ritz brothers. Legend has it that Louis B. Mayer once punched Sam Goldwyn in the showers.

The focal point of Hillcrest's exuberant lifestyle, however, was the "Round Table" in a corner of the dining room where the top comedians would gather for lunch every Friday. It was a comedy powerhouse, with each comic striving to outdo the others. The participants included such household names as the Marx brothers, Al Jolson, George Burns, and Jack Benny. Another habitué was George Jessel, the actor, comedian, singer, and Academy Award–winning producer. Jessel was perennially short of money; he also had a reputation for public speaking—he was nicknamed the "Toastmaster General"—and particularly for delivering classic eulogies at funerals. One day, when Jessel was sitting with all the regulars at the Round Table, an elderly businessman came up to him and said, "Mr. Jessel, my wife, Rosie, had a little poodle she was crazy about who just died. It would very much please her if you would do the eulogy at the dog's funeral." Jessel, greatly annoyed, shouted: "You want me to do a eulogy for a dog? I do people—not animals. Go away!" But the old man stood his ground and came back: "Look, Mr. Jessel, if you'll do me this favor, I'll pay you $2,500 in cash and donate $25,000 to the United Jewish Appeal." "That's different," exclaimed Jessel, closing the deal. "You didn't tell me the dog was Jewish!"

Although Groucho Marx had famously claimed he would never join any club that would take someone like himself, he was a prominent member of the Hillcrest and of the Round Table. Another was

Jack Benny. When the first non-Jewish member elected was Danny Thomas, a Catholic from Lebanon, Benny told him the least the club could have done was admit someone who looked like a gentile. George Burns visited the club every day to play bridge, right up until two days before he died. When a ban on smoking was imposed in the club, Burns complained. So a sign was put up that read: *Cigar smoking prohibited for anyone under 95.* That was a good encapsulation of the spirit of tolerance, wit, and idiosyncracy that has always characterized clubland. It is alive and well today in these sanctuaries of sociability.

Sanctuaries: The Enduring Tradition

In this book we have visited every variety of secret shrine, refuge, base for conspiracy, and bolt-hole for eccentrics. The venues have ranged from the sublime to the ridiculous; from the tabernacles of age-old religions to modern subterranean hideaways; from the satanic seedbed of genocide to the inner sanctums of conviviality. As these richly variegated examples have demonstrated, humanity's urge to squirrel itself away in inaccessible sanctuaries is an ingrained instinct from the womb—the initial human experience that such conduct may well subliminally seek to replicate. It is an interesting paradox that while this instinct is, at first blush, unsociable and isolationist, it usually expresses itself in a desire to gather in secret places with like-minded individuals, which actually constitutes a kind of communitarianism. Perhaps it is a genetic inheritance from primitive troglodyte society, where the extended family defended the territorial integrity of its own cave. Sometimes, as we have shown, there is a nefarious or evil purpose to such covert behavior. But, as we have also illustrated, there is a legitimate right to privacy that only a totalitarian society will invade. Secret rites and exclusive sanctuaries have been a feature of every civilization since history began. Human nature being what it is, we can safely predict they will endure as long as the species itself does.

INDEX

Abba (music group), 198
Abbey of Sainte-Madeleine du
    Barroux (France), 169–171
Academic fencing, 229–232
Acheson, Dean, 221
Adam, John, 240
Adamnan (Saint), 155
Aksum, Ethiopia, 53–54
Al-Aqsa Mosque (Jerusalem), 162
Alexander III (King of Scots),
    178–179
Alexander VI (Pope), 102
Alice ("Aliki," Princess), 166
Alien conspiracy theories, 130–134
Allende, Salvador, 56
Allen, Herbert & Mavin, 122
Allen, Woody, 25
Allori, Cristofano, 90
Al-Qaeda, 50
Amberger, J. Christopher, 232
American Free Press, 21
American private clubs, 247–251
Ancient Mystical Order Rosae
    Crucis (San José), 24–25
Angels and Demons (Brown), 3, 105
Anthroposophical movement,
    71–74
Anti-Semitism, 249–250
Apostolic Palace (Vatican), 163–165
Arctic Eden. *See* Svalbard Global
    Seed Vault (Norway)
Area 51 (Nevada), 129–134
Aretmisia (Montecristo), 143
Aristocratic charity, 3
Arizona, 132
Ark of the Covenant, 46, 53–54
Armenia, 194
Aryan race mythology, 68–69, 227
Ashley, Ralph, 115
Atatürk, Mustafa Kemal, 172
Atlantis, lost city of, 69
Attila the Hun, 101
Aureum Seculum Redivivum
    (Madatanus), 108
Australia, 136
Austria, 58, 64, 86, 96–97, 194
Autonomous Monastic Republic
    of Holy Mount Athos
    (Greece), 167–169

Bååtska Palace (Stockholm), 46–53
Baez, Joan, 43
Baigent, Michael, 8, 15, 59
Bailey, Charles W., 127

Bailiwick of Utrecht of the
    Teutonic Knights, 97
Balfour, Arthur, 244
Balliol, John (King of Scots), 179
Bandiera, Pietro Antonio, 106
Bank of England, 210
Banquiers Privés (Geneva), 205–206
Barbarossa, Heyreddin, 144
Baring Brothers & Co. bank,
    199–200
Bartels, Hermann, 65–66
Basel, Switzerland, 205
Beati Paoli (secret society), 3,
    109–112
The Beatles (singing group), 43
Benedict XV (Pope), 164
Benedictines (Order of St.
    Benedict), 81, 150, 155, 169,
    184
Benedict XVI (Pope), 54, 170, 231
Benét, Stephen Vincent, 223
Benny, Jack, 250–251
Bergman, Ingrid, 46
Berle, Milton, 250
Berlioz, Louis Hector, 203
Berne, Switzerland, 84
Bernhard (Prince of Netherlands),
    20
Bertie Wooster (fictional char-
    acter), 234–235
Berwart, Blasius, 95
Besant, Annie, 72
Bessemer Trust (New York), 203
Bevan, Aneurin, 238
Bezos, Jeff, 216
Big Sur, California, 41–44
Bilczewski, Jósef (Saint), 231
Bilderberg Group, 19–21
Bismarck, Otto von, 228
The Black Masked Knights (movie), 112
Blair, Tony, 21
Blanche (Queen of Castille), 14
Blavatsky, Helena Petrovna, 72
Bloem, Walter, 227
Bluemont, Virginia, 120–128
Blunt, Anthony, 213
Bob & Carol & Ted & Alice (movie),
    43
Bohemian Club (San Francisco),
    248
Boleyn, Anne, 112
Bollingen Tower (Switzerland),
    74–78
Bolt-holes, 120–129

Bolton, Josh, 201
Bonaparte, Napoleon (emperor),
    83, 96
Bonaparte, Napoleon (prince),
    141–142
Boniface VIII (Pope), 101
Bonn, Germany, 5
Boodle, Edwin, 238
Borbón, Juan Carlos, 83
Borghese Palace (Rome), 246
Borri, Guiseppe Francesco, 106–107
Borussia House (Germany), 5
Brandford, Ontario, 173
Branson, Richard, 203
Brant, Joseph, 173–174
Bray, Leslie, 125–126
Britain. *See* England
Bromley, Henry, 115
Brook club (New York), 248–249
Brotherhood (Bloem), 227
Brown Brothers Harriman & Co.
    (Philadelphia), 209–210
Brown, Dan, 15–16
Brummell, Beau, 236–237, 239
Bryce, David, 12
Buckley, Christopher, 219
Buckmaster, Herbert, 244–245
Budapest, Hungary, 185
Burgess, Guy, 213
Burgoyne, John, 239
Burisch, Dan (aka Dan Crain), 132
Burns, George, 250–251
Bush, George W., 219, 220
Bush, Prescott, 209

California, U.S.A., 24–26, 41–44,
    166
Calvet, Gerard, 169
Calvi, Roberto, 55
Cambridge University, 213–214
Cameron, David, 214
Campaign for Nuclear
    Disarmament, 136
Canada, 172–175, 188–189
Candleshoe (movie), 117
Cantor, Eddie, 250
Cardi, Ludovico, 90
Carl XVI Gustaf (King of Sweden),
    47
Carter, Jimmy, 188
Casa di Rodi (Rome), 85
Castel Sant'Angelo (Rome),
    101–105, 109
Castro, Fidel, 175

Catherine of Aragon, 112
Catholic Church
  liturgy, 54–55, 170–171
  memento mori symbols, 224
  prejudice against, 16
  survival in England, 112–118
  university "corps," 225, 231
Caves/catacombs, 99
Cecil, Robert, 115
Celestine II (Pope), 164
Cellini, Benvenuto, 104
Central Intelligence Agency, 22–23
Chapel of St. Oran (Scotland), 156
Chapel of the Ark (Ethiopia),
  53–54
Chapel of the Holy Grail (Spain),
  54–55
Chapels Royal of the British
  Crown, 172–175
Charitable brotherhoods, 3
Charlemagne, 192–193
Charles (Prince of Wales), 166, 168,
  169–170
Charles I (King of England),
  155, 195
Charles III (Constable de
  Bourbon), 100
Charles V (emperor), 100
Charles VIII (King of France), 102
Charles X (King of France), 191
Cheney, Dick, 120, 122, 127–128
Chérisey, Philippe de, 14
Chesterton, G. K., 16
Cheyenne Mountain (Colorado),
  129
Chivalry, sanctuaries of, 80–81
C. Hoare & Co. (London), 210
Chopin, Frédéric, 203
Christian chivalry, 3
Christina (Queen of Sweden), 106
Churchill, Pamela, 209
Churchill, Randolph, 237
Churchill, Winston, 31, 195, 205,
  243
Church of Sant'Eusebio (Rome),
  105
Church of Sinai (Egypt), 166
Church of St. Katherine
  (Nuremberg), 194
Ciaia, Azzolino Bernardino
  della, 90
Circolo della Caccia (Rome),
  246–247
Clancy, Tom, 128
Clark, Mark, 194
Clement VII (Pope), 100, 103
Clifton, Walter de, 11
Clinton, William J., 21, 209
Club 33 (Disneyland), 26
Clubland (gentlemen's clubs),
  234–235
The Colleges of Oxford (Jebb), 168–169
Collegiate Church of St. Matthew
  (Scotland), 9
Collegiate clubs. *See also*
  Fraternities
  Cambridge, 213–214
  German "corps," 224–229
  Harvard University, 216–217
  Mensur (fencing), 229–232
  Oxford University, 214

Princeton University, 215–216
  Yale University, 217–224
Colorado, 129
Columba (Saint), 155, 178
Columbus, Christopher, 86
Combes, Emil, 191
Compton, Spencer, 117
Conrad, Joseph, 20
Conspiracy theories
  "Doomsday Seed Vault,"
  157–158
  extraterrestrial, 130–134
  investigative media, 5–6
  Opus Dei, 17–19
  Templar and Masonic, 8
  Walt Disney cryonics, 25
Constantinople, Turkey, 171
Conventual Church of St. Stephen
  (Pisa), 89–93
Conversion of Saul (Michelangelo),
  163
Conway, Martin, 193
Cook, Robin, 23
Coolidge, Calvin, 123
Cooper, Anderson, 222
Corbu, Noël, 14
Cornwallis, Charles, 239
Corps Borussia, 5
Corps Hannovera, 5
Corridore di Borgo (Rome), 102
Corycian Caves (Greece), 41–42
Corzine, Jon, 201
The Count of Monte Cristo (Dumas),
  141–142
Coutts & Co. ("Queen's bankers"),
  197 (photo), 203–204
Coward, Noël, 241
Cracow, Poland, 194
Credit Suisse (Zurich), 204
Croker, John Wilson, 241
Cromwell, Oliver, 9, 195–196
Cronberg, Walther von, 95
Crowley, Aleister, 1
Crucifixion of St. Peter (Michelangelo),
  163
Crusades, 50, 80–81, 89
Culpeper, Virginia, 129
Curtis, Margaret, 154
Czech Republic, 86, 96, 136–137

Dagobert II (Merovingian King), 14
Dante (Italian poet), 92
D'Appiani, Alessandro &
  Elisabetta, 148
Dartmouth University, 218
Darwin, Charles, 241
David-Weill, Michel, 202
The Da Vinci Code (Brown), 2, 8–9,
  15–16, 50, 59
Davos, Switzerland, 20
Dawkins, Richard, 56
Decline and Fall of the Roman Empire
  (Gibbon), 239
Defense of the Faith (Stuber), 95
De Gaulle, Charles, 87, 211
Deism, 57
Delpech, Auguste, 56
Delphi, Greece, 36–41
De Molay, Jacques, 49
Deseronto, Ontario, 173
Deutschordensschloss

  (Mergentheim), 95–96
Dickens, Charles, 241
Dillon, Read & Co. bank (New
  York), 200
Disneyland (Anaheim), 25–26
Disney, Walt, 25
Disraeli, Benjamin, 237
Divine Comedy (Dante), 92
Dome of the Rock (Jerusalem), 162
"Doomsday Seed Vault," 4, 156–158
Dornach, Switzerland, 71–74
Drummond, George, 237
Duitse Huis (Utrecht), 97
Dumas, Alexandre, 141–142
Dumas, Roland, 56
Dunmuir, James, 189
Dylan, Bob, 43
Dzerzhinsky, Felix, 23

Easter Island, 150–153
Easter Island: The Mystery Solved
  (Heyerdahl), 151
The Economist (magazine), 50
Eco, Umberto, 106
Edward I (King of England), 179
Edward VI (King of England), 112
Edward VIII (King of England), 238
Egypt, 165–166
Eisenhower, Dwight D., 194
Elgar, Edward, 240
Eliot, T. S., 217
Elizabeth I (Queen of England),
  112–113
Elizabeth II (Queen of England),
  174, 182, 211
*The Emperor Constantine's Vision of the
  Cross* (Stuber), 95
England. *See also* London, England
  Ark of the Covenant in, 53
  British Royal Family, 166, 168,
  169–170
  Canada contingency, 188–189
  chapels royal, 173–175
  freemasonry in, 55
  grand lodge of Masonry, 49
  priest holes, 3, 112–118
  RAF Menwith Hill, 134–138
  Stone of Destiny, 179–183
Esalen Institute (Big Sur), 41–44
Escrivá de Balaguer y Albás,
  Josemaría (Saint), 17
Estulin, Daniel, 21
Ethiopia, 53–54
Et in Arcadia Ego (Poussin), 15
Etschmiadzin, Armenia, 194
Evlogios (bishop of Milan), 59
Extraterrestrial theories, 130–134
"Extricating Young Gussie"
  (Wodehouse), 234n

Farrell, Terry, 22
Fawkes, Guy, 115
Federal Relocation Arc, 128–129
Feuchtwangen, Siegfried von, 93
Finian (Saint), 155
Fir Bhreig stone sculpture, 153–154
Fitzgerald, F. Scott, 215
Fleming, Ian, 23, 239
Fonda, Jane, 43
Food Lover's Guide to France, 169
Forster, E. M., 213

Forsyth, Michael, 182
Fort Knox, Kentucky, 187
Fort Ritchie, Pennsylvania, 128
Foster, Jodie, 117, 222
Fox, Charles James, 240
Fox-Strangways, John, 238
France
  Abbey of Sainte-Madeleine du
    Barroux, 169–171
  freemasonry in, 56
  Lazard Frères bank, 201–202
  private clubs of, 246
  Rennes-le-Château, 2, 12–16
  Sante Ampoule, 190–192
  Sword of Charlemagne, 192–193
Francis de Paola (Saint), 110
Francis I (King of France), 100
Francis of Assisi (Saint), 165
Franklin, Benjamin, 174
Fraternities, 1, 214–215, 217, 225. See
    also Collegiate clubs
Freemasonry
  as brotherhood, 55–59
  conspiracy theories, 8
  Goetheanum and, 72–74
  lore of Rosslyn Chapel, 8–12
  Rosicrucians as origin of, 11–12,
    25, 72, 106, 108–109
  Swedish Order of, 47–49
  Templar association, 46, 49–53
  university clubs, 214–215
  in university clubs, 223–224

Galt, William, 111
Gardner, Gerald, 57
Garnet, Henry, 115
Gates, Bill, 157, 217
Gates, Henry Louis, Jr., 222
Geneva, Switzerland, 4, 205–206
George II (King of Greece), 59
George III (King of England),
    173–174, 203, 239
George V (King of England), 195
Geraldtown, Australia, 136
Gerard, John, 114–115
Gergen, David, 222
Germany
  after World War I, 31, 227
  concentration camps, 62–63, 68
  freemasonry in, 208
  origins of Templar myth, 50
  private bank services, 207–209
  secret bank accounts, 205, 207
  Teutonic Knights of, 95–96
  university "corps" and dueling
    societies, 4–5, 224–232
  Wewelsburg Castle, 2–3, 62–71,
    80
Getty Center (Los Angeles), 166
Giamatti, Bart, 221
Gibbon, Edward, 239
Ginsberg, Allen, 43
Glasgow Cathedral (Scotland),
    11–12
Glenmede Trust (Pennsylvania),
    203
Gnosticism, 57, 59–60
The God Delusion (Dawkins), 56
Goetheanum (Switzerland), 71–74
Gold bullion as asset, 210–211
Göldli, Hercules, 101

Goldman Sachs bank (New York),
    201
Goldwyn, Sam, 250
Goodhue, Bertram Grosvenor, 223
Göring, Hermann, 208
Goss, Porter, 222
Government bolt-holes. See Bolt-
    holes
Goy, Jean, 191–192
Grand Orient of France, 56
Grand Orient of Italy, 55–56
Great Church of the Holy Wisdom
    (Hagia Sophia), 171–172
Greece, 36–42, 167–169
Greenbrier Hotel (White Sulfur
    Springs), 128–129
Greenpeace, 136
Greer, John Michael, 170
Gregory the Great (Saint), 143
Grottoes, 99
Grotto of the Beati Paoli
    (Palermo), 109–112
Guidi, Camillo, 90

Hadrian (emperor), 102
Hagia Sophia (Istanbul), 171–172
Haile Selassie (emperor of
    Ethiopia), 53
Hambros (bank, London), 211
Handcock, Sarah Butler, 90
Harkness, Edward, 222
Harriman, Averell W., 209
Harrison, George, 43
Harvard University, 216–217
Hassell, Ulrich von, 227
Hatley Castle (British Columbia),
    189
Healey, Denis, 20
Heine, Heinrich, 198, 229
Heinrich I (Saxon King), 66
Henry VIII (King of England), 112
Her Majesty's Chapels Royal of the
    Mohawks (Ontario), 172–175
Heydrich, Reinhard, 68
Heyerdahl, Thor, 151
Hildebrand, Dietrich von, 170
Hillcrest Country Club (Los
    Angeles), 249–250
Himmler, Heinrich, 2–3, 61
    (photo), 62–71
Hirohito (emperor of Japan), 30–31
Hitler, Adolph, 31, 66, 170, 175,
    194, 226
Hohenzollern, Albrecht von, 95
Holland, 97
Holland, Henry, 240
Holmes, Oliver Wendell, 217
The Holy Blood and the Holy Grail
    (Baigent, Leigh & Lincoln), 2,
    8, 15, 59, 108
Holy Crown of St. Stephen
    (Hungary), 176 (photo),
    183–188
Holy Grail, 8–12, 46, 54–55, 69
Holy Lance of St. Longinus
    (Austria), 193–195
Holy Roman Empire, 63, 93–95,
    193–194
Hong Kong, 136
Hoover, Herbert, 123
Hoover, J. Edgar, 124

Hotel de Bilderberg (Netherlands),
    2, 19–21
Hourelle, Philippe, 191
House of Lazard bank (New York),
    201–202
House of Morgan bank (New
    York), 200–201
Hrzistie, Georg Skrbensky von, 96
Human instinct, to seek sanctuary,
    1–6
Hume, David, 239
Hund, Karl Gotthelf von, 50, 57
Hungary, 183–188
Huxley, Aldous, 42

I Beati Paoli (Galt), 111–112
Iona (Scotland), 4, 155–156, 178
Iran, 137, 208
Irei no Izumi (Tokyo), 33
Ireland, 155, 177–183, 245–246
Irminism, 64
Ise Jingu shrine (Japan), 28–30
Islam, 143–147, 162, 165–166
Island of the Day Before (Eco), 106
Islands as sanctuary, 4, 140–153
Isle of Lewis (Scottish Hebrides),
    153–154
Istanbul, Turkey, 171–172
Italy, 4, 55–56, 81–93, 109–112,
    141–150. See also Rome, Italy

James Bond (fictional character),
    22–23, 239
James I (King of England), 115
Japan, 28–34
Jebb, Miles, 168
Jerusalem, 10, 13, 162, 166
Jessel, George, 250
Jett, Joseph, 200
Jockey Club (Paris), 246
Johnson, Boris, 214
Johnson, George Frederick, 50
Johnson, Paul, 211
John XXIII (Pope), 165
Jolson, Al, 250
Joyeuse, the Sword of
    Charlemagne (France),
    192–193
J.P. Morgan Chase (New York), 200
J-Rod (Reticulan being), 132–134
Juan Carlos I (King of Spain), 83
Jung, Carl, 74–78
Justinian (emperor), 171

Karl Maria Weisthor (pseud-
    onym), 64
Kedl, Rudolph, 58
Kennedy, John F., 124, 217
Kennedy, Robert, 217
Kennedy, Theodore ("Ted"), 217
Kerouac, Jack, 43
Kerry, John, 219
Keynes, John Maynard, 213
KGB (Soviet secret service), 23
Kidder, Peabody & Co.
    (Massachusetts), 200
Kieran (Saint), 154
Kildare Street Club (Ireland), 245
Kingman, Arizona, 132
Kingsley Trust Association, 221
Kipling, Rudyard, 244

Kircher, Athanasius, 106
Kissinger, Henry, 20
Knebel, Fletcher, 127
Knickerbocker club (New York), 5, 248–249
Knights Hospitaller of St. John, 80–81, 88, 145
Knights of Malta (Rome), 81–88
Knights of St. Stephen, 88–93, 148
Knights Templar. *See* Templars
Kuhn, Loeb & Co. (New York), 209

Lampoon magazine (Harvard), 216
Lance of St. Maurice, 193
Last Judgment (Michelangelo), 163
Lateran Palace (Rome), 161–162
Lawrence, T. E. (aka Lawrence of Arabia), 80
Lawrence, Thomas, 241
Lazar, Bob, 131–132
Lazard Brothers (London), 201–202
Lazard Frères (Paris), 201–202
Leary, Timothy, 25
Lebanon, 80, 145–147
Le Barroux, France, 169–171
Le Crac des Chavaliers (Syria), 80
Lee, Robert E., 174
Leeson, Nick, 200
Lehman Brothers (New York), 209
Lehrman, Lew, 223
Lenhoff, Eugen, 48
Leo I (Pope), 101
Leo IV (Pope), 102
Leo X (Pope), 100
Lewis, H. Spencer, 24–25
Lexington, Virginia, 174
Lhasa, Tibet, 34–36
Lieberman, Joe, 222
Liechtenstein, 206–207
Liegh, Richard, 8, 15
Ligozzi, Jacopo, 90
Linares, Vincenzo, 111
Lincoln, Henry, 8, 15
List, Guido von, 64, 69
Ljokhang Temple (Tibet), 34–36
Lohengrin (Wagner), 54
Lombard Odier Darier Hentsch (Geneva), 206
London, England. *See also* England
 aristocratic clubs, 5, 234–247
 Baring Brothers, 199–200
 C. Hoare & Co., 210
 Coutts & Co., 203–204
 Lazard Brothers bank, 201–202
 Rothschild banks, 198–199
 St. Catherine Foundation, 166
 Vauxhall Cross, 22–24
Longinus (Saint), 193
Looney, James B., 126
L'Or de Rennes (Séde), 14–15
Los Angeles, California, 166
Louis VIII (King of France), 14
Louis XI (King of France), 190
The Loved One (Waugh), 25
Lubyanka Prison (Moscow), 23
Luttrell, Henry, 236
Lutyens, Edwin, 200
Luxembourg, 207

MacArthur, Douglas, 31
Macher, Heinz, 70–71

Macmillan, Harold, 237
Mafia, 109, 112
Magic Door (Rome), 105–109
Maistre, Joseph de, 57
Major, John, 182
Malachy (Saint), 164–165
Malta, Republic of, 87–88
Mamiliano (Saint), 143, 150
Maria de' Medici Embarking on her Journey to Wed Henri IV, King of France (Allori), 90
Marienburg/Malbork, Poland, 94–95
Martin, Malachi, 163–164
The Martyrdom of St. Stephen, Pope (Vasari), 90
Marx, Groucho, 250
Marx, Karl, 229
Mary Magadlen (Saint), 15
Mary (Queen of England), 113
Masonic Chapel (Russia), 58–59
Masons. *See* Freemasonry
Mature, Victor, 249
Mayer, Louis B., 250
McKenna, Terence, 44
Medici, Cosimo de (Cosimo I), 88–89, 92–93, 148
Medici, Guiliano de', 100
Medici, Lorenzo de', 100
Mellon, Paul, 221
Memories, Dreams, Reflections (Jung), 75
Mensur (academic fencing), 229–232
Mergentheim, Germany, 95–96
MI6 (British Secret Intelligence Service), 22–24
Michelangelo, 163
Middleton, William de, 11
Midlothian, Scotland, 2, 8–12
Mindszenty, Jósef, 187
M. M. Warburg & CO (Hamburg), 207–208
Moai stone sculptures, 151–153
Mollet, Guy, 21
Molnar, Thomas, 161
Monastery of St. Catherine of Sinai (Egypt), 165–166
Montecristo (Italy), 4, 139 (photo), 141–150
Monty Python (comedian group), 198
Morals and Dogma (Pike), 58
More, Thomas (Saint), 174
Morgan, J. P., 248
Morgan Stanley (New York), 200
Morwenstow, England, 136
Moscow, Russia, 23
Mount Athos (Greece), 167–169
Mount of Olives (Jerusalem), 166
Mount Sinai (Egypt), 165–166
Mount Weather Emergency Operations Center (Virginia), 120–128
Muhammad (Prophet), 166
Murphy, Michael, 42–43
Mynsicht, Adrian von, 108

Nader, Ralph, 216
Nakahira, Fumio, 34
Naples, Italy, 86
Natoli, Luigi, 111–112

Nazism, 2–3, 62–71, 170–171, 205, 208–209, 226–227
Netherlands, 2, 19–21, 97
Nevada, 129–134
New Age, Esalen Institute, 41–44
New Club (Scotland), 246
New Mexico, 165
New Zealand, 136
Nicholas III (Pope), 102
Nichols, Aidan, 60
9/11 Terrorist attacks, 50, 120–122, 126–127, 128–129
Niven, David, 117, 239
Nixon, Richard, 124
N.M. Rothschild & Sons (London), 198–199
Noble Sanctuary (aka Temple Mount), 162
Norman, Montagu, 210
Northern Trust (Illinois), 203
North Korea, 137
Norway, 4, 156–158

Oakeshott, Ewart, 193
Obolensky, Serge, 59
Occult theology, 57, 62–64, 72
Odinism, 69
Oglasa (Montecristo), 143
Oldcorne, Edward, 115
O'Neill, Thomas P. ("Tip"), 129
Ontario, Canada, 172–175
Oppe, John Russell, 57–58
Oppenheim, Friedrich Carl von, 207
Opus Dei, 16–19
Oracle of Apollo at Delphi (Greece), 36–41
Order of Knights Canopy Bearers of the Holy Ampoule, 190–192
Order of Malta (Rome), 81–88
Order of Schutzstaffel, 62–64
Order of St. Benedict. *See* Benedictines (Order of St. Benedict)
Order of St. Stephen (Pisa), 88–93
Order of the New Temple (*Ordo Novi Templi*), 64
Orthodox Church, 53–55, 59, 83, 166, 168, 171
Ottoman Empire, 89
Owen, Nicholas (Saint), 113–117
Oxbrow, Mark, 10–11
Oxford University, 168–169, 170, 214

Palermo, Sicily, 3, 109–112
Palombara, Massimiliano, 105, 107
Paris, France. *See* France
Parsifal (Wagner), 54
Pasha, Ali, 90
Passetto di Borgo (Rome), 3, 79 (photo), 99–105
Paul I (Czar of Russia), 83
Pauline Chapel (Vatican), 163–165
Paulson, Henry, 201
Paul VI (Pope), 116
Peale, Charles Wilson, 174
Pei, I. M., 201
Pendennis (Thackeray), 241
Pennsylvania, 128

People's right to know, 6
Petrie, Charles, 246–247
Philby, Kim, 171
Philip (Duke of Edinburgh), 168
Philippe, (Crown Prince of
 Belgium), 20
Philippines, 34
Philip the Fair (King of France), 51
Pictet & Cie (Geneva), 206
Pike, Albert, 58
Pinay, Antoine, 21
Pinochet, Augusto, 56
Piola, Carmelo, 111
Piranesi, Giovanni Battista, 85
Pisa, Italy, 88–93
Pius XII (Pope), 231
Plantard, Pierre, 14
Plimpton, George, 217
Pliny the Younger, 143
Poland
 freemasonry in, 224
 Holy Lance of St. Longinus, 194
 missile defense site, 136–137
 Teutonic Knights in, 93–95
 university "corps," 224, 231
 during WWII, 20, 67, 189
Ponting, Gerald, 154
Porter, Cole, 221
Portugal, 51
Poussin, Nicolas, 15
Prague, Czechoslovakia, 86
Present Laughter (Coward), 241
Price, Richard, 42–43
Priest holes of England, 3, 112–118
Princeton University, 215–216
Prioral Palace (St. Petersburg), 83
Privacy, right to, 6
Privatbankhaus Schacht & Co.
 (Düsseldorf), 208
Privatbankiers (Geneva), 205–206
Private clubs
 Europe and British Isles, 245–247
 London, 235–245
 United States, 247–251
Prophecies of St. Malachy, 164–165
Pushkin, Russia, 58–59

Quattromani, Gabriele, 111

Rachel, Nevada, 133
RAF Menwith Hill (Yorkshire),
 134–138
Reagan, Ronald, 43
Religious wars/conflict, 50, 80–81,
 89, 100–105, 112–118, 143–147
Remi (Saint), 190–192
Rennes-le-Château (France), 2,
 12–16
Retinger, Jósef, 20, 22
The Return of the Fleet of the Order After
 the Battle of Lepanto (Ligozzi), 90
Rheims, France, 190–192
Rhodes, Cecil, 174–175
Riley-Smith, Jonathan, 50–51, 54
Robertson, Ian, 10–11
The Robing of Cosimo I as Grand Master
 (Cardi), 90
Robinson, Geoffrey, 223
Rockefeller, David, 20
Rockefeller Foundation, 157
Roist, Kaspar, 101, 103–104

Rome, Italy. See also Italy
 Borghese Palace, 246
 Casa di Rodi, 85
 Castel Sant'Angelo, 101–105, 109
 Corridore di Borgo, 102
 Holy Lance of St. Longinus, 194
 Magic Door, 105–109
 Passetto di Borgo, 3, 99–105
 Pauline Chapel, 163–165
 private clubs of, 246–247
 Sancta Sanctorum, 161–162
 Vatican during WWII, 189
 Villa Malta, 85
 Villa Tevere, 2, 16–19
Romney, George, 173
Roosevelt, Franklin D., 33, 175, 217
Roosevelt, Theodore, 217
Rosa, Samuel, 50
Rosicrucian Park (San José), 24–25
Rosicrucians, 11–12, 72, 106,
 108–109
Rosslyn and the Grail (Oxbrow &
 Robertson), 10–11
Rosslyn Chapel (Scotland), 2,
 8–12, 54
Rothschild bank (London),
 198–199
Royal Bank of Scotland, 203–204
Royal City of the Holy Faith of St.
 Francis of Assisi, 165
RTA Incorporated, 219–220
Rubin, Robert, 201
Rudelsburg Castle (Germany), 5
Rumsfeld, Donald, 20, 127, 216
Russell, Bertrand, 213
Russell, William, 223
Russia, 58–59, 83, 122, 129

Sacred Military Order of St.
 Stephen Pope and Martyr,
 88–93
Sacred treasures. See Totems/
 talisman
Salmon Oppenheim jr. & Cie
 (Luxembourg), 207
Sancta Sanctorum (Rome), 159
 (photo), 161–162
Sanctuary/secrecy, defining, 1–6
San Francisco, California, 248
Santa Fe, New Mexico, 165
Sante Ampoule (France), 190–192
Saunière, Bérenger, 13–14, 108
Schacht, Hjalmar, 208, 210
Schlosshotel Rosenau (Austria), 58
Schmidt, Benno, 223
Schmoke, Kurt, 223
Schumann, Robert, 229
Schwarzman, Stephen, 219
Scotland
 Glasgow Cathedral, 11–12
 Iona, island of, 4, 155–156
 Isle of Lewis, 153–154
 private clubs of, 246
 Rosslyn Chapel, 2, 8–12
 Royal Bank of Scotland, 203–204
 Stone of Destiny, 177–183
Scottish Hebrides, 153–154
Scott, Walter, 241
The Secret History of the Sword
 (Amberger), 232
Séde, Gérard de, 14

September 11 attacks. See 9/11 ter-
 rorist attacks
Seraine, Jules Armand, 191
Seven Days in May (Knebel & Bailey),
 127
Seymour-Conway, Henry, 246
Shields, Brooke, 216
Shriver, Sargent, 221
Sicily, Italy, 86, 109–112
Sigismund (emperor), 193
Sigismund of Tuscany, 90
Sikorski, Radoslaw ("Radek"), 214
Sikorski, Wladysaw, 20
Simpson, Wallis, 238
Sinai, Egypt, 165–166
Sinclair, William. See St. Clair,
 William
Sire, H. J. A., 81
Sirhan, Sirhan, 25
Sistine Chapel (Vatican), 163
Site R (Raven Rock), 122, 128
Skull and Bones society (Yale), 209,
 212 (photo), 213, 215, 218
Sleeper (movie), 25
Slessor, John, 238
Smith, Adam, 239
Smith-Cumming, George
 Mansfield, 23
Smith, F. E., 241
Smith, Fred, 219
Society of Jesus (Jesuits), 106,
 113–114, 163–165, 175, 208
Sontag, Susan, 43
Sovereign Military Hospitaller
 Order of St. John of
 Jerusalem, of Rhodes, and of
 Malta, 80–81
Soviet Union, 160–161. See also
 Russia
Spain, 2, 18, 54–55, 83
Spear of Destiny (Austria), 193–195
Spencer, Herbert, 241
Spencer, Robert, 237
Spiegelberg, Frederic, 42
Spock, Benjamin, 221
Starck, Philippe, 200
St. Clair, Henry, 11
St. Clair, Plantard, 14
St. Clair, William, 9–12
Steiner, Rudolph, 71–74
Stephen (King of Hungary), 183
Stern, Edouard, 202
Stevenson, Adlai, 188
Stevenson, Robert Louis, 140
Stockholm, Sweden, 46–53
Stockmeyer, E. A. Karl, 73–74
Stoker, Bram, 203
Stone of Destiny, 177–183
St. Stephen I (Pope), 89–90
St. Stephen's Cathedral
 (Budapest), 185
Stuart, Gilbert, 173
Stuber, Nikolaus Gottfried, 95
Sugar Grove, West Virginia, 136
Suhard, Emmanuel Célestin, 191
Suleiman the Magnificent, 145
The Sum of All Fears (movie), 128
Svalbard Global Seed Vault
 (Norway), 4, 156–158
Svenska Frimurare Orden, 47–53
Sweden, 46–53

Swift, Jonathan, 236
Switzerland, 4, 20, 71–78, 84, 200,
    204–207
Szent-Györgi, Albert, 188

Talleyrand-Périgord, Charles
    Maurice de, 241
Teller, Edward, 132
Templars, 2, 8–16, 46–54
Temple Mount, 162
Temple of Jerusalem, 162
Temple of Solomon, 10
Tennyson, Alfred, 203
Teutonic Order of St. Mary in
    Jerusalem, 93–97
Thackeray, William Makepeace,
    241
Thatcher, Margaret, 20
Theodoracopulos, Taki, 202
Theosophical Society, 72
Theosophy, 69
Thirteen Days (movie), 128
Thomas, Danny, 251
Thompson, Hunter S., 43
The Three Musketeers (Dumas), 142
Thule Society, 69
Tibet, 34–36, 69
Tiffany & Co. (New York), 215
Time travel, 28
Tokyo, Japan, 31–34
Totems/talisman
    Charlemagne's sword, 192–193
    Cromwell's head, 195–196
    crown jewels as, 188–192
    Holy Crown of St. Stephen,
        183–188
    Holy Lance of St. Longinus,
        193–195
    Sainte Ampoule, 190–192
    Stone of Destiny, 177–183
Totila (Ostrogoth King), 102
Toumanoff, Cyril, 30
A Tramp Abroad (Twain), 232
Travellers Club of Paris, 246
Tripoli, Lebanon, 80, 145–147
Trudeau, Garry, 221
The True Story of the Bilderberg Group
    (Estulin), 21
Tucker, James P. ("Big Jim"), 21
Tunney, John, 125
Turgut Reis (Dragut Rais), 144–147
Turkey, 171–172
Turnbull, Malcolm, 201
Twain, Mark, 232

UBS bank (Zurich), 200, 204
Uhouse, Bill, 132
Unidentified Flying Objects (UFO),
    131–134
Union Club (New York), 248
United Kingdom (UK). See
    England

United Nations, 84
United Nations Educational,
    Scientific, and Cultural
    Organization (UNESCO),
    165, 167
United States. See individual state
    names
University Club (Ireland), 246
University of California, 218
University of Jena, 231
University of Leipzig, 231
University of North Carolina, 218
University societies. See Collegiate
    clubs
U.S. Air Force Flight Test Center,
    129–134
U.S. Bullion Depository (Ft.
    Knox), 187
U.S. Department of Homeland
    Security, 126
U.S. Federal Reserve Bank, 208
U.S. government
    Area 51 (Nevada), 129–134
    CIA headquarters, 23
    Federal Relocation Arc, 128–129
    Mount Weather Emergency
        Operations Center, 120–128
    NSA "Big Ear" facility, 134–138
    Site R (Raven Rock), 122, 128
U.S. National Security Agency,
    134–138
U.S. Trust (New York), 203
Utrecht, Netherlands, 97

Valencia Cathedral (Spain), 2, 45
    (photo), 54–55
Vance, Cyrus, 188
Vanderbilt, Cornelius, 221
Vasari, Giorgio, 89–90
Vatican City. See Rome, Italy
Vauxhall Cross (London), 7
    (photo), 22–24
Venice, Italy, 86, 93–94
Vermehren, Erich (aka Eric Maria
    de Saventhem), 170
Victor Emmanuel III (King of
    Italy), 149
Victoria (Queen of England), 174
Vienna, Austria, 72, 84, 86, 95–97,
    193–194
Villa Malta (Rome), 85
Villa Tevere (Rome), 2, 16–19
Virginia, U.S.A., 23, 120–128
Vorontzov Palace (St. Petersburg),
    83

Wagner, Richard, 54, 62, 229
Waihopai, New Zealand, 136
War and Peace (Tolstoy), 58
Warburg, Max, 207–208
Warburg, Paul, 208
Warburg, Siegmund, 208

Washington, D.C., 57–58
Washington, George, 173–175
Washington, state of, 136
Watson-Taylor, George, 149
Watson, Willie, 250
Waugh, Evelyn, 25, 53, 237
Westphalia, Germany, 2–3, 62–71
West Virginia, 128–129, 136
Wewelsburg Castle (Germany),
    2–3, 61 (photo), 62–71, 80
While, Stanford, 248
White, Francis (Francesco Bianco),
    236
White Sulfur Springs, W.Va.,
    128–129
White, Victor, 60
Wiccan movement, 57
Wilhelm II (kaiser of Germany),
    208, 229
Wiligut, Karl Maria, 64–65, 69–70
Wilmington Trust (Delaware), 203
Windswept (Martin), 163
Wiseman, William, 209
Wittgenstein, Ludwig, 213
Wodehouse, P. G., 234–235
Wolff, Karl, 68, 70
Wolfowitz, Paul, 20
Woodward, Bob, 222
World Economic Forum, 20
World Heritage Sites (UNESCO),
    165, 167–169
The World is Not Enough (movie),
    22–23
World War I, 164, 186, 227
World War II, 33–34, 67, 70, 187,
    188–189, 194
World War III, 160–161
Wright, Frank Lloyd, 31
Wright, Peter, 23

The X-Files (TV program), 128

Yad Vashem (Holocaust memo-
    rial), 166
Yakima, Washington, 136
Yale University, 209, 213, 217–224
Yamantau Mountain (Russia), 129
Yasukuni Shrine (Tokyo), 27
    (photo), 31–34
Yorkshire, England, 134–138
Yushukan museum (Tokyo), 33

Zakaria, Fareed, 221
Zander, Helmut, 71
Zeffirini, Onofrio, 90
Zimbabwe (Rhodesia), 175
Zoellick, Bob, 201
Zurich, Switzerland, 74–78,
    204–205

ABOUT THE AUTHORS

Stephen Klimczuk is a world traveler and corporate strategist who recently served as head of strategy for late billionaire Sir John Templeton's main private foundation. In addition to his current external faculty appointment at Oxford University, he advises philanthropies and companies in more than a dozen countries. Earlier in his career, he was a director and board member of the prestigious World Economic Forum in Geneva, Switzerland, and a member of the Davos program committee. He has also been a principal of the consulting firm A.T. Kearney. He started his career at Goldman Sachs and Bain & Company in New York and San Francisco in the 1980s, and was named a "World Young Leader" by the BMW Foundation in Munich.

The son of Polish political exiles who settled in North America, Stephen received an MBA from Harvard Business School, and is also a Phi Beta Kappa graduate of UCLA. Given the facts of birth and marriage, he has United States, Canadian, Polish, and Swiss citizenship. In his off-hours, he has explored many of the obscure places covered in this book—sometimes dragging his disapproving wife and three daughters along against their better judgment.

Gerald Warner of Craigenmaddie is a well-known Scottish newspaper columnist, broadcaster, and former policy adviser to a UK cabinet minister. His *Telegraph* blog "Is it just me?" is one of Britain's most popular. Apart from his many appearances on radio and television, he has authored six books, mostly on specialized historical subjects, folklore, and curiosities—including *Homelands of the Clans* (Collins, 1980). He graduated MA (Honours) in Medieval and Modern History at Glasgow University, after which he pursued three years of postgraduate research in Irish history.

During his distinguished writing career, Gerald has been social diarist and a columnist for *The Sunday Times* (of London); a columnist and leader (i.e., editorial) writer for *Scotland on Sunday,* Scotland's leading quality Sunday paper; and a leader writer for the *Scottish Daily Mail.* From 1995 to 1997, he left journalism to become Special Adviser to the Secretary of State of Scotland, a member of the British cabinet. He has also been a Parliamentary candidate himself. The Much Honoured the Laird of Craigenmaddie (to give him his full feudal title) holds several distinguished European orders of knighthood. His recreations include heraldry, genealogy, and wine-bibbing in congenial company.